Series Editors: Yvonne Rydin and Andrew Thornley

The context in which planning operates has changed dramatically in recent years. Economic processes have become increasingly globalized and economic fortunes have fluctuated. Administrations in various countries have not only changed, but old ideologies have been swept away and new ones have tentatively emerged. A new environmental agenda has prioritized the goal of sustainable development, requiring continued action at international, national and local levels.

Cities are today faced with new pressures for economic competitiveness, greater accountability and participation, improved quality of life for citizens and global environmental responsibilities. These pressures are often contradictory and create difficult dilemmas for policy-makers, especially in the context of fiscal austerity.

In these changing circumstances, planners, from many backgrounds, in many different organizations, have come to re-evaluate their work. They have to engage with actors in government, the private sector and non-governmental organization in discussions over the role of planning in relation to the environment and cities. The intention of the *Planning, Environment, Cities* series is to explore the changing nature of planning and contribute to the debate about its future.

This series is primarily aimed at students and practitioners of planning and such related professions as estate management, housing and architecture, as well as those in politics, public and social administration, geography and urban studies. It comprises both general texts and books designed to make a more particular contribution, in both cases characterized by: an international approach; extensive use of case studies; and emphasis on contemporary relevance and the application of theory to advance planning practice.

planning • environment • cities

Series Editors: Yvonne Rydin and Andrew Thornley

Published

Philip Allmendinger
  Planning Theory (2nd edn)
Ruth Fincher and Kurt Iveson
  Planning and Diversity in the City: Redistribution, Recognition and Encounter
Cliff Hague, Euan Hague and Carrie Breitbach
  Regional and Local Economic Development
Patsy Healey
  Collaborative Planning (2nd edn)
Patsy Healey
  Making Better Places: The Planning Project in the 21st Century
Ted Kitchen
  Skills for Planning Practice
Ali Madanipour
  Urban Design, Space and Society
Peter Newman and Andrew Thornley
  Planning World Cities (2nd edn)
Michael Oxley
  Economics, Planning and Housing
Yvonne Rydin
  Urban and Environmental Planning in the UK (2nd edn)
Mark Tewdwr-Jones
  Spatial Planning and Governance: Understanding UK Planning
Geoff Vigar, Patsy Healey and Angela Hull, with Simin Davoudi
  Planning, Governance and Spatial Strategy in Britain
Iain White
  Environmental Planning in Context

Forthcoming

Luca Bertolini: **Planning the Mobile Metropolis**
Jon Coaffee and Peter Lee: **Urban Resilience: Planning the Shock-Proof City**
Chris Couch: **Urban Planning: Theory and Practice**
Ed Ferrari: **GIS and Planning for the Built Environment**
Simon Joss: **Sustainable Cities**
Dory Reeves: **Management Skills for Planners: Success in the Workplace**

Planning, Environment, Cities
Series Standing Order ISBN 978–0–333–71703–5 hardback
Series Standing Order ISBN 978–0–333–69346–9 paperback
(*outside North America only*)

You can receive future titles in this series as they are published. To place a standing order please contact your bookseller or, in the case of difficulty, write to us at the address below with your name and address, the title of the series and the ISBN quoted above. Customer Services Department, Macmillan Distribution Ltd, Houndmills, Basingstoke, Hampshire, RG21 6XS, UK.

Environmental Planning in Context

Iain White ·

First published 2015 by
PALGRAVE

Palgrave in the UK is an imprint of Macmillan Publishers Limited,
registered in England, company number 785998, of 4 Crinan Street,
London N1 9XW

Palgrave Macmillan in the US is a division of St Martin's Press LLC,
175 Fifth Avenue, New York, NY 10010.

Palgrave is the global imprint of the above companies and is represented
throughout the world.

Palgrave® and Macmillan® are registered trademarks in the United States,
the United Kingdom, Europe and other countries

ISBN 978-0-230-30327-0   ISBN 978-1-137-31566-3 (eBook)
DOI 10.1007/978-1-137-31566-3

This book is printed on paper suitable for recycling and made from fully
managed and sustained forest sources. Logging, pulping and manufacturing
processes are expected to conform to the environmental regulations of the
country of origin.

A catalogue record for this book is available from the British Library.

A catalog record for this book is available from the Library of Congress.

Typeset by Cambrian Typesetters, Camberley, Surrey, England, UK

Contents

List of Illustrative Material

Boxes

Figures

Tables

Preface

The rationale and positioning of this book is explained most easily by the discussions that emerged after a question from a student: a kind of question that those of us who lecture on the environment find very familiar. I had just given a lecture on climate science and outlined the various options for mitigation and adaptation in planning, and the student wanted to understand why society hasn't prevented climate change. As the conversation developed it was clear that while the disarmingly simple question was hugely relevant to planning, elements of the answer were not necessarily a core part of our teaching. Rather, they were related to fundamental societal issues, such as how the environment is perceived, the ways that it is governed, the framing role of politics or the inherent constraints of science, as well as more mainstream planning elements of policy and decision-making. In presenting questions such as this in lectures I found it unsatisfactory to have to draw on material from geography, politics, philosophy or sociology, and then reinterpret these within a planning context. Like many, I ended up writing the book that I couldn't find on the bookshelves, but one that I felt both my students and I would find valuable.

Traditionally, planning has had a strong remit to consider the environment, from designating land, to controlling development, and to regulating certain activities. As part of their education, students acquire sophisticated knowledge of the theory, process and regulation of planning. However, many years of teaching planning has made it clear to me that the societal context within which these are applied exerts a significant influence on the ability of planning to be effective. As such, I believe that students need a deeper appreciation of the nature of the reality within which planning takes place. Put differently, this book differs from existing texts as it is less focused on the wording of policy X within country Y, and more about how societies frame, develop and operationalize the management of planning concerns.

The content in this book is organized to explore three nested scales within which environmental planning debates occur: society; public policy; and planning itself. The text is designed so that each successive chapter builds on the previous material to provide readers with an increasingly sophisticated understanding of the theory and practice of planning. It begins with Chapters 1–4 initially introducing the subject, before focusing on the broader milieu of environmental planning, and in particular on the intellectual legacies that affect the value placed on the natural world, the governance and power structures in operation, and the opinion-shaping forces of politics and the media. Understanding these key societal frames allows a fuller understanding of the discussion contained in Chapters 5–7. These unpack the process of public policy intervention, first exploring the pathways of logic associated with the concepts being applied, before using these to appreciate the constraints associated with the nature of scientific inquiry, and then how these elements influence the development and scope of policy and regulation. In turn, this foundation of knowledge enables us to better appreciate Chapters 8–10, which are focused on the arena of decision-making in planning, where we outline issues related to the effectiveness of the various decision support tools, and the nuances of the engagement process, before ending with a discussion of the inevitable social justice implications of the final decision. The concluding chapter summarizes the argument thus far and provides wider insights into the nature of contemporary environmental planning. This framework allows us to explore planning issues without being tied to any particular problem, nation or regulatory framework, as it focuses on the principles upon which planning operates and how societies organize themselves. Overall, the approach is designed to answer the 'why' questions, such as the one detailed at the outset.

The originality of this book is not just a matter of the content, but also of its interdisciplinary organization and synthesis, as each chapter develops the discussion progressively, to reflect the weekly demands of an undergraduate or postgraduate environmental planning course. Alternatively, its broad scope means that it is suitable for a variety of teaching and learning contexts, from introductory modules to more advanced theoretical courses. In summary, this book draws on geography, politics, sociology, history and philosophy, and reinterprets these from a planning context. Just as contemporary environmental problems do not mesh well with administrative boundaries, so too does understanding these issues challenge traditional disciplinary silos.

IAIN WHITE

Acknowledgements

There are a number of people who must be thanked for their kindness and support. First, I am grateful to the incredibly capable Dr Angela Connelly, who has provided consistently insightful comments and has proved to be a great sounding board throughout the process. I would also like to thank Professor Michael Hebbert and Dr Paul O'Hare, who have given valuable feedback on individual chapters; and Max Oulton, who drafted the figures. Finally, Stephen Wenham from Palgrave and Professor Yvonne Rydin both provided very constructive comments on the book.

Above all, I would like to thank my family for their incredible support: academics stand on the shoulders of giants in their personal life as well as their professional one.

IAIN WHITE

The author and publishers would like to thank the following who have kindly given permission for the use of copyright material: Taylor & Francis for Figures 1.2 and 8.2, the latter originally published in *Introduction to Environmental Impact Assessment* by J. Glasson, R. Therivel and A. Chadwick (2012), p. 4; Labour Archive (http://www.labourarchive.com/843/) for Figure 2.2; Elsevier Ltd for Figure 6.1; Oxford University Press for Figure 8.1; AICPA (American Institute of Certified Public Accountants) for Figure 9.1; and Cambridge University Press for Table 4.2, originally from Mike Hulme's *Why We Disagree about Climate Change* (2009).

Chapter 1

Introducing Environmental Planning

'We enjoy the fruits of the plains and of the mountains, the rivers and the lakes are ours, we sow corn, we plant trees, we fertilize the soil by irrigation, we confine the rivers and straighten or divert their courses. In fine, by means of our hands we essay to create as it were a second world within the world of nature.'

(Cicero, *De Natura Deorum II*, 45 BC)

The environment is in a constant state of flux: from frequent local changes to global scale variations between glacial ages. As nature operates continuously in this manner, and on such far-reaching geological timeframes, it can seem almost ahistoric, set apart from the ordinary rhythms of daily life. This sweeping scope and self-renewing character can influence perceptions concerning the extent of humanity's ability to enact significant environmental change in the pursuit of short-term economic and social benefit. Yet, pick up any newspaper or watch any news channel and there is a good chance there will be a story connected with the environment, many of them framed in negative or even catastrophic terms. Shrinking ice caps, biodiversity loss or devastating floods serve to remind us that humanity can be both subject to powerful natural events and exert its own potent forces in return. Using land and resources modifies the environment, but the relationship is not just in one direction. This process changes perceptions of the natural environment and can impact upon societies more generally, from the value of goods or services to the loss of lives and livelihoods. An awareness of this cyclical relationship is at the heart of managing the environment: we affect nature just as it affects us.

The interdependency between social and natural systems was recognized by the philosopher and socialist Karl Marx, who argued that nature is: 'man's inorganic body' (1975: 328). Not only does it supply the direct means of life, but since our labour changes the

1

natural world, it also provides the material for human activity. Therefore, in addition to our connectivity, we also have powers to create anew. The Roman philosopher Cicero discussed this point in the opening quote, as did the geographer Neil Smith describing how the ability to exert a transformative force means that societies can produce a 'second nature', a phrase designed to distinguish human changes from the untouched original. With reference to capitalism, Smith (1990: xiv) states: 'capital transforms the shape of the entire world. No God-given stone is left unturned, no original relation with nature is unaltered, no living thing unaffected'.

Contemporary examples are abundant, from geoengineering to genetically modified crops, and it is clear that the way societies operate can have long-lasting effects that can alter systems as well as operate within them. The relationship is therefore a little more complex than a two-way feedback; the fundamental desire to both use and transform also means that environmental systems, which may be considered instinctively to be too large or plenteous to be affected, are firmly within the scope of humanity's power. Nature is therefore both our entire surroundings and a human construction; and as such we should take care in how we interact with it.

People may feel more intuitively linked to 'human' problems than 'environmental' ones, but there are intrinsic connections between environmental, social and economic systems. The BP Deepwater Horizon oil spill provides an illustrative case. In 2010, an oil rig explosion killed 11 crew members and ruptured a well-head that released millions of gallons of crude oil into the Gulf of Mexico. This pollution caused a massive loss of marine wildlife, and the battle to control the oil dominated the global news media for weeks. The official White House report into the causes of the incident makes for interesting reading. Inadequate safety practices and cost-cutting decisions were cited as a cause, and the report even suggested that this problem might be systemic within the petroleum industry more generally (National Commission on the BP Deepwater Horizon Oil Spill and Offshore Drilling, 2011). This means that the most high-profile *environmental* issue of recent years had a clear *socio-economic* origin and, in addition to wildlife and biodiversity impacts, it had a great affect on both people's lives and the balance sheets of multinational companies. So the all-too-frequent demarcation of problems as 'environmental' or 'social' or 'economic' is neither helpful nor accurate as the boundaries between these spheres are difficult to distinguish. Therefore, to fully appreciate 'environmental problems' there is a need to understand the societies within which the environment is constructed, valued and managed. The case also demonstrates that while environmental concerns may naturally lead to the discussion of intervention strategies, such as new regulations or policies, to be effective the wider societal context within which the problem is embedded may need to be considered.

The task of environmental planning is to reflect on the relationship between these aspects and to consider environmental impacts alongside the worldviews and the methods of production that help to determine the role and value of land and resources. Environmental planning scholars have tended to engage increasingly with politics and policy; in reality there are opposing arguments, morals and values within any potential issue, and to engender change these distinctive stances need to be understood and addressed. That is not to say that those concerned with environmental planning should focus on targeting policy-makers. Though seductive as a means of exerting influence, it can mean that any intervention may be directed down institutionally agreeable pathways, or the analysis targeted at more easily understood fixes, rather than the complex underpinning structures and processes apparent in the Deepwater Horizon incident. This requirement suggests a strong link between what some may have initially considered to be distinct topics: the *environment, planning, politics* and *policy* – an aspect this book is designed to address. In short, to conduct successful environmental planning necessitates an understanding not just of an impact, but also of an awareness of why this has happened, what mechanisms are available to elicit change, and how these can be implemented.

This book essentially concerns the broad topic of environmental planning, an interdisciplinary subject encompassing aspects of the natural and social sciences. It has relevance within a host of discrete subjects, from environmental studies to sociology, and to geography, but is aimed most directly at a planning audience. I would urge readers to resist donning any disciplinary straitjacket or studying aspects in strict isolation, however. As we shall learn, the complexity of many environmental issues reinforces the need for a subtle erosion of knowledge and expertise silos, with issues integrated within societies more generally and how the 'environment' may be perceived. I would therefore encourage at least some small engagement with disciplines outside your chosen field or specialism. Consequently, this book will deliberately encompass a wider array of literature than might be expected within a typical environmental planning text, touching on aspects such as history, geography, politics and sociology, as well as more mainstream planning and environmental management. There are two key messages running through this book: environmental problems are also social ones; and that to have effective environmental planning you need to consider broader questions, such as how we live and how decisions are made. Let us now begin to investigate this fascinating subject in more depth by looking at the importance of the discipline, its inherent complexities, and how difficult it can be to intervene effectively.

The importance of environmental planning

You can easily devote entire books to discussing the various meanings and applicability of the term 'environment' without achieving a firm consensus, or indeed, any substantial pedagogical value. Equally 'planning' can find itself subject to lengthy discussion about precisely what it should encompass, or is frequently pigeonholed lazily as something procedural or bureaucratic that only 'planners' do. In practice, both terms can be defined from a narrow managerial or regulatory perspective, as perhaps a rule to be applied or a law adhered to, but it is when they are considered alongside wider social and economic systems that the terms really come alive.

Here, we sidestep the temptation to become bogged down in the entangled ontology of unequivocal definitions and instead provide a simple answer that encompasses what this book aims to cover. While environmental planning is a hybrid of two separate terms, together they are: 'concerned with society's collective stewardship of the Earth's resources' (Selman, 2000: 1). And it is related to these general principles of informed spatial intervention over time that this book is positioned. There are critical questions that fundamentally influence any engagement with this topic regardless of *where* you are in the world or even *when* you may be reading the book: how is 'the environment' understood? How are these frames of reference interpreted? And how does this lead to judgements, from moral ones to aesthetic, to economic? This book will focus on the contexts, principles and complexity that will gradually give environmental planning more colour and meaning. In this sense, the words environment and planning are framing devices that provide the focus of discussion: in short, they are the lens as well as the subject.

In addition to its encompassing scope, the scale of environmental planning is also noteworthy. As knowledge concerning the extensive influence of human activity has changed over time, so have the requirements for the subject to be conducted across different administrative or political boundaries: from what were initially very local issues to what are now major international concerns. However, this brings new difficulties in gaining political agreement on both possible strategies and the spatial distribution and scale of any threat. To some, particularly those connected with the climate change agenda, we may be in an 'age of crisis', where catastrophe is only a few decades away, yet on the other side of the coin, we have powerful short-term concerns about the impact that any remedial measures might have on economies. In reality, most environmental issues are subject to similarly competing viewpoints and a key aim of the book will be to help readers to understand and navigate these.

The argument that environmental regulation or protection may be a barrier to economic growth is well understood; it is a pervasive message of the political and policy spheres and a common discussion in the media throughout the world. As such, environmental planning is often subject to attack and there are frequent calls for its power to be reduced or altered. Yet its contribution to society is immense. The easiest way to appreciate the value of environmental planning is to consider what would happen in its absence. Think about your local neighbourhood or city and reflect on how space and resources would be utilized differently, or how businesses may operate. Green spaces may be built on, buildings constructed to a cheaper standard, watercourses polluted, or cities would operate without the necessary strategic planning to make the whole function more effectively. Now think about the effect, from neighbourly disputes resulting from insensitive house extensions to unchecked urban sprawl, to the degradation of the global commons.

It is also illustrative to consider, when reflecting on these debates, who would *benefit* from an absence of planning. Would it be you, or another group? Would it be a multinational corporation with little concern for local well-being, or perhaps a company that makes money from exploiting environmental resources? In this sense, planning may stake a strong claim to be a 'public good' – one of those rare mechanisms whose existence can benefit society as a whole. It is more than merely an ability to control development in the present, however; the inherent potential to plan for the future can bring social benefits for generations, as may be seen in the formation of the garden city movement, the establishment of national parks, or the creation of valued civic spaces in any city in the world. Taking a step back and considering this larger perspective, the entire rationale for the planning system may be considered to be a way to prevent the worst excesses of capitalism and its systemic desire for cheap land, low costs and maximum profit.

A final aspect of note with regard to the subject of environmental planning is that it is inevitably a growing concern; in the twenty-first century there will be more pressures on the natural world and a greater need to plan places and spaces that effectively consider the natural and built environments while enabling increases to the quality of life for humankind. There will be more people, more urbanization, an ever-increasing demand for resources, and new pressures on the natural environment. There will also be more knowledge than ever before on the impact of humanity on the planet and a need to balance this with the requirement for growth to proceed and standards of living to rise. The connection between nature and humanity over differing scales means that environmental planning is also a complex subject that argues against a reductionist and fragmented approach. With this in mind, the next section will introduce some of the bigger environmental planning problems, and demonstrate how they are integrated.

The complexity of environmental planning

One of the reasons why humanity has the potential to transform the environment to a degree never previously seen is the sheer number of people on the planet. We shall use this fundamental aspect to trace how impacts occur and how they, in turn, lead to other environmental issues, and so on. Understanding this connectivity is at the heart of successful environmental planning.

During the vast proportion of human history the global population has been estimated to be less than a few million people. Among other factors, this total was constrained by the limited availability of basic resources, poor health and welfare provision, a lack of technological advancement, and local environmental constraints, most notably the restricted supply of energy (Mumford, 1961). The past few centuries have seen an explosion of progress in all of these areas and, as a result, a steep upward trend in global population. At the start of the twentieth century the number of

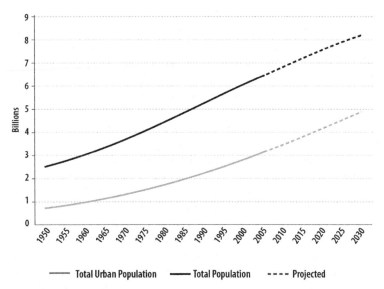

Figure 1.1 *World population change*
Source: Adapted from United Nations (2011).

people in the world was estimated to be 1.65 billion. This figure has since increased dramatically, and by 2012 the Earth's population was estimated to be around 7 billion. The number of people on the planet has doubled in the last 40 years and this growth is expected to continue over the coming decades. Dependent on factors such as fertility, the total global population is predicted to be around 9.3 billion by 2050 (United Nations, 2011) (see Figure 1.1).

These people will all have an impact. They build settlements and roads, consume natural resources and require water and land for crops. This means that the extent of the reach of humanity on the Earth's surface is also expanding. It is estimated that over 75 per cent of the ice-free land area can no longer be considered wild (Ellis and Ramankutty, 2008) with the pace of change accelerating alongside population increases. Compare the heavily forested sight of Manhattan that Henry Hudson might have seen as he sailed into the natural harbour in 1609 with the presentday configuration of New York City, and take a moment to reflect on the enormous ecological changes that have been wrought in the equivalent of an eyeblink in geological time. The virgin land has been transformed beyond all recognition: the soil has been levelled, the ponds drained, the trees chopped down, and biodiversity largely eradicated. Then think about what has been created; indisputably one of the greatest cities in the world, and one with an amazing social and cultural richness. The exercise also serves to illustrate that land use change is not necessarily 'bad', since benefits may accrue alongside costs. It is the nature of environmental planning to navigate this tricky juncture.

The discussion over the number of people and their demand for resources logically leads to related environmental planning issues, such as population density. The term 'sprawl' (later called 'urban sprawl') was first used in 1937 by an early planner in the USA to describe the flight of the affluent from the industrial city to more desirable surroundings (Black, 1996). While early cities needed people and industries to be located nearby, advances in fields from energy to infrastructure to technology gradually extended this distance, with daily commutes or remote working now a common feature of modernity. Reflecting on the nature of sprawl over the twentieth century we can also start to appreciate cultural differences in the use of land. For example, density levels in Europe or Asia tend to be much higher than in countries such as the USA, Australia or Canada, related to aspects such as land availability and value, cultural norms and planning constraints. In addition to the social and economic impacts of this trend – from inequality to social homogeneity, to higher financial costs for infrastructure – the environmental effects are also significant, not least with regard to pollution, habitat fragmentation and reducing the viability of public transport options.

Considering this factor also allows us to turn the discussion to the next related issue: energy. Land use is very static; uses do not tend to change much over time and can serve to 'lock' trajectories of behaviour decades into the future (Guy *et al.*, 2011). A low density model of living relies on the cheap availability of power to function effectively, which is fine for the fossil-fuel-rich late twentieth and early twenty-first centuries. However, world energy consumption is predicted to grow by 56 per cent between 2010 and 2040, and during this time around 80 per cent of energy will be derived from fossil fuels (US Energy Information Administration, 2013). Regardless of the environmental impacts of extraction, production and consumption, what will be the results of this model from a socio-economic perspective as the price of these fuels rises inexorably because of limited supplies and higher demand associated with the rapid industrialization of countries such as India or

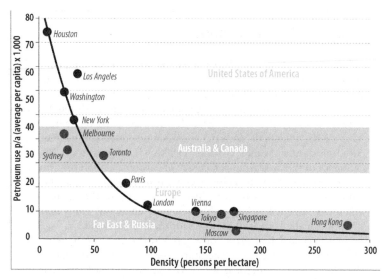

Figure 1.2 *Gasoline use per capita and population density*
Source: Newman and Kenworthy (1989).

China? Figure 1.2 explores this spatial and temporal aspect by linking land use patterns with gasoline use. Here, you can imagine how
historic decisions on ways to use land may result in citizens in
certain countries paying significant amounts of money to move
around for many decades into the future.

The use of fossil fuels is also central to managing what is possibly the most critical environmental issue of our time: climate
change. It is argued that carbon dioxide (CO_2) emissions need to
be strictly limited to keep the increase in temperature to less than
two degrees Celsius, at which point dangerous changes are
projected to occur (United Nations, 2009). The impacts on the
environment from climate change may be significant and encompassing, from species extinction to ocean acidification to biodiversity loss. Yet humanity is so dependent on fossil fuels for energy,
and international negotiations do not appear to be making significant political progress. Environmental planning has a dual role
here, both in limiting emissions by thinking about architecture,
travel or energy use, and enabling adaptation to manage the effects
of a changing climate. Box 1.1 provides a small case study of the
development of this particular environmental planning problem.

This small section raises a number of environmental planning
concerns that are individually pressing, but collectively compelling.

Box 1.1 Climate change

While climate change can be presented as an intensely complex and disputed topic, at its heart this is an uncontroversial science, and the basic physics of the effect of greenhouse gases in the atmosphere have been established for a surprisingly long time. Although the degree to which this should be welcomed has hardened since the start of the twentieth century, as this quote from the pioneering Swedish scientist, Svante Arrhenius (1908: 63) demonstrates: 'By the influence of the increasing percentage of carbonic acid in the atmosphere, we may hope to enjoy ages with more equable and better climates, especially as regards the colder regions of the earth, ages when the earth will bring forth much more abundant crops than at present, for the benefit of rapidly propagating mankind.'

It is accepted that greenhouse gases warm the planet, without which we would have a temperature closer to that of the moon or the planet Mars. Indeed, it was way back in the early nineteenth century that the principle of the greenhouse effect, whereby the Earth's atmosphere acts as an insulator, was discovered by Joseph Fourier (1768–1830). Physicist John Tyndall (1820–93) further established that CO_2 was a 'greenhouse gas'. The next step was to investigate more deeply the relationship of the gas to temperature, and in the early twentieth century scientists, most notably the chemist Svante Arrhenius, argued that if CO_2 content changed, so could temperature, calculating that a doubling of CO_2 would lead to an increase of between 1.5°C and 4.5°C. In the 1930s a British engineer, Guy Callendar (1938: 223), further developed this argument by presenting evidence that the burning of fossil fuels can increase the concentration of atmospheric CO_2, which in turn can warm the Earth. He started a seminal article with the striking words: 'Few of those familiar with the natural heat exchanges of the atmosphere, which go into the making of our climates and weather, would be prepared to admit that the activities of man could have any influence upon phenomena of so vast a scale. In the following paper I hope to show that such influence is not only possible, but is actually happening at the present time.'

In 1956, a *Time* magazine story entitled 'Science: One Big Greenhouse' discussed global warming and interviewed Roger Revelle, one of the leading scholars of the emerging science of climate change. The article argued that the rise in temperature could not only have damaging impacts, such as the melting of ice caps and flooding of coastal cities, but warming may produce further climate forcing within the system. Despite the seemingly catastrophic

→

→

content, the article struck a conservative, neutral tone, with the scientist going on to state that he will keep watching and recording to observe whether: 'man's factory chimneys and auto exhausts will eventually cause salt water to flow in the streets of New York and London' (Roberts, 1956).

This may now be an opportune moment to reflect on the science of climate change and its operationalization within environmental planning. If there has been evidence for well over 50 years that increasing CO_2 levels from burning fossil fuels can cause global warming, and that this can lead to dangerous secondary effects that may be difficult to reverse, why haven't societies acted? Why does climate change appear to be so contemporary; an arch-twenty-first century problem with such high-profile antagonism? Despite the perceived certainty of the basic tenets of climate science, it is important to note that science does not operate in a vacuum; it is intertwined with economics and politics – and the relationship between these aspects can be murky and contested. For example, while you may assume there is a trend towards evidence-based policy, with scientific research used objectively to provide a clear rationale for public policy change, in cases where the data has potentially significant effects on economic and social norms, information can be ignored or appropriated selectively to support political ideologies or long-held worldviews. This issue will be discussed in more depth in Chapter 4.

The disagreement essentially comes down to *one* key issue with which scientists are still grappling, and may not even establish in the foreseeable future: the precise extent to which humans are forcing the climate, essentially creating the 'second nature' introduced at the start of the chapter. And the reason why this is relevant is because it influences how societies respond politically, with potentially far-reaching consequences. Imagine, for example, the effect of altering taxation regimes in a country to make fossil fuels more expensive, and the concomitant impact on productivity or energy costs. However, if one nation acts alone there is a possibility that business and capital will simply move to other countries where there may be lower burdens on industry. This emphasizes the need for global agreements, but these require strong arguments and if we wait for absolute proof then the impacts may be impossible to prevent or already be widely experienced. In this sense, climate change science has become politicized, which is a critical point to bear in mind when considering how similar issues are discussed in environmental planning.

The world is becoming increasingly interconnected, and just as the actions of one nation can affect another, the impact of a single global trend – in this case that of population growth – can have wide consequences for energy requirements, resource use, food production, deforestation or space for crops and living. Contemporary civilization is centred on the consumption of resources and production of waste, a practice that is exaggerated in more advanced cities. As the rise in urbanization is predicted to be concentrated in less developed countries that understandably want to replicate the consumption-intensive lifestyles enjoyed in affluent countries, this will create a huge demand for effective environmental planning.

This discussion shows that environmental planning is far more than a narrow focus on regulation or policy. Reading this section, the description of these impacts and their possible long-term effect on people and the environment may seem very persuasive. If this is the case, then why does significant action seem not to occur? This is where the political and policy angles become really interesting and relevant. This argument also highlights how this subject is interwoven with variable spatial and temporal dimensions, a challenging perspective to accept. Fundamentally, environmental planning concerns how we use *space* over *time* – to live on this planet is to affect it: societies need to develop on land and consume resources, and there will be impacts from this, but where, who or what is affected, and to what extent? To develop this point further we shall now briefly explore how environmental challenges may be prioritized differently between people and places.

Ascertaining environmental "priorities"

'The warnings about global warming have been extremely clear for a long time. We are facing a global climate crisis. It is deepening. We are entering a period of consequences.'

(Al Gore, 2005)

'With all the hysteria, all the fear, all the phony science, could it be that manmade global warming is the greatest hoax ever perpetrated on the American people? I believe it is.'

(United States Senator James Inhofe, 2003)

Carrying forward the climate change example from earlier in this chapter, it is clear that the topic has received a great deal of attention, particularly in the USA, a country perceived to be critical to the success of any global initiatives. However, it is also where those in public office hold particularly fervent and polarized views: for example, former Democrat vice-president, Al Gore, became the focus for the film 'An Inconvenient Truth' and received the Nobel Peace Prize for his efforts in disseminating knowledge about man-made climate change. Meanwhile, his Republican counterpart, Senator Inhofe, made his well-known 'hoax' remark while chairman of the influential Senate Select Committee on Environment and Public Works. Widely divergent opinions such as these are common-place when discussing issues connected with environmental plan-ning. Disagreement is not only limited to the importance or value of individual concerns, but also between the severity of competing environmental issues and those who argue for a policy focus on economic or social priorities instead. We shall now investigate this matter by looking at that initial step for most environmental plan-ning activities: establishing the nature and severity of the issue to be addressed, whether it is a global concern, the protection of a much loved local space, or even a threat that has yet to materialize.

Imagine you are in charge of your country and have the power to set the agenda regarding what should be the top environmental concerns. Quite quickly you should appreciate the difficulties in assigning priorities; readers from differing cultural backgrounds may find themselves caught among a host of contending issues such as biodiversity, climate change, urban sprawl or even overfishing. They all seem to be very important, but in a world of competing priorities, 'beauty' may well exist in the eye of the beholder and problems can change over time as new evidence emerges. To help illustrate this argument, let us now turn to the 'answer' to our exer-cise, the top environmental priorities of selected countries and agencies at local, national and global levels.

Reflecting on a selection of publications designed to provide a geographical and scalar contrast, from the United Nations (UNEP 2012), China (Ministry of Environmental Protection of the People's Republic of China 2011), the UK (Environment Agency 2000), the USA (United States Environmental Protection Agency 2010) and Glasgow City Council (2010) in Scotland there are a few noticeable factors. First, not only is there no consensus, but it is illuminating to reflect on which issues may be missing, and why. For example, climate change is not mentioned as a priority in China, which is consistent with their 'economy first' stance in international discus-sions on this topic (Dimitrov 2010). In addition, priorities are framed very differently: some are thematic, such as those pertaining to water and air, while others, such as health and well-being, are cross-cutting. However, there is less difference over scale than you might expect, with, for example, Glasgow City Council and the United Nations both identifying energy as a key consideration. There are some spatial and cultural aspects noticeable, with China being concerned about pollution, a growing problem in that nation, while the UK's Environment Agency aims to reduce the risk of flooding, which occurs frequently in Britain. The data also demonstrates that the way we have governed the environment shapes intervention; for example, the distinctive institutional remit of agencies appears to play a key role with both the US Environmental Protection Agency and the UK Environment Agency both designing agendas directly aligned to their specific political mandates. In this regard, every agency might have its own environmental priorities, from local councils, to the EU, to a non-governmental organization (NGO) or pressure group.

Moving from the priorities of decisionmakers to those of the public, we can see similar complexities are at play. In February 2011, a survey was conducted of over 18,675 adults in 24 countries. Respondents were asked: 'In your view, what are the three most important environmental issues facing your country today?' Table 1.1 details the results of five of those countries: the UK, the USA, China, Russia and Brazil.

Reflecting on this data we can see that environmental concerns differ spatially, temporally and culturally – or, more succinctly, it depends where, when and of whom you ask the question. For example, with regard to Brazil and China it may be expected that deforestation and air pollution would be their top selections, because at the start of the twenty-first century they are high profile issues in those nations. However, there are still common concerns that have stretched beyond the nation state perspective towards what we may call environmental citizenship, in particular, climate change and dealing with the amount of waste generated. The link to economic output and standards of living is a further factor: future energy supplies and depletion of natural resources both scored highly as environmental concerns, but could also be classified as strong economic issues. This supports the argument that fears of economic impacts can mobilize political support for environmental intervention.

When a particular issue is strongly aligned with public opinion, as reported by polls or gleaned from political focus groups, there is

Table 1.1 *Public surveys of the most important environmental issues*

Country	Top-ranking issue and percentage	Second-ranking issue and percentage	Third-ranking issue and percentage
Brazil	Deforestation (53%)	Global climate change (42%)	Water pollution (40%)
China	Air pollution (41%)	Reducing waste (37%)	Depletion of natural resources (31%)
Russia	Deforestation (42%)	Emissions (42%)	Air pollution (38%)
UK	Energy sources and supplies (50%)	Reducing waste (48%)	Overpopulation (41%)
USA	Depletion of natural resources (50%)	Energy sources and supplies (50%)	Reducing waste (41%)

Source: Ipsos MORI (2011).

a good chance that it may achieve saliency and command the attention of politicians. For example, there are often short-term spikes in interest after a major disaster permeates the news cycle, which sometimes crowd out other, less spectacular, concerns. Yet, even the results of polls themselves can influence public opinion, as they not only passively relay findings, but can also be used or reported in such a way as to influence other members of the public as well as politicians. Indeed, that is a reason why some polls are carried out, most notably those by news organizations. However, if legislature attention is drawn to a specific concern, this usually means that focus is being drawn away from another. So, if public opinion is given too much emphasis during policy-making, it runs the risk of making the process seem a fleeting, reactionary pursuit punctuated by quick fixes and staccato agenda shifting. Box 1.2 deepens the discussion of environmental problems to include a consideration of those wider societal pressures that may underpin their existence, as was apparent in the Deepwater Horizon example cited earlier in the chapter.

Given the importance of gaining agreement and mobilizing the political will to address many environmental challenges, the complexities apparent within the early stage of identifying targets and priorities make environmental planning challenging in practice. It is not just a matter of experiencing problems and then working

16

Box 1.2 Societal pressures

'Many women who do not dress modestly ... lead young men astray, corrupt their chastity and spread adultery in society, which increases earthquakes' (Hojjatol-eslam Kazem Sediqi). This quote is from an Iranian cleric, who argued that the real reason why Iran suffered an earthquake in 2003 was not because of any natural movement of the Earth's plates but was because of women wearing revealing clothing (*The Guardian*, 2010). Similar observations have been made regarding many natural disasters throughout history. One Church of England bishop claimed that the 2007 UK floods were caused by 'moral decadence' (Wynne-Jones, 2007), while a US state senator blamed the prevalence of 'gambling, sin and wickedness' for bringing God's judgement to bear on New Orleans via Hurricane Katrina (ABC News, 2005). In the more distant past, the philosopher Voltaire even criticized God for causing the 1755 Lisbon earthquake (Glacken, 1967). While these examples are extreme, they demonstrate a disconnect between cause and effect; a division that provides a real challenge for environmental planning.

We have just seen how the existence, severity and priority of environmental problems is subjective and contested, and we now build on that debate by exploring how similar uncertainties are visible when ascertaining those aspects of everyday life and society more generally that place the environment under pressure. These can include any relevant factor, from the number of people on the planet and how they behave, to the use and preference for certain types of energy or transportation. To take the example of the UK, research in this field reveals some interesting findings. With regard to the singular risk of flooding, 23 *societal* aspects were highlighted that could have an impact on the future ability to manage this *environmental* risk, such as urbanization and public attitudes (Evans *et al.*, 2004). More generally, the UK Environment Agency (2006) identified 51 broad drivers and prioritized 19 that they considered would place the most significant pressure on the environment up to the year 2030. To give an idea of the nature, scope and scale of key societal pressures, these critical issues were:

1. A rise in global population.
2. Globalization.
3. The uncertain future of international governance.

→

→

4. The future of Europe.
5. The changing nature of environmental legislation.
6. Increasing consumer environmental awareness.
7. The role of self-interest in responding to climate change.
8. A consumption culture.
9. The rise of personal mobility.
10. Increased focus on well-being.
11. Changing household arrangements.
12. GRIN (Genetics, Robotics, IT and Nanotechnology technologies).
13. Developing and implementing environmental technologies.
14. Increased pressure on public spending.
15. Increasingly stressed infrastructure.
16. Changing patterns of land use and food production.
17. Climate change and social response.
18. Resource-constrained growth.
19. Increasing scientific understanding of systems that underpin ecological change.

The first element to note is that these forces are almost entirely anthropogenic and therefore, in theory, we have the ability to change them. It should also be recognized that not all societal pressures damage the environment: new technologies, increasing education or changes in consumption patterns are trends that can exert a positive effect. The text in this box does, however, reveal how difficult it can be to place boundaries around aspects that put pressure on the environment: from how many should be selected, to their scale, or their relationship with politics, economics or society. They also interact and are dynamic, making it difficult to isolate issues or extrapolate influence precisely.

Significantly, when we reflect on their cross-cutting qualities, it is apparent that they do not map on to existing remits and influence of existing environmental agencies, which may be organized thematically, such as improving water quality or forestry, or with a focus on managing the impacts, such as through promoting agricultural best practice. This means that the institutions designed to *manage* the environment may have very little influence over the *forces* that cause environmental pressures, as these are embedded in society more generally. Instead, they are more suited to addressing the impacts of change and attempting to lobby where possible to influence elements such as the pressure on public spending.

rationally towards a solution; in reality, each concern is constructed and propelled into a vibrant political environment that may raise or lower priorities in a continuous manner. And all the time the societal pressures that drive problems remain tantalizingly out of reach of environmental agencies, which commonly tend to have much narrower remits. Consequently, environmental planning is not just a matter of using sound science to identify what to target. It is also influenced by the political sphere, public opinion and general societal pressures. This will inevitably lead to considerations such as the ability to make a difference, and at what cost. Do we address all aspects, or just the 'easier' ones that may be clear, quick and cheap? Connected with this is the need for reliable data, which is important both to pushing one specific concern over another and in designing indicators to measure progress, an aspect discussed further in Chapter 8. Finally, we should ask how many priorities there ought to be: five, seven or nine? Why stop there? Clearly, resources and finance also have a significant influence, which muddies the water even further.

Environmental concerns are therefore highly political and subjective; not just with regard to what is selected but even what is defined as current, emerging or able to be quantified as an efficient use of financial resources.

Conclusion

> 'Climate change is not "a problem" waiting for "a solution". It is an environmental, cultural and political phenomenon which is reshaping the way we think about ourselves, our societies and humanity's place on Earth.'
>
> (Hulme, 2009: v)

We frequently talk about the environment as being a 'problem' – whether it is a problem of climate change, air quality or biodiversity loss. When the discussion inevitably turns to what should be done, the criticality and severity of the issue automatically comes to the fore. And this chapter has deliberately followed this view until now. As the opening quote concerning climate change highlights, while almost any environmental concern can be thought of as a problem, this terminology is value laden, as it essentially packages climate change as an issue that not only requires 'solving' but can actually be 'solved'. Many simple and local environmental issues can perhaps be prevented by a simple technical outcome. However, this binary characterization can be simplistic and unhelpful as it ignores the wider social, economic and cultural processes that influence the way that the environment is perceived and comes under pressure.

This introductory chapter is designed to emphasize that the environment and our societies can be understood in many different ways: spatially, temporally and culturally. It also highlights that environmental planning is well-suited to reductionism, where a gamut of interconnected issues can be broken down into manageable parts, but this is both a strength and a weakness. While it shows synergies with the political tendency to allocate responsibility to specific agencies, it can inhibit a wider appreciation of the nature of problems and their links to societal pressures that serve to make the topic more interesting and valuable. The chapter posits that the key to effective environmental planning is not just about appreciating both people and places, but also involves a knowledge of the broad forces, practices and philosophies that influence how environmental concerns are managed. As a result, we shall take a wide view of the factors that both place pressure on the environment and affect the ability to intervene effectively.

Having provided an overview of environmental planning, it is now an opportune time to introduce the scope of the book, its style and its structure. The discussion so far has established that environmental planning is much more than a focus on the nuances of policy X within country Y, as the societal context within which these are framed, developed and operationalized exerts a significant influence on their ability to be effective. As such, the content is organized to explore the nested scales within which environmental planning debates tend to occur: wider society and politics, the process of policy-making, and within the practices of planning itself. In short, the book aims to foster a deeper appreciation of the nature of the reality within which planning takes place.

The text is designed so that each successive chapter builds on the previous material to provide readers with an increasingly sophisticated understanding of the theory and practice of planning. It begins with three chapters focusing on the broader milieu of environmental planning. The first of these (Chapter 2), 'The Intellectual Legacies', provides a foundation for understanding the subject in more depth by providing a historical overview of the developing interactions between humanity and the environment, and the dominant ways of thinking that both pull us closer together and drive us apart. Present-day issues begin by examining broad societal factors within chapters on 'Governance and Power' (Chapter 3) and 'Politics and the Media' (Chapter 4), both of which emphasize their ability to exert influence over a host of subsequent debates, from the focus of science to the scope of regulation. Understanding these key societal frames allows a fuller understanding of the discussion contained within the following three chapters. These unpack the process of public policy intervention, initially exploring the pathways of logic inherent in the selection of 'Framing Concepts' (Chapter 5), before examining the constraints associated with the nature of scientific inquiry in 'The Role of Science' (Chapter 6), and how these elements subsequently influence the development and scope of 'Policy and Regulation' (Chapter 7). In turn, this foundation of knowledge enables us to better appreciate the final three chapters, focused on the arena of decision-making in planning, where we outline issues related to the effectiveness of 'Decision Support Tools' (Chapter 8) and the nuances of 'Engaging with Stakeholders' (Chapter 9), before ending with a discussion of 'The Question of Justice' (Chapter 10) regarding the implications of the final decision. This framework allows us to explore the context of planning issues without being tied to any particular problem, nation or regulatory framework, as it focuses on the principles on which planning operates and how societies organize themselves.

The originality of this book is not just a matter of the content, but also of its interdisciplinary organization and synthesis, as each chapter develops the discussion progressively to reflect the weekly demands of an undergraduate or postgraduate environmental planning course. Alternatively, its broad scope means that it is suitable for a variety of teaching and learning contexts, from introductory modules to more advanced theoretical courses. In summary, the book draws on geography, politics, sociology, history and philosophy, and reinterprets these fields within a planning context. Just as contemporary environmental problems do not mesh well with administrative boundaries, so too does the understanding of these issues challenge traditional disciplinary silos.

All too often the environment is seen as a contemporary problem, with the onus on examining the impacts on the present time. Chapter 2 should provide a check against falling back on short-term answers, as we shall see how an appreciation of the past, and the intellectual legacies of previous centuries, inescapably hold relevance for the future. And it is with a clearer view of a collective future that any discussion of environmental planning is inextricably linked.

Chapter 2

The Intellectual Legacies

'Like a stranger that has blown into town, ecology seems a presence without a past. Before committing ourselves too firmly to its tutelage, however, we might do some digging into its previous life – not in the expectation of uncovering grisly deeds, but simply that we may know our teacher better.'

(Worster, 1977, ix)

This chapter provides a deeper insight into how the environment has been understood and engaged with over space and time. It does this for a number of reasons. First, while it may be tempting to pigeonhole this part of the book as the 'history' section, I'd urge you to resist this. As the opening quote emphasizes, while a number of aspects will inevitably have a museum-like quality, others will contain underlying truths still whispered on the breeze that serve to shed light on current problems. The primacy of science, the dualistic separation of human and natural environments, and the engagement with technological solutions all have their roots in history; critically, therefore, this chapter will help to foster a more sophisticated understanding of *contemporary* environmental issues, many of which have a legacy that stems from long-standing worldviews and frames of reference.

Second, changes in social history have altered not only the relationship to the natural world but also created new environmental concerns. So the boundaries between social and environmental developments are blurred, and appreciating these links brings a valuable integrated perspective. Contextual histories such as this stress the importance of paying attention to the *reasons* for environmental pressures, which are the product of social, economic or cultural factors far removed from a simple understanding of site-based impacts or specific regulations that can occupy many concerned with environmental planning.

The history of Western environmental thought has recurring themes that authors have used to provide a degree of organizational

21

clarity to help navigate the past 2,000 years or so. Some authors take a thematic stance: for example, highlighting the critical role of technology (Stine and Tarr, 1998) or agriculture (Crosby, 1995) in shaping socio-environmental relationships. This book adopts a slightly different approach. Cronon (1993) suggested that attempts to categorize environmental history either focus on changing relationships between societies and the natural world, or they consider culture and how this influences interactions with the environment. Hughes (2006) similarly argued that the key elements are the influence of the environment on humans and vice versa, and the history of human thought as it relates to these aspects. By including both an appreciation of impacts and a more critical view of the thinking that drives such practices, a deeper appreciation of both the *what* and the *why* is fostered. This perspective acknowledges that it is essential to recognize the driving forces that are critical in causing and exacerbating problems – without which measures have a tendency to drift towards 'sticking plaster' or 'end of pipe' solutions. This chapter can be viewed as running in a loose chronological manner, where for example, the emergence of the strong reliance on technological solutions can be better appreciated when attention is paid to parallel advances in scientific thought.

Environmental impacts are an inevitable feature of human society: to interact with the environment is to change it, and the first half of the chapter emphasizes this *connection*: from the reasons for environmental pressures; from resources to economics to cultural issues; and the measures taken to manage changing relationships. It will first investigate the beginnings of environmental concerns and reveal how our understanding of the biosphere developed as humans explored and exploited resources. We shall tackle the onset on the industrial age, with its burgeoning discoveries of new lands, new technologies and new ways of living. Finally, we shall focus on the increased awareness of the interdependencies, feedbacks and societal impacts that are feature of modernity. Together these issues will reveal the gradual increase in impacts towards the multi-scalar effects familiar in the present day. The second half of the chapter will explore the key advances in thought that influenced these relationships. It is within these frames of deed and thought that we shall then follow the advice of Worster (1977: ix) and begin to uncover the past of this 'stranger blown into town'.

The history of environmental planning

Common misconceptions regarding environmental concern are that either it began as a reaction to the visible impacts and pollution of the Industrial Revolution or it is a political response deriving from the growing awareness since the 1960s of the environmental impacts of humanity. The reality is a little different. Early cave paintings, for example, demonstrate an ongoing, symbiotic affinity with nature, while the Greek philosopher and polymath, Aristotle (384–322 BC), may rightly be described as the father of natural history. He was awarded a grant of 800 talents of silver (worth around US$15m in 2014) by his former pupil, Alexander the Great, to enable him (1965 [350 BC]) to compile his classic text *Historia Animalium*, the first attempt to observe, record and interpret the natural world. A fact Aristotle was all too aware of, as he stated in the introduction: 'I found no basis prepared; no models to copy. Mine is the first step, and therefore a small one, though worked out with much thought and hard labour. It must be looked at as a first step and judged with indulgence.' His contribution includes advances in taxonomy and his rational proto-scientific approach was the forerunner of Francis Bacon's scientific method. This humble quote reveals more than his pioneering status; it also emphasizes that new scientific knowledge is generated continuously. In a sense we shall always be standing on the shoulders of giants.

Texts from the distant past also display evidence of the long-standing nature of certain aspects of environmental concern. The availability of resources and the development of technology to access and exploit them were just as critical to prosperity as they are in the present, and the results of mining and deforestation provided the seeds of the first environmental concerns. Fears of soil erosion and deforestation were present in Classical Greece, Imperial Rome and Mauryan India (Grove 1995). For example, in *Critias*, Plato (429–347 BC) evocatively compares the land after deforestation and the resulting soil erosion as being like a body wasted by disease with: 'all the richer and softer parts of the soil having fallen away, and the mere skeleton of the land being left' (2008 [360 BC]). Pliny the Elder (AD 23–79) also spoke out against certain mining practices in his book *Natural History* because of the impact on the environment (2012 [77–79]).

It is no coincidence that Rome, Greece and Asia Minor, home to many of the first cities, should also be at the forefront of examining evidence of environmental changes wrought by civilization. Classical authors also display a concern for nature in tune with much contemporary debate. They tend to focus, for example, on aspects such as amenity and beauty, and express a distaste for 'scars' on landscape – features that have been at the forefront of modern public critique. Equally, as in the present day, economic aspects played an important role and there was evidence of the now familiar tension between these competing priorities. For example, the Roman general Agricola defended the vital role of mining for social and economic purposes, while the Greek historian Thucydides (460–395 BC) drew attention to how crucial natural resources were for projecting power, in this case timber for shipbuilding (Hughes, 2006).

Early measures to mitigate the impacts of change were also evident. After observing the effects of extensive deforestation, the Chinese philosopher Mencius (372–298 BC) highlighted the need for effective stewardship of land, not only arguing for alternative forestry and grazing practices but also suggesting that it should be monitored by the state. Xenophon (430–354 BC), a Greek historian, similarly recorded that, when travelling through his lands, the Persian king would give rewards or reprimands depending upon how effectively land was managed (Hughes, 2009). As in current debates, good management was therefore perceived as being critical not just to avoid environmental degradation, but also to maximize socio-economic benefits.

There was also evidence of early environmental planning on a strategic scale. In Ancient Greece there was an unwillingness to encourage excessive growth, and new colonies were established around the Aegean and Mediterranean to avoid overcrowding. Further, Aristotle's *Politics* (1977 [350 BC]) discusses the size, construction and function of the ideal city state, while the Greek architect, Hippodamus of Miletus (498–408 BC), was reputed to be the first city planner, introducing concepts still in use today, such as grid patterns and land zoning (Jowett, 1977).

These examples demonstrate that the need to manage the environment for the benefit of citizens is not a modern phenomenon, and, as today, it relies on knowledge, both of cause and effect and the potential of any remedial measures. The concerns at this time were characterized by both scale and utility. Indeed, one of the reasons why forestry and mining were at the forefront of environmental discussions is that these visible and local impacts were more noticeable than changes in the soils, atmosphere or ecology. The perceived trade-off between the environment and economy central to much modern debate was also in evidence. In this regard, a philosophy centred on the procurement and usage of resources was a direct function of the economic and political outlook of both the Hellenistic and the Roman periods. As today, effective governance structures is a further factor; it is no coincidence that states with laws, regulations and a means to enforce change were at the forefront of early environmental management.

The debate now skips forward to a fertile period often invoked to illustrate the transformative relationship between humanity and the environment: the onset of the Industrial Revolution, the huge growth of urbanity and the Age of Discovery.

The Age of Discovery

From around the beginning of the sixteenth to the end of the nineteenth centuries, new knowledge ushered in a step change in the relationship between humanity and the environment. There was a growing awareness of the power of human endeavour, exemplified by the ability to travel around the globe, to better understand nature and to transform landscapes fundamentally. In many ways it could be seen as the beginning of a prolonged 'Age of Discovery' – of lands, technologies, philosophies and scientific understanding. But these advances also increased the pressure on the environment: new technologies demanded and consumed resources, and human influence now stretched into lands previously largely untouched. There was also startling economic growth and significant progress in areas such as health, agricultural mechanization and sanitation, all of which served to increase the human population and place further demands on the environment.

The Industrial Revolution began in this period in the UK and spread throughout Europe and beyond. It marks a key shift in the relationship between humanity and the environment, introducing the large-scale use of fossil fuels, a greater consumption of natural resources, and increased pollution and resource depletion. Alterations to the landscape were also now occurring on a larger scale, with rivers diverted for power, reservoirs created and cities expanded.

It can be tempting to see the period of the Industrial Revolution as simply a time of environmental degradation, epitomized vividly in William Blake's poem 'Jerusalem', where England's 'green and pleasant land' contrasted with 'dark Satanic mills' that ruthlessly exploited resources and caused pollution. However, modern environmental protection also has a debt to the fecundity of this era. There was a vast increase in information concerning the natural world and how societies may impact on it. Many countries started to compile data on their own natural environments and there were works that tried to synthesize, compile and organize this new knowledge. Perhaps the most significant development from this perspective was the work of a Swedish botanist, Carl von Linné, more widely known as Linnaeus, who devised a method of plant classification called the 'Systema Naturae'. It formed the foundation of all binomial nomenclature (the process by which Latin names are given to all living things) and created a common taxonomic scientific language that proved critical for gathering evidence concerning the environment across different countries and researchers. Charles Darwin's (1859) *Origin of the Species* also changed our perception of the world and helped to turn ecology into a scientific field in its own right. By placing humanity firmly as being connected to nature rather than separate from it, Darwinism maintained that humanity was not divinely favoured, challenged anthropocentric thinking and became a key influence for later notions of biocentricism.

While this was a time of intensive progress and optimism, it is incorrect to picture a reality where no real thought was given to the consequences. Indeed, there was a strong thread of Victorian pessimism as anxieties concerning faith, morals and the speed of change led to concerns about the future. For example, it was during the nineteenth century that the first conservation groups were established and discussions of 'limits', a perennial environmental issue, began to permeate political discourse. The reaction against deteriorating social conditions also led to some critical thinking about how societies could live differently. Thomas More invented the term 'Utopia' in his book of the same name (1982 [1516]), and philanthropists later began to develop model villages, such as Saltaire and Port Sunlight, while Ebenezer Howard designed the garden city at the start of the twentieth century.

European colonial expansion in Asia, Africa and the Americas brought further developments in understanding human–environment interactions. Not only did explorers such as Captain James Cook help to unveil new landscapes, flora and fauna, but particularly from the discovery of the 'New World' in the eighteenth century, knowledge regarding the ability to influence the environment grew. The pristine nature of the newly explored landscapes essentially provided a huge field laboratory for study. If swathes of forest were cleared it was possible to observe the effect on the climate, soil or drainage. However, the explorers' main concern was generally framed by a managerialist requirement to maximize productivity rather than a purely environmental focus. For example, Pierre Poivre, the French governor of Mauritius in the mid-eighteenth century, noted that extensive deforestation had reduced rainfall vital for crops, and, as a consequence, advised that preservation practices should be introduced (Grove, 1995).

At this juncture it was becoming clear that the extent to which societies impacted on the natural world was becoming the subject of common debate. There is, however, an opposite view that was beginning to gain traction at this time, one where the environment is thought to influence and shape humanity rather than vice versa. The contentious issue of environmental determinism is explored in more depth in Box 2.1.

The examples given in Box 2.1 provide an appropriate point from which to revisit the notion of contextual histories, where behaviour is grounded in a time and place. For example, Worster (1977: 53) suggests that the Linnaean view of classification 'dove-tailed neatly with the needs of the new factory society'. It held synergies with trends in political thought that privileged utilitarian-ism, and information on nature created the potential to exploit as well as preserve. Equally, Darwin's theory was a product of its time and culture; with the role of natural selection reflecting Victorian England's competitive, laissez-faire nature. Practices in the colonies also had a pragmatic resourcist and political perspective: if colonies were unthinkingly deforested, the land would be less productive and local employment would fall, thus making it more difficult to maintain order. Therefore, conservation could be linked to the need to maintain a political regime rather than being an environmental ideology. As Grove (1992: 47) states:

> If a single lesson can be drawn from the early history of conser-
> vation, it is that states will act to prevent environmental degra-
> dation only when their economic interests are shown to be
> directly threatened. Philosophical ideas, science, indigenous
> knowledge and people and species are, unfortunately, not
> enough to precipitate such decisions.

To give an example, the issue of air quality, discussed in more depth in Box 2.2, received early attention because it fitted within these socio-economic parameters.

28

Box 2.1 Environmental determinism

There are natural laws that affect everyone, but a strong emphasis on the formative role of geography and climate rather than human choice in influencing the outlook and behaviour of people has a long, persistent and rather worrying history. This notion of environmental determinism was present in the writings of the classical philosophers, for example in *On Airs, Waters and Places* written around the 4th century BC Hippocrates (460–370 BC) argued that variances in climate, solar exposure and winds influence a host of factors, from the success of cities to fertility rates to individual temperaments (Hippocrates 1881). A view similar to the Roman Pliny (2012 [77–9]), who in his *Natural History* suggested that the people of the cold north are fierce because of the harsh climate, and that temperate areas are inherently more suited for the pursuance of civilization. Further, in his influential fourteenth century text *Muqaddimah*, the Arab scholar Ibn Khaldun (1969 [1377]) ascribed characteristics of peoples to their climatic zones, as did the Italian Giovanni Botero (1956 [1589]) in his sixteenth century book *Reason of State* who, for example, while discussing geographical influences on people suggested that those of the north are bold but lack cunning, while southerners are the opposite.

As travel expanded and colonies were established, the exposure to differing cultures and climates led to a surge in geographical knowledge and a new desire for explanation concerning the huge differences between societies. The US geographer Ellen Churchill Semple (1911: 1) summarized succinctly the belief that human and physical geographers should carry out their studies in unison, stating: 'Man is a product of the earth's surface' and expanded her argument to cover aspects such as the influence of natural barriers and climate. There were counter-arguments however. David Hume (1987 [1742]) critiqued this position in a eighteenth century essay 'Of National Characters' where he argued that determinism based on physical causes does not adequately consider societal, cultural or moral factors, and the US geographer Carl Sauer argued similarly from the 1920s onwards. More recently, Diamond (1997) posited that the differing geographical and environmental factors may even explain why the Eurasian continent became hegemonic over peoples inhabiting other parts of the Earth. For example, the spatial variability in the availability of seeds and animals for domestication created the potential for larger populations and specialization,

→

→

which accelerated the change from hunter-gatherer to agrarian societies and beyond. A similar, but contrasting, view is provided by the theory of cultural determinism, an approach championed from the Romantic period onwards, which argued that it was not the physical environment but rather the culture in which a person was raised that affects their worldview and behaviour. Possessing a similar perspective of geographical causation, but occupying a contrasting cultural standpoint, proponents suggest that nature is a human invention, and that culture determines how individuals might relate to it (Cronon, 1995).

This section provides a good illustration of how seemingly benign views of the environment may influence social beliefs and wider national policies, and therefore be relevant for effective environmental planning. For example, opponents of environmental deterministic views highlight how it can lead to nationalism and racism and may, for example, justify acts of imperialist violence or domination of peoples (Peet, 1985), or serve to justify disadvantage as being an accident of geography rather than the product of powerful social and economic forces (Correia, 2013). The use of geographical ideas in this vein to pursue social policies is also present within notions of colonialism, with, for example, Semple (1911: 21) further arguing that it was people possessing: 'superior qualities of mind and character' who made the voyage overseas, and perhaps more shockingly by Miller (1947: 2), who wrote that 'the enervating monotonous climates of much of the tropical zone, together with the abundant and easily obtained food supply, produces a lazy and indolent people, indisposed to labour for hire and therefore in the past subjected to coercion culminating in slavery'.

These deterministic views display a degree of social Darwinism, drawing on evolution theory to outline how it is believed that humanity might have adapted to conditions, and perhaps more ominously, advocating a survival of the fittest mentality that could be used to explain why some social groupings are superior to others. A controversial topic, environmental determinism faded from its zenith around the start of the twentieth century, becoming replaced by environmental possibilism, rooted in the work of Lucien Febvre in 1925, who held a more recognizably contemporary view emphasizing the role of choice and creativity, where the environment established possibilities for societies – while nature may supply opportunities and constraints, it is humans who hold the ultimate power.

Box 2.2 Air quality

Air quality may seem to be a more contemporary problem, given the association with the use of coal-fired power stations or heavy traffic in dense urban environments. However, its relationship to the production and use of energy, and the need to regulate to control its effects, is surprisingly long-established. The huge expansion of the city of Rome as the empire expanded provides a case in point, as not only did the Roman poet Horace (65–8 BC) complain about air pollution caused by wood-burning fires and copper smelting, but the authorities also allowed civil lawsuits that could help to regulate the effects (Jacobson, 2002). John Evelyn's 'Fumifugium, or the Inconvenience of the Aer and Smoake of London Dissipated', published in 1661, is also a forceful attack on air pollution. It argues:

> The immoderate use of, and indulgence to Sea-coale alone in the city of London, exposes it to one of the fowlest Inconveniences and reproches, that can possibly befall so noble, and otherwise incomparable City ... Whilst they are belching it forth their sooty jaws[sic], the City of London resembles the face rather of Mount Aetna, the Court of Vulcan, Stromboli, or the Suburbs of Hell, than an Assembly of Rational Creatures. (Wall, 1994: 45)

This vivid account is also noteworthy because of its engagement with potential remediation strategies, and in particular the need to change the nature of places to be greener, with an increase in the size and number of public parks, and the relocation of polluting industries (for example, brewers, dyers, lime-burners) outside the core of the city. As a final example demonstrating early knowledge regarding the relationship between air quality and health, in 1731 an English doctor, John Arbuthnot, published 'An Essay Concerning the Effects of Air on Human Bodies', explicitly linking poor air quality with disease and suggesting that cities should adapt to be 'open, airy, and well perflated' (Glacken, 1967: 563).

As the availability of coal gradually replaced wood as the main source of heat and energy, the impacts became more pronounced. In 1898, the Coal Smoke Abatement Society was formed in England as industrialization exerted a more noticeable effect on the surroundings. Smog continued to affect the health of city dwellers, with, for example, 4,000 people dying in London in 1952 from this pollution, which eventually led to the 1956 Clean Air Act. Perhaps surprisingly, given its detrimental effects, the imagery of smoke belching

→

→

Figure 2.1 *'Smoke of chimneys is the breath of Soviet Russia'*
Source: http://commons.wikimedia.org/ wiki/File:Smoke_of_chimneys_is_the_ breath_of_Soviet_Russia.jpg).

Figure 2.2 *'Smoke from chimneys not from guns'*
Source: Labour Archive (2014).

from a chimney can also be used for positive propaganda, a sign of progress and optimism for the future. Karl Marx rallied people to marvel at the industrial age as it would give societies more control over the natural world (Sutton, 2007). Figures 2.1 and 2.2 provide excellent examples of this positive angle, with an early Soviet poster claiming that 'Smoke of chimneys is the breath of Soviet Russia', while a 1935 campaign poster from the British Labour Party gives a comparable economic view of the need to emit 'Smoke from chimneys not from guns'.

These examples highlight a number of important issues. First is the enduring nature of some environmental issues and the need for regulation, with, for example, the first smoke abatement law being passed in England in 1273 prohibiting the use of sea coal. This does, however, rely on the ability to link cause and effect, which was relatively straightforward in earlier times, given the visibility and local effect of air quality. Second, the proximity between the concentration of people and the means of production has historically been a factor; the lack of distance between people and pollution emissions means that Ancient Rome may have experienced similar problems

→

→

to those of modern-day Beijing or Lagos. Third, there is a need to consider the relationship between the natural and the built environments. The zoning of industry and the potential of green infrastructure as a mitigation tool is relatively long-standing, as demonstrated in the earlier example given of John Evelyn, who advocated the principles, if not the terminology, familiar to contemporary environmental planners. Fourth, and most critically, is the inveterate perceived trade-off between the political imperatives to maintain energy supply and increase production and jobs, and the environmental effects. As air pollution becomes less visible and localized, the latter issue is growing in importance, with its management becoming increasingly difficult. This may be seen when considering the burning of fossil fuels – a seemingly twenty-first-century problem but one that can essentially be traced back to the discovery of fire.

The period briefly described here emphasizes how more advanced societies have the potential to leave more significant impacts and the genus of the mode of thinking where environmental resources can be exploited on an industrial scale and traded around the world. Throughout this period an increasing knowledge of the impacts and consequences of change, both spatially and temporally, created the potential for the modern environmental outlook, where, for example, there is a greater focus on understanding *pressures* and the rise of environment as a *political* concern.

Towards modernity

From the nineteenth century onwards, the pressures of population and human activity have become increasingly apparent; this was not just a case of expanding cities or intensified resource extraction but also of the wide-scale settlement of new lands. For example, in North America, the population was spreading westwards, adapting to harsh conditions and, as with colonial expansion, the pristine nature of the new world environments provided a case study of how landscapes can be hugely transformed over a relatively short time. This process of new development also further subtly influenced environmental and social thought. For example, by the second half of the nineteenth century, overhunting and habitat destruction was threatening the existence of the once populous bison on the North American plains. In response, controls on hunting were established and a view of the environment as something to be 'conserved' by regulation began to emerge. It was in the relatively new country of the USA that the roots of conservation as both a social movement and a regulatory authority started to emerge. Here, Yellowstone was established as the world's first National Park in 1872, and the US Forest Service was created as far back as 1905.

While the protection of natural spaces within new administrative boundaries such as these signifies a key development in environmental planning, equally significantly this also marks the rise of an emerging professional class – one equipped with expert knowledge concerning environmental change and a capability and mandate to highlight any impacts. For example, in 1949, the American ecologist and former Forestry Service employee, Aldo Leopold, published 'A Sand Country Almanac'. A skilful blend of natural history and personal philosophy, it still exerts an influence over current environmental movements. Leopold (1949: 262) famously advocated a 'land ethic' – a way to co-exist in a more harmonious way with nature, stating: 'A thing is right when it tends to preserve the integrity, stability, and beauty of the biotic community. It is wrong when it tends otherwise.' He further argued that humans have a responsibility to nature similar to that we should hold for each other, exemplifying the dawn of a more widespread ethical debate that has been present ever since.

Perhaps counter-intuitively, the development of some technologies also helped to foster similar environmentally sensitive views. Alongside rises in education and standards of living, Hays (1982) identifies how the automobile helped to foster a new valuing of protected places by enabling travel to unspoiled wilderness areas. Post-1945 also saw the establishment of National Parks in many countries, and legislation to protect species and regulate impacts was becoming more common. In this sense there was a shift from a slightly narrow 'conservation' emphasis associated with land management, protection or preservation to the more recognizable frameworks in operation today.

So far, we have discussed much about interest in the environment for economic, social or philosophical reasons. A key factor emerging initially from the nineteenth century, and then much more noticeably from the mid-twentieth onwards, was the politicization of the environment. The rise of the professional class, the growth in knowledge concerning the impacts of development, and a desire to conserve important natural environments created the foundation for *environmentalism*, a shift that represented more than a simple adjustment in nomenclature. The 1960s signalled the birth of environmental concern as a distinct social and political movement, able to influence political parties and wider public opinion – an issue that is discussed in more depth in Chapter 4. This period of time may be encapsulated by the publication of Rachel Carson's influential book, 'Silent Spring' (1962), which outlined how the increased use of pesticides was not only having an effect on insects but also on the animals higher up the food chain that feed on them. The title referred to the unpalatable possibility of a spring without birdsong and captured mainstream public opinion on the environment in a more populist manner than ever before, helping to create the political momentum for new regulation.

Whereas the earlier conservation movement had a concern with preservation, the 1960s and 1970s started to shake off this paternalistic view, and wider environmental regulation and proactive management became more commonplace. Further, a burgeoning ecology movement, which differed from the mainstream environmental view as it was more about nature in itself rather than human interaction with it, was questioning the entire basis of socio-environmental relations, and in doing so challenged norms within both the government and the private sector. Research was also starting to engage with more global concerns, such as population (Ehrlich, 1968) or critical resources (Meadows *et al.*, 1972). Many of these took an apocalyptic stance, which not only helped to politicize the environment further but also in some respects served to depict the field as a radical one. As Worster (1977: 355) outlined: 'The discovery of nature's vulnerability came as so great a shock that, for many ... the only appropriate response was talk of revolution.' New phrases such as 'ecopolitics' and 'ecocatastrophe' entered the lexicon, and philosophies challenging the scale and sustainability of many economic practices were mooted (Schumacher, 1973). Perhaps surprisingly for some readers familiar with current environmental planning, at this time ecology was highlighted as a 'subversive subject' as it contested widely held social, political and economic premises (Sears, 1964: 11).

Environmental concerns and their associated politics were now extending on to a global scale. The problems challenged existing administrative and national boundaries and led to what appears to be a more consensual turn, characterized by supra-national discussion, partnership working and new discourses regarding equity – between nations, generations and species. However, the need for widespread agreement prior to action has caused problems in finding an ambitious enough common ground that can address environmental concerns effectively, and create the requisite international political momentum to enact transformative change.

The differences between this period and previous times were in regard to scale, social organization, information and capacity. It also marked the birth of the political era, and it is noteworthy that the initial view of conservation is not necessarily comparable to contemporary environmentalism. For example, the rationale for early measures fitted well with dominant modes of thought centred on managerialism and utilitarianism, where resources were protected because they have quantifiable worth for society. Knowledge of the extent to which changes may impact on the quality of life can be powerful argument, particularly if a failure to act might have severe economic consequences. In contrast, environmentalism was much more challenging, demanding different ways of viewing the natural world and questioning the commonly accepted activities and worldviews that place it under pressure. As a consequence, this outlook can also frame environmental protection to appear to be in opposition with economic and social norms in a way that conservation may not.

Reflecting on the discussion so far, it is clear that humanity is part of nature – changing landscapes, exploiting resources and receiving feedback in return. The environment and humans are interconnected; an interdependent relationship in evidence from the earliest civilizations to the present day. The past clearly offers case studies of environmental change, and in particular how *contextual* activities are, highlighting the need to understand the underlying causes of an environmental problem, the social forces that may serve to normalize such activity, and how there are opposing economic forces that may inhibit the ability to conserve, protect or regulate. Equally, the lessons of the past indicate a number of times when real progress has been made, from the creation of national parks to the controlling of pollution. It may be easy simply to hark back to a pre-industrial view of nature as an Arcadian paradise and reject contemporary politics and the desire for consensus, but when economic, social and environmental arguments have synergy, the path to positive change is noticeably smoother. In addition to an awareness of the impacts of development, this places an onus on understanding more about the nature of politics and decision-making generally. In reality, studying the past helps to identify environmental planning as a means of managing rates of change pushed by dominant social and economic paradigms, from capitalism to consumerism and beyond.

Yet, while the argument to date displays a significant degree of *connectivity* and *commonality* between humanity and the natural world, as the rest of the chapter will emphasize, this is not only largely unacknowledged, but in many ways appears to be almost actively disputed. Despite the arguments so far of interdependence, in practice there are powerful philosophical, scientific, economic and cultural forces that underpin an opposing paradigm of *separation* and *superiority* in evidence throughout the past 2,000 years. It is this contrast that shows the value of both understanding impacts and the thinking behind them that was mooted in the chapter introduction. The following discussion outlining key advances in social thought will now provide a complementary counter focus and reveal much about the origin and power of contemporary environmental problems.

The history of environmental planning thought

> 'The end of our foundation is the knowledge of causes, and secret motions of things; and the enlarging of the bounds of human empire, to the effecting of all things possible.'
> (Francis Bacon, *New Atlantis*, 1627)

In world history, certain clusters of thought signify changes in direction that resonate far into the future. This section will attempt to navigate a meaningful passage through these deviating strands and provide a lens through which to view current issues in the environment with more clarity. The thinking of the past may frequently be ascribed as esoteric accounts of yesteryear with relevance mainly to historical scholars. However, our current worldviews that influence how the environment is perceived and valued stem from longstanding frames of reference that enjoy a surprising malleability to maintain relevance through huge social transformations. To a greater or lesser degree, influences such as religion, science and technology have all had an effect on the environment for millennia.

Despite the critical importance of science in environmental planning, this tale is not one penned solely under this single disciplinary influence; religious beliefs, artists and economists all contribute to the richness of the story. The focus is centred mainly on Western perspectives (European and US) mainly because of its dominance within this canon of literature, and this has in turn shaped my knowledge down similar pathways. This approach also has the result of better reflecting the undercurrents steering the current direction of travel, as the world has become increasingly in tune with the values of the global West and North concerning the environment, science, technology and capitalism.

The section starts with an analysis of the early and ongoing role of religion, before discussing how advances in science and philosophy associated with the Enlightenment gradually undermined these beliefs but retained much of the hierarchal thinking in evidence. This, in turn, created the foundation for the next themes, characterized by a faith in empiricism and technology, and a seemingly inevitable, incremental progress in the ability of humans to control and master the natural world, with humanity becoming ever more free from the constraints experienced by other species. Finally, we investigate the contemporary economic frames of capitalism and consumerism that exert an equally powerful influence upon how governments, people and corporations currently perceive the environment.

It is important to note that these worldviews do not succeed each other neatly, with each development in thought replacing the previous one chronologically; rather, they represent differing understandings that may run in parallel. Equally, they should also not simply be considered as acting in competition with, for example, science being seen as simply debunking the faith in a creator. In reality, humanity has a remarkable capacity for interpreting new information as conforming to already existing understandings, and many scientists, from the scientific revolution to the present day, see no conflict between these worldviews.

As we shall see, the dominant ways of viewing the environment represented in this chapter have a strong narrative theme, which appears to be present in each of the main strands of thought of the last 2,000 years – and it is this that provides the overarching message to bind the seemingly disparate elements together. As outlined in the introductory quote from *New Atlantis*, Francis Bacon's final utopian novel, aspects of humanity have long held themselves to be both *separate* and *superior*, regardless of their philosophical or societal influences: in this sense, the sections of this chapter will argue progressively that hierarchal thought, empiricism, human exemptionalism and notions of unending 'progress' and growth are not such different masters.

A sense of hierarchy

> 'The clearest proof of man's rule is afforded by what goes on before our eyes. Sometimes vast numbers of cattle are led by one quite ordinary man ... and all the prowess and strength of all those well-armed animals ... cower before him like slaves before a master, and do his bidding.'
>
> (Philo of Alexandria, *On the Creation*, 20 BC to AD 50)

Philo's view is characteristic of the intensely hierarchal worldview in evidence in much early Western thought. Humanity was seen as superior and, as such, held natural dominion over other creatures. The view was replicated in some religious worldviews which suggest that Man was created in His image, with, for example, many early Christians believing that the Earth's bounty was provided by a beneficent master for His subjects. The opening quote above reveals much of the tenor of some environmental critiques concerning Deism – the belief in a creator. In contrast to earlier, and still ongoing, pagan animism as espoused by Plato and many indigenous peoples, where humans are strongly connected to the natural world, Deism elevated humanity as 'closest to God', an example of a hierarchal view that can provide a rationale for much environmental exploitation and degradation.

The early belief that nature was not only God's creation but a gift to humanity was particularly dominant up to the dawn of the Enlightenment and the associated Scientific Revolution. The view that nature had generously been provided to serve humanity's needs not only facilitated a clear *ranking* in the ordained order, but also a division between humans and the wider environment; separate from the whole and effectively acting as steward. Worster (1977: 26) uses the example of 'Christian Pastoralism' to highlight how shepherds do not see themselves as equal parts of a system, but rather as protectors of their flocks against the hostile forces of nature. From this perspective, the control over nature is determined by a higher position on the scale of being, and a consequent role as overseer, husbandman or even a finisher of nature (Glacken, 1967). Figure 2.3 articulates this stance by depicting the Great Chain of Being delineated by Didicus Valades in 1579. This image describes a religious hierarchy of all matter and life – with humanity on the third rank behind God and Angels, and with animals, plants and minerals lower down.

Figure 2.3 *The Great Chain of Being*
Source: http://commons.wikimedia.org/wiki/File:Great_Chain_of_Being_2.png.

Analysing a religious viewpoint from an environmental impact perspective can lead to challenging ideological discussions. This was notably expressed in Lynn White, Jr's (1967) article 'The Historical Roots of our Ecological Crisis', in which he argued provocatively that Christianity was a highly anthropocentric religion, with Man positioning himself as being created in the image of God, having dominion over all living things and receiving explicit instruction to multiply. Glacken (1967) further suggests that in much Christian theology there has been a Contemptus Mundi; a distaste for, and a lack of interest in, nature. However, it should be noted that this anti-environmentalism critique of Christianity is a little blunt, particularly given the propensity of religious texts to be interpreted in contradictory or extreme ways. For example, 'dominion' may also have positive connotations of careful and sensitive stewardship, reflecting values more synergous with mainstream conservation movements or even sustainability debates.

Equally, figures such as St Francis of Assisi have demonstrated a holism and Arcadian view of nature that may satisfy even the fiercest critics. The designation of humanity as being subservient to God could also be used to argue against technology or the disruption of nature. For example, Herodotus (484–425 BC) thought that massive works such as bridges and canals demonstrated an overreaching human pride that might call forth divine punishment – a view that still holds traction over two thousand years later as can be frequently seen in the aftermath of natural disasters.

We should therefore be cautious in applying potentially sweeping arguments. The complexities of religious faith may take divergent paths and operate in differing contexts, and it should be noted that this does not mean that all religions are subject to the same critique. For example, Taoism, Buddhism, Hindu and Jaina all stress natural harmony and hold continual attraction to environmentalists because of their marked contrasts with the predominant Western religious view of the primacy of man. Equally, it does not suggest that atheist or non-religious societies take a more desirable, opposing view – the environmental degradation in communist Russia or China provides ample evidence of this point.

The most important idea to take from this section regards the tendency to *order* beings with humanity usually elevated above other species. And, critically, this is not just a religious characteristic. While we have used certain religious thought as a case study of this perception, hierarchal thinking can also be seen within Aristotle's concept of higher and lower order creatures in his *History of Animals* written in the mid-third century BC, Linnaeus's *Systema Naturae* 2,000 years later and many contemporary perspectives where the environment is seen in a utilitarian manner. The key issue is that hierarchal thought, as evident in this religious example, can influence perceptions of the natural world, shaping relationships and interactions in a way that may operate in a largely unseen manner. Moreover, as we shall see within the following sections, the instrumental perspective that elevates humanity as separate and superior may not be tied so easily to a particular ontology or time period. Its existence in non-religious or modern societies demonstrates it is a relational historiography that may well prove to have a persistent influence upon our interaction with the environment regardless of any future religious, social, cultural or philosophical developments.

The authority of empiricism

From the seventeenth century onwards, great leaps in knowledge and culture occurred, causing a change in the relationship between environment and humanity. This shift is known as the 'Enlightenment', signifying an awakening and liberation of humans from the perceived superstition, dogma and corruption of the Church. This development was driven by a whole host of scientific, philosophical and cultural advances that effectively challenged the hegemony of theology and instead promoted the seemingly competing secular authority of human reason, rationality and ingenuity.

Significant progress in multiple branches of science ushered in a scientific revolution, transforming the relationship between the environment and humanity. In astronomy and physics, Copernicus, Galileo and Kepler all helped to demonstrate that the Sun, and not the Earth, was at the centre of the solar system, thus shifting understanding of the place of human beings in the universe. Similarly, developments in mapping, exploration, anatomy and mathematics all created a burgeoning belief in the power of human ingenuity. Advances in meta-physics and philosophy were also linked to breakthroughs in science; in *Discourse on the Method*, René Descartes advocated the importance of scepticism, while Francis Bacon designed a robust scientific method as an ideal procedure for investigating phenomena (Jacob, 2009). Both of these examples assisted the drive towards the objective, detached empiricism that resonates strongly in the present. Indeed, one of the key reasons for the success of Charles Darwin's (1859) *The Origin of the Species* was that it gained the support of the foremost authority of the age: science.

Yet it is too simplistic to see science in dialectic opposition to, or as a replacement for, theology. Bacon's philosophy of attaining control over nature via scientific inquiry is perceived to be a vital part of his interpretation of religion, with ignorance being seen as similar to: 'a second fall of man' (Glacken, 1967: 472). Indeed, in Bacon's (2001 [1627]) work *The New Atlantis*, Eden was to be built by scientists; essentially secularizing a moral vision and justifying the extensive transformation of landscapes. Therefore, while science challenged the dominance of a religiously inspired hierarchal worldview, crucially, the relative position of humanity was unchanged. In this sense, it was humans' ability to think, to perform science and to control nature that made humanity superior. For example, Descartes argued that, as thinking beings, humans were distinctly separate from the rest of the natural world: a dualism that could justify exploitation and subservience just as effectively as religion (Pepper, 1996). As Ralph Waldo Emerson (2009: 18) put it in 1836: 'Nature is thoroughly mediate. It is made to serve. It receives the dominion of man as meekly as the ass on which the Saviour rode.'

There are also ongoing parallels in how science and religion affected relationships with the environment; just as God creates unity, order and hierarchy, so does science. In many ways, the scientific revolution may be seen not as a reaction to theology, but rather a product of its mindset, retaining subtle underlying influences that shape how and why science is conducted. Indeed, Berdyaev (1962) highlights that rather than usurping religion as a rival authority, Western science, from its very beginning, was infused with a Christian approach to nature, maintaining the same detached, separated and dualistic worldview.

However, the discovery of more knowledge about nature can lead to the development of technologies to control and exploit the environment for the benefit of humanity. The great expansion in science and the establishment of certain laws governing nature facilitated a more *mechanistic* view of the natural world. Living organisms were thought to be part of a vast machine that could similarly be isolated, examined and deconstructed. However, such a detached perception of nature had more ominous undertones. Science's reductive, atomizing tendencies tended to view nature through a narrow utilitarian lens that effectively gave it no moral rights. Here: 'by reducing plants and animals to insensate matter, mere conglomerates of atomic particles devoid of internal purpose or intelligence, the naturalist was removing the remaining barriers to unrestrained economic exploitation' (Worster, 1994: 40).

While the intellectual freedom from dogma provided by scientific enterprise was initially attractive to many naturalists, the exploitative potential of science and its intertwined relationship with industry and mechanization increasingly became apparent. During the eighteenth and nineteenth centuries in particular, the cool, objective nature of science became contrasted with a more romantic turn linked to artists and creatives of the time, such as Wordsworth or Goethe. Romanticism emphasized how the organic holism of nature evokes wonder and influences our affections. Many naturalists instinctively shared this view, with the American, Henry David Thoreau, and the English pastor, Gilbert White, both being examples of those who advocated a more humble existence and harmony with nature, speaking out in a quiet way against its burgeoning monetization.

Despite these opposing stances, advances in reason and rationality meant that the environment became known more *empirically*, as well as emotionally or religiously. Perceiving the environment as a machine to be understood essentially frames nature as the backdrop to human activity and can justify environmental damage (Merchant, 1982). This concerns the ideology of science more generally; how it operates and what it could, or indeed should, achieve. Here empiricism refers to a dominant philosophy of science traceable to the scientific method whereby evidence and testing, such as from experiments, holds the sway of power. This tendency can be seen clearly in many aspects of environmental planning, such as evidence-based decision-making or cost–benefit analysis. In this sense, empirical rationality has a power that is comparable to theology and can determine multiple aspects of environmental intervention, from the existence and scale of a problem to the stringency of regulation. Moreover, the absence of evidence is frequently used as a rationale for inaction, regardless of how difficult information may be to obtain, or the possible impact of any activity. Therefore, advances in science did not just impact on the environment; they also began to exert an authority over how humans interact with it – from how decisions are made to how value is allocated. Crucially, it also influenced us, as the next section will discuss.

The rise of human exemptionalism

There is little doubt that scientific advances changed societies in a positive manner, increasing knowledge about humanity and its surroundings, raising standards of living and improving productivity. Related to this, new technologies, from the axe to the plough to the internal combustion engine, also transformed the relationship between societies and the environment. Yet it is critical to note that these scientific and technological developments did not merely create a simple vehicle that delivers potentially detrimental change to be managed, but a more ethereal sense of an emerging power to control nature – and it is this lingering influence in *thought*, in particular the ability to master nature and ignore constraints, that may be overlooked in comparison to more physical outcomes.

Advances in a host of fields helped to foster an 'imperial' view of nature as a target for control, and greatly expanded the scale at which this could occur – from the Victorian parks and gardens, with their imported exotic plants and highly manicured lawns, to the cultivation and management of resources in far-flung European colonies. The growing understanding of natural laws and other advances not only assisted in rationalizing human mastery over the environment, but as with the other issues discussed so far, helped to elevate the perception of *Homo sapiens* to be above the constraints experienced by other creatures. Characteristics such as human culture, language and sophisticated social organization created a sense that other, seemingly fixed constraints, did not apply to human beings. This perceived 'human exemptionalism' (Catton and Dunlap, 1978) fostered a view that humans are unique and could be exempt from the laws that govern most of nature – with technology, for example, enabling anyone to fly high above the Earth, live in previously uninhabitable conditions, or circumvent the limitations to which other species are subject (Sutton, 2007).

This brings a common paradox to light. Most people would accept instinctively that humans are part of a variety of wider natural systems operating at various scales, such as those relating to catchments or even the planet Earth itself. This view is widely reflected in most literature pertaining to sustainability, resources or limits, for example. Yet, while this may be commonly accepted, societies tend to operate as if it was not the case, with economic and political systems fuelling short-term and fragmented practices and processes. The widely held view of the exemptional nature of humanity, with its inventiveness and unquestionable progress, has impacts not only on the environment but also on how humans perceive problems and construct possible options for intervention. For instance, contemporary issues such as scarcity, carrying capacities or ecological limits provide examples of similar 'natural laws' from which key societal groups feel excepted, while some adaptive responses to climate change suggest a reliance on technology that may prove to be unable to offer an effective solution for many. Arguments that challenge this standpoint can be resisted innately because of humans' strong sense of 'ontological security' (Giddens, 1984) – a feeling of confidence and trust that the natural and social worlds are as they appear to be. This sense of permanence and order is important to maintain a sense of stability, structure and meaning between individuals and the wider world.

Combined with this cultural stance was a new belief that technological progress will provide new frontiers, energy sources and managerial solutions. Such techno-optimism has been embedded strongly in society and its institutions ever since. Indeed, the philosopher John Gray (2009) argues that there is essentially a secular 'faith' in endless advancement and progress that resonates with humankind's most unappetizing traits of destruction, transience and conspicuous consumption. This can foster an internal logic where technological advances are seen as being automatically desirable, perhaps even unstoppable, regardless of their potential application and impact. We only need to look at the resources spent on technological advances for waging war to see ample evidence of this technological imperative. The related issue of technological determinism, and its undertones of inevitability, is explored in more depth in Box 2.3.

As a consequence, the pervasive sense of inevitable human progress over time should not be accepted uncritically. With regard to sanitation, Mumford (1961: 289) argues:

> as far as usable open spaces go, the typical medieval town had at its foundation and through most of its existence a far higher standard for the mass of the population than any later form of town, down to the first romantic suburbs of the 19th century.

Advances in agriculture, soil fertility, drainage, health and construction all took place, but 'progress' is not just confined to the technological sphere, and the benefits are not distributed equally and universally. For example, inequality is a feature of modernity, with huge disparities apparent both within and between countries.

Technology specifically, and progress more abstractly, are problematic subjects for those concerned with environmental planning. While it is tempting to see technological advances from a negative perspective, creating the potential for impacts that are now reaching a global scale, it is important to note that they have also bought enormous social and economic benefits over thousands of years. Indeed, to argue against technology may appear to be an unreasonable position more akin to the Luddites of the nineteenth century, who vainly protested against the mechanization of the Industrial Revolution, than a realistic position to affect positive change. This issue is now so powerful that cultures measure progress by this means, effectively positing a hegemonic 'technological imperative' driven by the industrialized global North (Jamieson, 2001). Even

Box 2.3 Technological determinism

Technological determinism holds that social and cultural values are driven by technology, or, that technology's power as a crucial agent of change has a prominent place in the culture of modernity (Smith and Marx, 1994). The social theorist, Karl Marx, exemplified this view when he said that 'the hand-mill gives you society with the feudal lord; the steam-mill, society with the industrial capitalist' (Marx et al., 1910 [1847]: 119). There are two main strands to this; one sanguine and the other cynical. Techno-optimists emphasize the benefits that technology brings and, in its most naïve versions, support 'technological fixes' as a solution to social problems. This should be contrasted with techno-pessimism, where the supposed benefits of technology are thought to bring about a future detraction in the human condition.

Science fiction literature provides a route into understanding these themes. When one speaks of a 'Wellsian' world view, the analogy is to the science fiction writer, H. G. Wells. Wells is generally thought to offer a utopian view of technological progress, but in reality he took a fairly ambivalent stance and was preoccupied with overpopulation; some commentators even consider him to be the 'father of Green Politics' (Carey, 2000: 372). In his *Shape of Things to Come* (1933) Wells projects to a world where humanity lives in a 'world garden' where population size is controlled to 2 billion and biological research produces new plant species. This tempered optimism of human evolution through technological development is also clearly stated in *The World Set Free* (1914), where nuclear war, famine, plague and other illnesses were necessary catastrophic preludes to the establishment of Utopia.

Yet the promise of technology is not always regarded so benignly. Aldous Huxley's *Brave New World* (1932) presents a 'World State' that has dispensed with art and literature. Though medicine has rid the world of hunger and disease, all social life is driven by technology; babies are produced in test tubes and genetically engineered to produce five grades of human being suitable for certain tasks. Humans, in effect, become deadened and are depicted as unthinking automatons. Further, in George Orwell's (1949) classic dystopian vision of authoritarianism, *1984*, the inhabitants of Oceania are subject to the machinations of 'Big Brother' and his 'World Party', where technology is used to control society through mass surveillance and the manipulation of leisure and language.

→

→

What these examples should alert you to is that multiple positions are susceptible to the charges of technological determinism. Whether in their optimistic or pessimistic forms, these renderings all assume a linear, or teleological, path. Effectively, an end point or goal is envisioned, whether it is Armageddon or Utopia, towards which technology unstoppably propels human society. Yet, technology does not simply drive society and culture. Indeed, some scholars point to how science and technology are rooted in social and cultural practices (Latour and Woolgar, 1986).

Though the horrors experienced during the two world wars dented the belief in continual technological and human progress, these positions of optimism and pessimism in technology still resurface. In the late 1950s, the 'space race' engendered all sorts of technologies beneficial to humans. As politicians were quick to recognize, technological progress could be harnessed for economic growth – a link that should not be overlooked with regard to environmental planning.

The influence of technology also permeates into society and its institutions. For example, with regard to the planning profession, a modernist rationality prevailed at this time through large-scale plans that swept away much of the urban landscape to replace it with new road infrastructure that would supposedly liberate humans and raise their standard of living. Even so, many people were rejecting such futuristic movements, and the 1960s also saw the beginnings of the 'New Age' movements and increasing awareness of environmental problems caused by technology.

Similar debates can be seen today. Climate change is a good example, with technological fixes always seemingly on the near horizon, and routinely seized upon as a more desirable solution than behavioural change, which is not only much more difficult to achieve but also slightly mundane in comparison. As we shall see as the book progresses, the perceived risks, benefits and faith in technology varies historically, culturally and socially. On one hand, such solutions raise anxieties, and attention is drawn to the underlying failure to change existing patterns of human consumption. Others point to technologies that are technically possible but are not always developed, or when they are developed, are rejected. For example, the shift towards alternative energy sources is influenced by a seeming lack of political commitment and a concern about cost.

sustainability or environmental debates can become enmeshed with the pervasive desire for technical solutions. This progressive view of the *potential* of technology is important to note as it signals the possibility of a beguiling future of incremental betterment and exemptionalism that is not only attractive in itself but meshes smoothly with predominant modes of capitalism and consumerism that shape more contemporary worldviews. On reflection, it may do this in a similarly authoritative, but more subtle vein to the hierarchal dogma of medieval times.

The power of economic systems

Environmental damage and the pressures placed upon nature more generally are not just a result of the processes of industrialization; they are also related to the inherent functioning of capitalist market economies that have been such an established feature of the last few hundred years. There are a number of variants of capitalism, but simply put they largely rely on competition for resources, labour, markets and profits, and the attachment of prices to goods and services. The central role of profit within this economic system places pressure on reducing the costs of production and increasing demand, ensuring that consumerism is an inevitable by-product. Indeed, industries that facilitate the growth of consumption are a necessity of this model, with sectors such as marketing and advertising being designed to artificially create and boost demand for products and promote materialistic, high-consumption lifestyles.

Some may question the paralleling of economic growth, capitalism and consumerism with the other influences on environmental thinking outlined in this chapter. Yet there is a strong argument that it does operate as both a comparable 'belief' system and a lens through which to view the world. The overwhelming reliance on economic growth by governments and stock markets around the globe means that the environment can easily be seen through a capitalist lens, with its value to society determined by its ability to deliver growth and jobs. While consumerism may be described as 'a way of thinking, a mentality or even an ideology' (Sutton, 2007: 68) and has frequently been compared in operation as almost a modern religion, where luxury goods are seen as an indicator of social status, and carbon-intensive lifestyles are equated with 'success'. In this sense, capitalism is, like religion and science, a worldview that may operate in tandem with other influential modes of thought to shape environmental interactions. This perspective also helps to bring the journey towards the present: as for example, early conservationists may have focused on economically efficient production, while later environmentalists may attempt to address ecologically responsible consumption.

The principles of capitalism and the desire for economic growth means that it can be visibly connected to environmental impacts with resources frequently used in an insensitive manner, but its influence on thought, in particular regarding the role of the environment within society, is equally critical. While a number of contemporary social movements have questioned the global dominance of capitalism in a high-profile manner, the economic system is not just a product of recent times; its foundations are traceable to the rise of mercantilism and the merchant class in the Middle Ages. Like technology, though, capitalism is a thorny subject to discuss, and it would be remiss not to acknowledge that this economic system has brought huge benefits to societies, from improved standards of living to health care to social organization, or indeed, the seeming lack of viable alternatives.

With regard to capitalism, the overriding theme of a separation between humanity and nature encompasses a number of aspects. There is an initial detachment between production and consumption as the system serves to mask environmental cause and effect, both with regard to the physical product as well as to the more abstract materialism in maintaining an affluent lifestyle. Capitalism also enables a physical separation of humans from polluted landscapes, with impacts typically experienced by those unconnected with the pursuit of profit. Here, recipients of wealth have tended to insulate themselves physically from the social and environmental impacts of the conditions created by capitalism, such as by their initial flight to the suburbs in the early days of industrialization to homes in the country in more recent times. In this sense, the division created by capitalism is not just regarding people and nature, but between humans and other humans, with labour being seen as a component raw material alongside natural resources, and where wealth and power are distributed unevenly.

Technological advances, mechanization and the more sophisticated organization of labour can all feed what Schnaiberg (1980) referred to as the 'treadmill of production', an explanation of how environmental problems can expand over time. In seeking more profit, shareholders or owners wish to drive both productivity and consumption, leading to a circuitous need for more production and potentially generating increased pollution and environmental pressures. And so the cycle continues. Furthermore, all sectors of society rely on the ability of economic growth to continue eternally, with the aftermath of the global credit crisis demonstrating how only a few quarters of negative growth can generate shock waves that reverberate around many seemingly unconnected areas.

This worldview may also lead to the attachment of an artificial economic value to elements of nature – but crucially this may be either zero or unrepresentative of its intrinsic value or impact. For example, unless there is a price placed on pollution that can be factored in to the production process, this may be generated alongside profits; however, pollution may affect local residents rather than those corporations receiving the financial benefit. Further, economic concepts such as offsetting that permeate environmental planning can link the natural world to policy, but this trade may not be comparable to the potential effect. These issues link to debates touched on throughout the book, from the price of pollution or the acknowledgement of the value of ecosystem services to environmental justice. More fundamentally, there is a question over the ability of a capitalist economic system to facilitate the effective protection of the environment within defining structures that value low regulation. Again, this demonstrates how environmental planning, with its 'red tape' of rules, regulations and policies, may be seen as a mechanism to influence capital for the wider societal good. Or, perhaps more controversially, from a Marxist perspective, it provides a figleaf just big enough to mask the multiple social and environmental injustices inherent in capitalism that may otherwise precipitate public revolt against the injustices of the economic system.

The final separation is more conceptual: that between economics and ecology, an intellectual division where the power is heavily weighted towards the former. Where the Enlightenment was characterized by the pursuit of natural laws driven by science, society now adheres to the equally authoritative demands of the constructed laws of economic systems, where hegemonic notions of market liberalization and incessant growth remain as unchallenged as the religious dogma of the Middle Ages. Therefore, not only have advances in science, technology and industry made products that can exploit the environment, we have also made societies that rationalize these practices within powerful economic belief systems and social norms.

Conclusion

'The civilised man directs his exploitation of the earth with a mastery which has ceased to astonish him, but which, when we reflect on it for a moment, is singularly disturbing.'

(Febvre, 1925: 355)

From an environmental planning perspective, it can be all too easy to be centred in the here and now, and consumed by current concerns, localized issues or the nuances in domestic regulation. The sheer volume of information regarding the interaction between humans and the environment, from new data on ice sheet loss to local recycling practices, can be both daunting and divide attention. In the midst of this cacophony of competing signals it can be difficult to take a step back, to deliberately reduce the background noise and to consider the wider picture. As the above quote from Febvre emphasizes, when we do so we can look afresh and cogitate anew on the most fundamental of relationships: that between humanity and its surroundings, with a view to increasing the depth of our understanding when we are inevitably enticed back by the siren call of the present.

This chapter has been designed to highlight key historical developments that affect the way that the environment is thought about, what its role is, and how it relates to humanity – all factors that influence our ability to manage it. Previous changes in this regard help us to both understand the present and plot the future. Yet this chapter has also demonstrated that any forthcoming trends may be likely to morph into dominant frames of thought, much like a meandering river eternally flows to the sea, rather than fundamentally changing the course of how people behave with regard to the natural world. As Hughes (2006: 8) observed: 'people are skilful at adapting their attitudes ... to their needs and desires'. This historical overview also lends weight to the argument that there may be no 'eureka' moment where the weight of evidence demanding an entirely new paradigm between humanity and nature becomes a rational inevitability.

Indeed, an overview of the history of environmental thought reveals that there are themes that echo throughout the ages, regardless of changes in beliefs concerning the possible role of a creator, the incredible ability of science and technology to transform landscapes, or the power of economic systems to influence behaviour. It is clear that, despite the physical evidence of connectivity and commonality, the opposing threads of separate and superior reverberate loudly, being not simply the product of the advances of the Industrial Revolution, but rather encompassing a powerful amalgam of religious, scientific, social, cultural and economic thought. Overall, the idea of a higher place for humanity in some grand scheme imbues power, whether via the teleological argument that the existence and order of nature implies a hierarchy, the ability of science to foster human exemptionalism, or the more recent secular 'faith' in technology and capitalism. This dualism is now institutionalized and normalized to the extent that it is difficult to picture society outside these frames. There is a counter-argument, however, that humanity had to consider nature as a separate entity in order to understand it, a step that necessitated an independent, rational mindset that could observe and experiment on this isolated entity. The results of this have paved the way for social progress and inevitably have a utilitarian outlook as a result of knowledge being used in a host of fields from increasing agricultural yields to medical advances. As Williams (1980: 75) puts it:

> to speak of man [*sic*] 'intervening' in natural processes is to suppose that he [*sic*] might find it possible not to do so, or to decide not to do so. Nature has to be thought of, that is to say, as separate from man, before any question of intervention or command, and the method and ethics of either, can arise.

The dualism does have consequences however, not just with how environmental impacts appear to be prioritized by how much they reflect back upon humanity but also, more generally, with regard to how perceptions of the environment operate within these dominant frames. For example, nature can frequently be understood as happening outside urban areas, or there may be a tendency to attach a low value to 'undeveloped' land. Even within this discipline, notions of 'town' and 'country' or distinct 'urban' and 'environmental' issues reflect this mode of thought.

Alternatively, one could adopt a more holist disposition that may be incumbent within ecological thinking, and acknowledge the complex interactions of nature over a number of scales. This view provides a counter-point to the fragmentary pressures of empiricist science. While it may have its lineage in Pagan, Arcadian or Romantic thought, it has recently gained sophistication by co-opting those very same rational scientific approaches to argue for greater consideration of more 'systemic' approaches. Terminology such as ecosystem services or resilient systems is a clear example of this. In reality, many human interventions in nature have gone uncurbed because scientists have not adequately understood how these might impact upon the broader whole (Commoner, 1966). Yet systems thinking itself might not provide the answer. As we shall see in later chapters, its complexity does not link well with many aspects of environmental planning, from disciplinary silos to cost–benefit analysis to prevailing ways of governance.

As a final point, it should be recognized that environmental histories can engender an unhelpful pessimism and powerlessness. Cronon (1993: 2) reflecting on his own experience in teaching this subject, singled out the overwhelmingly melancholy feedback from his students and remarked that: 'To conclude that the environmental past teaches the hopelessness of the environmental future struck me as a profoundly disempowering lesson.' He subsequently changed his lectures to better consider his own more optimistic views and avoid what he thought might become a self-fulfilling prophecy. In this positive sense, those very same aspects that have displayed tendencies to separate or elevate, such as elements of science or economics, may themselves offer solutions to protect, manage and improve the environment. History demonstrates that it may be that the most success could be gained from knowingly working within the existing dominant frames rather than trying to supersede them. While paradigm change may offer a seductive counter-position, this chapter lends weight to the argument that the timescales needed for this strategy may stretch far into the future and face huge opposition from powerfully entrenched positions.

It is now apparent that what we could at present call 'environmental problems' cannot be reducible to a single issue; instead they are a complex display of interconnectivity in deed and thought that not only defy the ability to easily ascertain cause and effect, but also challenge the ability of our institutional frameworks to agree on these problems, never mind resolve them. The move towards the politics of consensus with regard to environmental issues from the end of the twentieth century onwards also emphasizes the contemporary importance of governing and how power is used within environmental planning, an issue that forms the focus of the next chapter.

Chapter 3

Governance and Power

'How can anyone govern a nation that has two hundred and forty-six different kinds of cheese?'
(Charles de Gaulle (1890–1970), quoted in Mignon, 1962)

The French president, Charles de Gaulle, was reputed to have made the now infamous opening observation when discussing the travails of attaining unity within his native country. His references to the individuality and variety of something as mundane as cheesemaking was designed to draw parallels with the more combative and heterogeneous political landscape, within which a variety of political stances, agencies and actors can all hamper the efforts of the state to govern and wield power effectively. The broad societal issues discussed in this chapter are important, as essentially they serve to frame environmental planning, setting aspects such as the content and tone of debate, and the relationships and responsibilities of key stakeholders. It provides more than the background mood music, however, as the chapter also sheds light on how and why some environmental issues are addressed, and the differing means by which influence can be exerted.

The first question that may strike you is why *governance*, as opposed to the more familiar term, *government*. The latter typically refers to the executive body that governs a nation or state, with formal institutions that exert administrative control through legislation, regulation, taxes and so on. It plays a significant role within environmental planning but its powers are not absolute and in some ways can actually be very limited when compared to wider societal forces.

In contrast, governance is a:

descriptive label that is used to highlight the changing nature of the policy process in recent decades. In particular, it sensitizes us to the ever-increasing variety of terrains and actors involved in the making of public policy. Thus, governance demands that we consider all the actors and locations beyond the 'core executive' involved in the policy making process. (Richards and Smith, 2002: 15)

Here, the notion of the core executive refers to a range of formal and informal institutions and actors that co-ordinate across cabinet to ensure that decisions are enacted.

In simple terms, governance differs from government as it is related to the style in which decisions are made, the diversity of those involved, the manner by which power is exercised, or more simply, the act of 'governing'. As a concept, governance goes beyond traditional structures of authority to include other actors and agencies with power; most notably those connected with the market and civil society, and encompasses the variety of networks, interaction and collaboration between differing stakeholders over multiple scales. As Stoker (1998) points out, the outcomes are not so different from a traditional view of government, but the processes are.

The value of understanding the notion of governance lies in its ability to bring all of the actors and agencies involved into view and, consequently, to be able to analyse their interactions. Perhaps the best way of quickly understanding the importance of the topic is to consider it within the context of one particular concern. The complex problem of climate change offers a good example. While governments around the world broadly agree on the causes and the severity of potential impacts, action appears to be rather limited when compared to the possible consequences for citizens and the biosphere. But why should this be so? It is instructive to remind ourselves of the nature of the debate, and the stances of key stakeholders, to illustrate how governance is distinct from government. Generally speaking, in this case, scientists and academics may provide evidence that argues for a greater control of CO_2 emissions. Those engaged in more market-oriented activities are concerned about the effect of regulation on business, but may accept new measures such as carbon trading. The media and civil society may be worried about an increase in taxes or a restriction in liberty implied by climate change mitigation initiatives. While the comprehensive nature of stakeholder interest on this topic could potentially increase the take-up of measures, the multiplicity of influential views can also reduce the likelihood of agreeing common ground, or limit the level of intervention that is acceptable to all parties. A governance view sees the problem and its solution as not being an issue for *government*; rather, that effective actions may also lie beyond the scope of this sole agency and include other key parties.

As a consequence, governance is not simply about the maelstrom of competing opinions; it is connected with power. For example, in this situation governments are constrained in their ability to respond to the message from the scientific community, whether on political, financial or ideological grounds. Moreover, even if they act decisively there are a host of forces that will affect the success of climate change policies that lie outside the control of most, if not all, governments. Therefore, governance perspectives recognize the plural nature of views and power in modern society.

Reflecting on this case, we can start to appreciate why climate change has been described not as just an environmental problem, nor simply a danger stemming from the failure of the market, but rather as 'a crisis of governance' (Hulme, 2009: 310). From this perspective, the reason for our inaction on climate change is not scientific uncertainty as many may think, or a lack of technology or finance, but rather it could be considered a failure of collective action: essentially it is an issue that is not well served by the dispersal of power and influence that is characteristic of many contemporary societies. This also illustrates the difficulty in simply compartmentalizing a problem as an 'environmental' one, as in reality the potential consensus and solvability is considered by a wide array of stakeholders, each within its own subjective social, economic or political frame.

Therefore, in much the same way as environmental impacts could be considered a failure of the market, so too could the existence and severity of environmental concerns be considered a failure of governance. While there may be a familiar refrain of 'Why don't politicians do something?', often the focus seems to be on the political stances of dominant parties, the difficulty of the problems or the cost of intervention on business, rather than the inability of the *system* to 'govern' decisively. In reality, to govern the environment effectively there is a need to go beyond the agencies of government and engage with broader actors of governance. As Howlett (2000: 412) explains: 'Modern governments face a paradox in that, theoretically, their bureaucratic capacity for action in terms of knowledge, expertise, budgets and personnel resources is high, while, at the same time, phenomena such as globalization and democratization have severely undermined their ability to directly control social outcomes.'

The chapter strays a little into social theory, political theory and organizational studies, as all hold relevance for this aspect of environmental planning. It is not intended to cover all aspects of governance, nor the perspective of every stakeholder, rather those key elements that will help readers to grasp how governing has changed and what this may mean for discourses relating to environmental planning. As Stoker (1998: 18) explains: 'the value of the governance perspective rests in its capacity to provide a framework for understanding changing processes of governing'.

Before we explore this aspect of environmental planning it is useful to pause and reflect on what is understood by the term 'state'. Often it is characterized as a 'thing' that acts; however, definitions of the state will depend on particular theoretical persuasions. Neoliberals, for example, will advocate a minimal state, perhaps consisting of only institutions such as the judiciary and the police. Social democrats, on the other hand, would argue for a more expansive notion of the state that included significant aspects relating to human welfare, such as health care and unemployment benefits. More radically, for Socialists, the state is an apparatus controlled by the bourgeoisie in order to rule over the working classes; consequently, under Socialism, the state would be abolished (Miller, 2005). Clearly, in different times and different places, a definition of the state will change. However, it is usually strongly linked to legitimacy, coercion and a means to provide security. A key theorist in this area is Bob Jessop (2008: 9), who describes the state as a 'rational abstraction' that can be defined as a: 'distinct ensemble of institutions and organizations whose socially accepted function is to define and enforce collectively binding decisions on a given population in the name of their "common interest" or "general will"'. Given this, how one defines the common interest, particularly in the light of global challenges such as climate change, is a particular problem for environmental planning.

This chapter begins by examining the role of government more generally, investigating how influence in societies has transitioned from being the sole concern of a centralized state, usually termed the 'command and control' approach, to being a more pluralistic stance that takes into account the views and abilities of wider stakeholders and engages with forces such as neoliberalism, globalization and the private sector. The changes to key relationships, and how influence is exerted as a result, will then be explored before different modes and scales of governance are introduced. All of this has resulted in changes to the way that power is wielded and by whom, which provides the focus of the final section.

From government to governance

'The only way to erect such a common power, able to defend them from the invasion of foreigners, and the injuries of one another, and thereby to secure them in such sort as that by their own industry and by the fruits of the earth they may nourish themselves and live contentedly, is to confer all their power and strength upon one man, or upon one assembly of men, that may reduce all their wills, by plurality of voices, unto one will.'

(Thomas Hobbes (1588–1679), *Leviathan*, 1962 [1651])

Hobbes' quote is from a seminal work of seventeenth-century political thought that arguably helped to usher in the modern era of government as we know it today – one that is now so familiar that we rarely question it. The book was written in a time of great political instability; Hobbes lived in an England that, at the time, was in the midst of a terrible civil war. He went on to argue that, in the absence of a higher authority, the natural state of humanity would be one riven with anarchy because every individual would pursue his or her own ends, and the strong will subjugate the weak. The biblical Leviathan of the title was a metaphor that Hobbes used to refer to the need to overcome such anarchy through the rule of an absolute authority, a body with much greater power than any individual in order to bring peace and security. This is, perhaps, a realistic and more prosaic aim in contrast to the earlier utopianism and idealism of writers such as Plato or More.

Influenced by a Europe riddled with war that emphatically underscored the perils of an *absence* of political control, *Leviathan* is certainly a product of its time; however, the key themes remain resonant and it continues to be a foundational text of modern political philosophy. In particular, it was the first to introduce the idea explicitly of a 'social contract' between the individual and a sovereign ruler, essentially a hypothetical compact whereby rights would be ceded and gained for the 'public good'. This two-way process was vital to enable the creation of peace and laws, but Hobbes also argued for some individual rights to be reserved in order to constrain the ability of monarchs to exert absolute power.

Political theorists use the idea of the social contract as a tool that refers to a hypothetical relationship between citizens and the state rather than being an actual signed 'contract'. In addition to Hobbes, Jean-Jacques Rousseau (1923 [1762]) and, in the modern era, John Rawls (1971), have all invoked this idea in order to reflect on an appropriate relationship between citizens and the state; for example, what rights should be given up and what the state must be obliged to do in return. This is a discussion that provides the foundation to any debate concerning environmental planning, from the need for regulation, to its extent and possible impact on individual freedom. Regardless of the topic, it is influenced by one's view of society as a whole.

While not directly attributable to Hobbes, social contracts and limits to political obligation duly came about in many European nations, and the resulting greater democracy and stability helped to usher in the era of innovation and mercantilism characterized by the Industrial Revolution. For the purposes of this section it also marks the beginning of the discussion that moves us towards the present: more than an intellectual argument for government, it highlights that we need to understand a whole host of more nuanced aspects from the purpose of the executive, to its legitimacy, and to its ability to fulfil its end of any notional 'social contract'. It also helps to understand the relationship between the state, capital and society more generally: an area at the heart of environmental planning.

Early state intervention in the environment as described in Chapter 2 was similarly related to the need for an 'authority – an external body, similar to the Hobbesian 'Leviathan' that could help to manage public health, river quality or the planning of towns. As the twentieth century progressed, government intervention regarding the environment increased alongside the growing public profile of environmental concerns and the rise in scientific knowledge and evidence-based approaches that will be discussed in Chapters 6 and 7. From the 1960s onwards, the exploration of space, the rise of sustainability agendas and numerous international conferences all reinforced the view that societies are *connected* beyond national borders, and that social, economic and environmental issues are intertwined, raising challenges for governments around the world.

In addition, towards the end of the twentieth century in many Western countries, particularly the USA and the UK, the post-war consensus that had resulted in the large-scale governments seen in the 1960s and 1970s began to be fractured. A powerful right-wing politic critiqued the state as an inefficient monolith, which not only created social and economic problems, but could actually be part of their structural underpinning. It was not enough to legislate or regulate; rather, the scale and nature of state intervention itself was part of the problem. Protagonists preached privatization, deregulation and a 'smaller state', all arguing that the private and voluntary sectors could offer services in a more efficient manner than the public sector; for example, via performance-related pay, a reduction in waste and a smaller public subsidy.

The era of political decisions administered solely by institutional bureaucracies was waning, and an era of 'new public management' (Hood, 1991) emerged, based around modernization, a greater involvement of the market and a transformation of the public sector. Moreover, the post-war era of burgeoning globalization placed nation-state-centred approaches under significant reevaluation. These trends led to an argument demanding ever more international trade and free-market policies, with roles once performed by the state now filled by multiple stakeholders. According to Evans (2012: 32) globalization lends weight to the argument that: 'the old order of sovereign nation states, which divided territories and organized economies, ruled over populations and corporations, disciplined subjects and consolidated identities, is becoming irrelevant, replaced by organs of global governance, like the World Trade Organization, which set rules constraining the actions of national governments'. The traditional perception of the state as simply exerting sovereign authority over civil society does not address the practical limitations of this bounded spatiality and power in a globalized world and there is a strong view that government should be more concerned with organizing and guiding rather than commanding and controlling – in essence, a 'light-touch' or 'small' government that can enable others to act.

Many authors usefully describe the shift as being akin to a move from 'rowing' to 'steering' (see Bevir and Rhodes, 2003: 46), where the former was concerned with central service delivery and the latter relates to setting a focus on the direction of policy. From this perspective, co-ordination has become much more important, with the state pursuing facilitative roles, such as building partnerships, providing matched funding or promoting public–private collaborations. As a result, there is also a blurring of boundaries and responsibilities, with power now being held in relationships and interactions rather than by a sole agency or set of government institutions. Here the state is not simply reorganized but rolled back, a direction of travel that Rhodes (1994) popularized as the 'hollowing out of the state'.

While the perception that the state may be shrinking attracts attention, the shift in its role is equally interesting. Indeed, there were a lot of problems associated with the so-called 'command and control' methods of governing the environment that may now be lessened. For example, the traditional legislative or regulatory roles performed by states inevitably struggle to manage complex environmental problems that may be the result of the cumulative effect of millions of industries or people from around the world. Furthermore, we shall explore in Chapter 7 how this method of governing has led to issues such as the privileging of expert information, the selective availability of data, and the need for problems to have a good fit with the institutions charged with environmental protection. This original stance has proved to be useful in managing the environment, particularly where there are clear causal links, but it can often result in fragmented approaches that over time may produce a myriad of disparate guidance that is not always analogous with the interconnected nature of environmental problems. Lindblom (1979: 517) describes a flaw of this approach as being one of 'disjointed incrementalism', typified by a standpoint that reacts to problems and focuses on muddling through rather than working strategically towards positive goals.

Considering the changing scale, scope and complexity of environmental concerns, one could be forgiven for approaching a view that the nation state has become ever more unsuited to be the main means of managing the environment. Yet it is incorrect to dismiss it as one that is irrelevant and receding. Its role has adapted to become more appropriate to changing societal contexts and demands – ever more organizational, collaborative and networked. While the state may appear to be separate from society, it does reflect shifting societal trends. An economic crisis and the 'age of austerity' that has afflicted the early twenty-first century provides a good example of this continuously evolving relationship, and serves to heighten how environmental policy, regulation and resources may be influenced by short-term economic forces and electoral agendas. Regulatory tendencies at times like these can be difficult to reconcile with loud private sector voices often calling for a stripping away of 'red tape' or the design of ways to address environmental problems while stimulating the private sector.

Despite the changing role of the state within environmental planning, its importance remains. This is helped by its unique ability to perform roles that cannot easily be done elsewhere, in particular its capability to offset some of the worst excesses of wealth accumulation, and to organize, arbitrate and manage interconnected complexities. It is also a useful mechanism to serve capitalism and the demands of markets. Essentially, it is back to the central precepts of Hobbes: a higher authority with the remit to limit individual freedoms for the social good. Yet, as we shall see, it is too simplistic to see a 'smaller' state as one with less power, or as a consequence the environment is managed better or worse. Rather, environmental planning has evolved to be influenced by agencies beyond the state, with the long-standing agencies of government now wielding a softer, less direct power, in addition to conventional means.

Evolving influences and relationships

In a groundbreaking work *Economy and Society*, the German sociologist, Max Weber (1978 [1922]), highlighted how bureaucracy is essential for public administration, given that it is the most effective and logical means of carrying out the aims of the state. He stated that: 'The decisive reason for the advance of bureaucratic organization has always been its purely technical superiority over any other form of organization. The fully developed bureaucratic mechanism compares with other organizations exactly as does the machine with the non-mechanical modes of production' (Gerth and Wright Mills, 1948: 214). Rational lines of hierarchy and authority, specialization of functions and transparent codes of conduct that facilitate equal treatment are just three features of a bureaucracy Weber highlighted that help to organize societies in beneficial ways.

Weber also drew attention to how the superior efficiency of bureaucracy as a means of control can actually drive an irreversible impetus that will result in humanity being trapped in an 'iron cage', prisoners of the sheer value and instrumentalism of the organizational framework that has been created. Yet the trends in public administration described in the previous section challenged state efficiency and rationality, and in doing so, also its supremacy. In contrast to the claims of Weber, bureaucracy became regarded by some as being more akin to the works of the writer Franz Kafka, who commonly depicted it as faceless, irrational and incompetent. However, as we shall see, bureaucratic power and influence is not so easily diminished in any 'hollowing out' of the state.

Whereas discourses concerning governing via the state may link to notions of the ruled and the ruler, this binary opposition does not reflect adequately the pluralistic nature of twenty-first-century influence and relationships. In most Western democracies, public administration has been reconfigured not only to allow the involvement of the private and voluntary sectors, but also the formation of new public–private hybrids, resulting in a blurring of boundaries in the relationship between the state, the market and civil society. The involvement of multiple stakeholders essentially marks an expansion of influence and a shift in responsibilities that has implications for how the environment is managed.

Extending the scope of decisions to include wider stakeholders does offer a number of advantages, including the resultant increase in resources and the possibility of agreeing to act collectively. It is also useful as a means of addressing environmental concerns, particularly given how they may be caused, and addressed, beyond the core power of the state, whether by individual behaviour, the market or the forces of global capitalism. When considering the environment it can be easy to focus on the 'evils' of the private sector and its perceived inveterate lobbying of government to reduce regulation, but the more networked position of the state also allows it to exert an outward influence and involve the flexible and inventive potential of non-state actors to assist in managing environmental concerns.

The new plurality of environmental governance, in which the state is only one of many powers, results in a situation that is much more complex than the command and control relationship described in the previous section. Risks do, however, emerge from such structural changes, and effective environmental governance still stresses the requirement for 'rules' that can enable interaction to take place, but whose existence can still ultimately privilege some sections of society over others. Far from a view of the state acting 'in the public interest', it has adopted a more facilitative role that can oversee how relations occur; for example, by making it a statutory requirement to engage with community organizations, non-governmental organizations (NGOs) or specific actors in the private sector. This altered role enables decisions connected with the environment to be made, whether by individuals or the private sector in a voluntary fashion, within new partnerships, or via the more conventional and legislative mechanisms of the state. Significantly, it may also create the potential for decisions *not* to be taken.

The role of governments in managing the environment, or more specifically the interaction between humanity and the natural world, has clearly been very important. The state can address specific areas directly, from pollution to energy use to conservation. It also has the potential to establish agencies with a specific remit connected to aspects of environmental protection, or connected areas such as sustainability, climate change, agriculture or forestry. In addition to their visible operational influence, institutions also hold a wider power within society. Even without designing legislation governments can influence behaviour, set directions, distribute subsidies, or employ a host of other mechanisms that can set a general tone or a direction of travel to both industry and citizens. The use of indicators or the design of contract terms and conditions for external services provide two good examples of new forms of state influence. Here, control is exerted in much less obvious ways, encompassing aspects such as penalties for missing performance targets, or determining how projects and programmes are evaluated. Equally, the gradual acceptance and normalization of administration duties performed by the market or civil society in areas such as security, law, education, public health or pollution control is a form of behaviour conditioning exerted by the state without resorting to more visible levels of discipline.

Commissioning research or having an onus on 'best practice', which is endemic in environmental planning, can also help to propagate preferred spatio-technical measures of intervention, or even the desired social engagement processes. This central process of opening debates, goal setting or the contracting out of services creates a dialogue that encourages stakeholder 'buy-in'. For example, when bidding for a government tender, an organization implicitly assents to how the problem is framed, its scope and who should be involved. Importantly, it is also perceived to be the applicants' *choice* and within their power to accept or decline, so only willing participants should apply. This softer form of control still allows the state to set objectives, but these are realized through external agents rather than within its own institutions. Here, the government essentially frames the issue, the resulting debate and the means by which it can be addressed. Rydin (2011: 49) explains the evolving influences thus: 'particular government rationalities are promoted so that certain ways of understanding the world, its problems and its potentialities are taken for granted'. All of which may be seen as part of a shift in influence and responsibility with regard to the dynamic and, perhaps increasingly opaque, social contract that is part of how societies now function.

From this perspective, the 'rules' of government introduced at the start of this chapter are still in existence but are complemented by the subtle promotion of an agreeable self-discipline that aligns society with the aims of the state. The French social philosopher, Michel Foucault (1979), explained this objective through his notion of 'governmentality'. This term may be understood as concerning the 'governing of mentalities' and describes how modes of thought can be influenced by institutions and the state, not just in a hierarchal way by threats or coercion, but rather by guiding and shaping how individuals self-regulate and, in a sense, govern themselves (Lemke, 2002). Foucault (1979) uses the example of the Panopticon, a type of prison developed by the English philosopher Jeremy Bentham (1748–1832), to develop his argument. This building is cleverly designed with a ring of cells all facing a central watch tower, so the prisoners are never sure if they are being watched or not. As a consequence they modify their behaviour even if they are not under observation. The end result is that people are conditioned to govern themselves in a way that aligns with the aims of authority.

This is an interesting issue for environmental planning, as non-state actors and behavioural change are such critical issues. Rather than being merely a dualistic discussion about the merits of top-down government, or of bottom-up community-led approaches, it highlights a deeper level of connection. It further draws attention to the way that power may be inherent within institutional contexts, and that notions of 'the environment' may be internalized and constructed by various stakeholders, from private-sector organizations to individuals. The more subtle influencing of ethics, values and behaviour is not to be underestimated as a means of exerting authority and can serve to frame debates concerning science, policy or decision-making that will be discussed as this book progresses.

However, governance approaches such as these do highlight what could be argued to be a gradual emasculation of the state, in which nations now have a reduced role that is frequently concerned with influencing or implementing changes that may be determined elsewhere or by a wide range of groups. Consequently, this also undermines democracy. In contrast to the standards of transparency, accountability and legitimacy that society demands from more visible and formal government institutions, opaque, and potentially unaccountable, power is now held by numerous actors and agencies. As Peters (1993: 55, quoted in Stoker, 1998: 20) comments: 'We must be concerned with the extent to which complex structures linking the public and private sectors ... actually mask responsibility and add to the problems of citizens in understanding and influencing the actions of their governments.'

Indeed, this blurring of roles and responsibilities may create a degree of uncertainty as to who should be responsible and held accountable if action does not happen: 'blame avoidance and scapegoating are not new political phenomena but governance structures do extend the capacity for such activity' (Stoker, 1998: 22). Therefore, environmental planning is not just a matter of the exertion of central control but can depend on the compliance of others who allow power to be exercised and adhere to its implications. Significantly, in some cases people may have little knowledge of this happening or any control over the results. The transition in approach from government to governance has consequently led to an evolving relationship between the state and other stakeholders that has changed how decisions are made, by whom and over what scale.

Changing modes and scales

If we take the view that environmental planning concerns are not just about policy implementation or the level of government resources, but relate more broadly to how influence is exerted and how discourses are shaped, then the implications of changes in governance for those involved can be understood more readily. The unambiguous top-down hierarchies characterized by central, regional or local government bureaucracy have been supplemented with messy and changeable structures that are less linear and more focused on what are sometimes opaque networks and relationships. In understanding the nuances and implications of this difference it is useful to consider the variable 'modes' of governance pertaining to how governmental and non-governmental actors interact, and the scales on which these operate.

With specific regard to environmental planning, Evans (2012) highlights three modes of governance that have particular relevance. In addition to the familiar 'hierarchy' mode, there is also 'network governance', within which various empowered actors may coalesce in pursuit of a common goal. From an environmental planning perspective this could, for example, involve NGOs, international agencies, community groups and scientists all working in a flexible, collective manner to solve a particular problem in a decentralized fashion. While it can provide increased resources, a wider experience base and a means to adapt to uncertainty and complexity, to realize these benefits requires trust, efficient communication and effective knowledge transfer. A third example is 'market governance', which concerns influencing aspects of the production of goods and services, setting taxes, providing incentives or even creating entirely new market instruments, such as carbon trading. It can correct market failure and influence the private sector, but will be more visibly subject to forces such as lobbying, the vagaries of contract law or globalization.

In addition to these modes, governance can also operate on multiple scales: from small local interactions, to corporate governance within a company, to national and supra-national scales, with networks operating within and across these. Therefore it may be understood as being 'cross-scale', encompassing horizontal and vertical interactions, rather than simply local or international (Berkes, 2002). This is an important aspect as it enables new interactions to develop that may be better suited to the interdisciplinary, transboundary nature of environmental concerns, which can be simultaneously global and local, intragenerational, or even be related to a planet-wide 'commons'. Governance approaches are also well placed to help in achieving sustainability objectives, which may rely on behavioural change or new ways of working. Indeed, the Local Agenda 21 approach that emerged from the 1992 Rio Earth Summit could only be achieved by working closely with local-level partners. With regard to environmental planning, the agencies concerned will vary depending on the issue to be addressed, making it relatively fluid and potentially very effective in comparison to the inflexibility of the nation state.

While it creates a platform to address tricky international issues, expanding the scale does, however, increase the number of stakeholders and can create a complexity that pushes agreement towards the lowest common denominator acceptable to all parties. The Copenhagen Climate Change Conference (COP15) in 2009 provides a high-profile case study. Far from producing any legally binding agreement, in the wake of serious disagreements the summit culminated in a vague political declaration, the Copenhagen Accord, and a loose commitment to further talks. Despite a consensus on the threat posed by climate change, gaining a legally enforceable agreement involving all nation states that could detail the level of cuts to be achieved by a certain date proved impossible (see Dimitrov, 2010 for a review). Considering the unequal distribution of fossil fuels and their ability to enable economic growth and create wealth on a national scale, this impasse is not a complete surprise. This example also highlights how important the state remains, not just as an actor on an international scale, but with regard to its established authority and ability to set rules, steer and control.

In short, changes to the status quo may experience resistance in any mode or scale, whether by a failure to engage, a lack of cooperation or a difference of opinion. Therefore, while governance trends may facilitate new networks and discussions, they may also lack the simple leadership inherent in 'command and control' models. Significantly, it can create an absence of clear authority that may serve to delay action on pressing matters; democracy and pluralism can have its disadvantages.

An understanding of governance processes now leads the discussion logically towards our next section: where the power lies. This is particularly apparent when considering the outcomes of collective forms of decision-making. For example, why should those in the wealthy countries change their lifestyles for the greater 'good'? Or why should this generation go without so that those not yet born can use scarce resources? It is worth reminding ourselves that some countries are rich precisely because others are poor, and that resource exploitation and globalization bring an uneven distribution of benefits that some would like to see preserved. Chhotray and Stoker (2008: 209) even argue that the whole idea of environmental governance is 'fundamentally about how to use power to influence critical decisions about the environment'. We shall see that this bold claim holds great weight.

Power and legitimacy

Power is critical to understanding environmental governance, both as a theory and from there how it might have an impact on practice. Power can influence a whole host of factors, including the form (how governance is structured), content (how governance is imposed) and ethic (whether governance is fair) (Chhotray and Stoker, 2008: 208). One of the key messages from the previous sections is that, despite dispersing power and being in discussion with other actors within the broader environmental governance, states have tended to retain forms of power and still exert influence in a more sophisticated, and less obvious, fashion. While a wider array of stakeholders has been empowered, this does not necessarily equate to a similar reduction in the power of governments, or, indeed, an escape from authority: domination may occur by more adroit means. In simple terms, you may have 'power to' but are still subject to 'power over' (Pitkin, 1972).

Take a moment to think of a single environmental issue that is not subject to various opinions – a task that is much more difficult than it sounds. Climate change or fracking may be the most high-profile current examples of divergence, but even concerns within one's local neighbourhood would display opposing views that require dialogue. Disagreements here are frequently dismissed as 'Nimbyism', but using this terminology is a display of power in itself: it is too simple to view every individual perspective as one of utilitarian self-interest; people have a moral compass that can value concerns relating to the community, country or planet as higher than their own (Clegg, 1989). Moving up in scale, consider the contrasting approaches to the environment from nations such as the USA, Australia, China or those in the EU that frequently bring a degree of conflict. For example, whereas the EU has shown an appetite for legislating and harmonizing environmental management, the USA has recently experienced deregulatory pressures. Yet each of these actors will have to meet when discussing matters that merit international co-operation, and each will have regard for self-interest and the avoidance of unpalatable obligations. The harsh reality is that environmental planning is riddled with self-interest, and power struggles operate at all levels.

A variety of writers throughout history have discussed the concept of power, from Aristotle to Weber to Machiavelli, but its development into a distinct academic discipline began from the middle of the twentieth century. Though notions of power are contested, and within academia there is no single rarefied view, Lukes (2005) identified three dimensions of power that are useful in investigating the subject. The first is a positivistic definition that provides an initial platform for understanding the notion on a deeper level. Here, Dahl (1957: 202–3) famously defined the issue as being where: 'A has power over B to the extent that he can get B to do something that B would not otherwise do." The second dimension questions this simple focus on decision-making and openness, and focuses on more covert power struggles and agenda setting, where 'non-decisions' may occur or people may be excluded from the process. The final aspect concerns 'hidden' or 'invisible' power, which in contrast with the previous two interpretations may not be seen as a conflict or struggle. Here power can influence more subtly by persuasion and assent, or even by the very fabric of socialization. In this final example, A may also exercise power over B by: 'influencing, shaping or determining his very wants' (Lukes, 2005: 27).

Exploring this third dimension further is a useful exercise in understanding power. For example, the Marxist thinker, Antonio Gramsci (1995), argued that dominant stakeholders can create a cultural hegemony by aligning their values and worldviews with those of the good of society as a whole, in essence normalizing their position and embedding it within the cultural mainstream. Mitchell (1995: 103) extends this argument of hidden power further, citing the concept of 'culture', something that is usually accepted without question. He stated that there is no such thing, and instead culture should be regarded as an authoritative idea that has: 'developed under specific historical conditions and was later broadened as a means of explaining material differences, social order and relations of power'. The way that globalization or capitalism are seen as systems without alternatives offers a final illustration of hidden power. Here, the creation of a powerful ideological trope essentially argues for the citizen to merely adapt to the normal demands of capital and the state, at the expense of exploring any more transformative measures that can result in systemic change.

To sum up, 'hidden' power draws attention to the way that normality and culture can be socially constructed and deterministic. Here, the notion that becomes most dominant is actively (though not consciously) maintained and employed by dominant groups. With respect to the environment, Box 3.1 focuses on how perceptions of wilderness and nature can lead to a persuasive moralistic and ethical naturalism that demonstrates just how powerful cultural ideas can be.

Authoritarian ethics such as those connected with naturalism brook little right of debate and essentially are a process of internalizing external power. It is inaccurate to view ethical arguments as being just another strand of the 'natural' world, when in reality ethics is a societal choice happening all around us. As discussed in Chapter 2, the neo-deism of 'progress', the hegemony of capitalism, or the new 'religion' of consumerism are all competing frames of reference wielding the power to channel debate down prescribed pathways and greatly influence the relationship between humanity and the natural world.

Issues connected with legitimacy and authority also exert great weight in environmental planning, but again an understanding of power suggests that this should not be accepted meekly. Institutions may be seen to hold legitimate power, but this is: 'not simply an empirical statement. It is an implicitly normatively evaluative statement, endorsing certain political arrangements' (Clegg and Haugaard, 2009: 3). In simple terms, power does not only *confer* legitimacy, it can also *determine* it by defining reality, framing debates and managing information, which links to the discussion in Chapters 6 and 7 that discuss science, expertise and policy. Though trends in open access, knowledge networks and data sharing may appear to disperse this control somewhat, this only serves to heighten the importance of how information is constructed, gains influence, and the identity of the stakeholders performing this role. How environmental problems are understood and represented is connected inextricably to how they may be addressed. Therefore, though not as conspicuous a use of power as force, other displays associated with conferring legitimacy and authority can achieve similar ends.

Environmental impacts may be understood as a physical phenomenon, but here we can see that there is also a strong sociopolitical dimension. An awareness of power can help us to understand how and why some concerns are defined, highlighted and mitigated, while others may stubbornly persist or be ignored altogether. Consider some of the discussion in the book so far, from the failure to challenge the 'human exemptionalist' paradigm which separates humanity from nature, to the dominance of technological or market-based solutions, to agencies distorting or cherrypicking science to support their own arguments. Even some of those aspects of environmental planning that are taken for granted, such as rationality in decision-making, link the construction of rules, knowledge and practices that shape interpretation and outcomes, and can transform what may appear superficially to be in the public interest into the protection of special interests (Flyvbjerg, 1998). In sum, with regard to power, wider aspects such as the ability to produce and control information, subtly suppress agendas or even normalize problems should be considered alongside the more discernible displays of authority such as policy creation or enforcement of environmental penalties.

Box 3.1 Moralistic and naturalistic fallacies

In an essay entitled 'The trouble with wilderness; or, getting back to the wrong nature' the environmental historian, William Cronon (1995), offered an interesting perspective on the natural world. In an effort to encourage people to think differently about 'wilderness' he argued that the term is not fixed, and is rather a compelling and constructed notion that differs between cultures. For example, the idea of a *pristine* wilderness is central to much green activism and conservation movements. Here, a state of natural wilderness is automatically aligned as 'good' and any change to this is unnatural, and by extension 'bad'. But there is no real justification of why this is the case, it just seems persuasive in particular societies and operates in a largely unchallenged manner.

The implication of assuming a stance that nature offers us a clear ethical steer that should be obeyed is known as moral naturalism; a view positing that what is natural is automatically moral, and what is moral is right. Therefore, what is natural is right. But this is neither a fact nor an indisputable message; rather, it is an opinion that is a facet of society and culture. While some things are clearly identifiable as natural or not, there is no logical outcome that should flow from this position. Indeed, any notion of 'good' is impossible to establish categorically as it is a term of reference.

The British philosopher, G. E. Moore (1903 [2004]: 10), called positions where nature is employed within arguments in an ethical manner such as this a 'naturalistic fallacy' that almost unconsciously skews debate towards one side. While the idea of 'wilderness' being unequivocally desirable may instinctively ring true with many concerned with the environment, this view is: 'culturally fabricated, culturally specific and culturally variable' (Castree, 2005: 135). For example, if you were an early settler in the USA a few centuries ago you might hold a vastly different outlook from that of the present: a view that wilderness was unattractive; land that needed to be tamed for the good of all. In a similar vein, Cosgrove (1984) argued that 'landscapes' are not only physical environments but also a cultural construct that emerged from the European Renaissance period, when new ways of mapping, surveying and visualizing provided a highly aesthetic representation of nature, such as is apparent in much of the art of the time. In this case, the term represents both a 'physical environment' and a way of 'seeing' that influences people as to what land should look like.

These examples raise questions over *whose* way of seeing nature becomes dominant, and what the outcomes may be. Representing

→

→

and romanticizing the natural world in this manner exerts power and is frequently used disingenuously to exert moralistic authority in order to further particular interests. For example, from this perspective, wilderness should automatically be preserved. However, such a 'moralistic fallacy' (Pinker, 2002: 162) can exert a hidden cultural power to protect and maintain space in the interests of economic elites, with change clearly on the wrong end of the argument. Here, people who already own houses may campaign for the conservation of natural land, but what about those who may not yet be on the property ladder? And isn't development good for society and growth? The mere existence of a counter-argument proves that while nature implies fixity, it loses this quality on entry to the moral sphere.

Adopting a naturalistic perspective also impacts on environmental policy, where the argument automatically follows that human intervention should be minimized or techniques that mimic nature should be adopted. The seemingly self-evident logic in floodplain restoration provides a good example of this. Though counter-arguments concerning the social construction of nature habitually form in opposition, it should be noted that these views are also subject to critique. For example, social constructionism has been branded as a perspective that can be used to justify further exploitation of the natural world (Proctor, 1998).

The often used and relatively unchallenged standpoint that 'nature knows best' may resonate instinctively with some. However, it should be noted that tacit in this view is that ethics or morals are predicated from nature when in reality they vary temporally and spatially, and are a construct of social and cultural norms. A good illustration here is provided by the Gaia hypothesis developed by the British scientist, James Lovelock (2000). This proposition argues that the Earth is an enormous, single integrated system that operates in an ordered and naturally harmonious way. Implicit in this view is that self-regulating mechanisms react to human activity and as a result we may make the planet more uninhabitable by disrupting them. Accepting this powerful 'Mother Nature' frame logically leads to the need not merely to change behaviour but also to re-evaluate the entire human relationship with the biosphere. Therefore, it has strong ethical undertones leading inevitably to a core belief that natural limits should be imposed dictatorially on societies. The 'nature knows best' theory has a hidden moral power designed to strengthen a particular argument.

Conclusion

The US president Harry S. Truman famously kept a sign on his desk reading 'The buck stops here'. The phrase is essentially about responsibility, obligations, accountability and transparency – all aspects of effective environmental planning. But the way society is governed and power wielded can make this phrase one that could no longer be used in public office; a relic of the command and control era. The fragmentation of power, the creation of new networks and cross-scalar engagements means that there is rarely one single actor or agency with the unilateral power to solve problems, and each stakeholder may have different resources and agendas. This is both a function of how influence may be exerted over the environment and how far-reaching some problems may be. Even seemingly purely state-centred or market-orientated approaches do not operate in isolation; they are supported or undermined by a myriad of wider social interactions that are a feature of negotiations over space or resources. As the social contract described in *Leviathan* becomes more difficult to recognize, challenges and opportunities emerge for environmental planning.

The study of governance has become an academic field in itself. Indeed, there are different forms and iterations of 'governance', from network governance to economic governance, and even to 'good' governance, all of which have their own nuances (Evans, 2012). However, this chapter has been centred on using the term as a means of comprehending decisions relating to the environment; its value here is as an interpretive framework that allows us to better understand and analyse environmental planning. This is no one-off task – as the ways by which institutions are structured or power distributed in societies will continue to evolve – rather, the discussion has been designed to equip readers with an understanding of the most relevant aspects to allow a comprehension of the issues discussed in subsequent chapters in a deeper manner.

There is no doubt that state power in contemporary societies is altering, not that it is being reduced, rather it is different. We know that there has been a pluralist turn towards incorporating the views of a multitude of stakeholders, and that this transformation away from a purely hierarchal model holds a number of implications for the governance of environmental planning. Yet it is too simplistic to see a smaller state as being necessarily a weaker one. A counter-argument would say that the state has changed to be relevant to the interconnected and cross-scalar nature of many environmental problems, and is now better equipped than ever to influence civil society, the private sector and wider stakeholders. It has adapted to external changes, retained relevance and may actually be an expression of how societies now *prefer* government to operate. This move may also be more able to address problems which may have been endemic in a system that governs the environment from the narrow hierarchal perspective of the nation state. For example, the new co-ordination and engagement role associated with governance can mitigate some persistent issues associated with centralized approaches that 'can be – and historically is, in case after case – an instrument for protecting historically inherited inequalities' (Lindblom, 1979: 523).

In addition to conflict over unevenness, governing the environment necessarily raises tensions with notions of liberty, or the 'freedom' to act – whether overtly to pollute, consume or despoil, or engage in more unconscious activities that may bring indirect or inadvertent impacts, from air travel to materialism. The social contract discussed by Hobbes was an early acknowledgement of the need for a higher authority that could manage the trade-off between the needs of the individual and the collective in order to benefit society more generally. Yet alongside rights there are also obligations. The question is more connected to where the lines are drawn rather than whether the pen is picked up. And here, as with all interactions between humanity and the environment, there will be strong views based not just on personal ethics and values, but also on wider societal drivers from shareholder value to government priorities for economic growth.

While trends of governance in both the state and society more generally can frame and inhibit environmental planning, it should be noted there may be good reasons underpinning this. For example, there is no doubt that, despite their many benefits, systems of democracy and pluralistic modes of decision-making are limited in their ability to control environmental impacts (Eckersley, 2004). Equally, core principles of market-based economies, such as economic liberalism, deregulation, consumerism and non-interventionist government in many cases do not offer a solution to the protection of public goods. But there is still the potential to generate beneficial outcomes while working within these constraints. It is less about how strong is the role of the state; rather, the consideration of the – admittedly subjective – notions of good and bad governance. Indeed, not all environmental policies and agreements are effective, nor do they even have the interests of the environment at their heart.

Here, an understanding of power helps us to appreciate how poor environmental policies can emerge, and how non-decisions are 'made' where, for example, there is a latent cultural and social power to frame debate and exert control. Before reading this chapter you would have been aware of how well-networked interest groups can play a role in lobbying for or against measures, and through the process of consultation might even inform the scope and extent of any policy. But influence and power is much more pervasive, hidden and even misused. For example, we frequently hear of the strength of public opinion. But who is 'the public'? To what extent can a singular view represent the public? And who are using this argument as a way to achieve their own ends? We now develop this mode of thought further by investigating a related subject with the power to frame environmental planning: politics and the media.

Chapter 4

Politics and the Media

'Political conflicts distort and disturb the people's sense of distinction between matters of importance and matters of urgency. What is vital is disguised by what is merely a matter of wellbeing; the ulterior is disguised by the imminent; the badly needed by what is readily felt.'

(Paul Valéry, quoted in Keynes, 1933)

The above quotation by French polymath Paul Valéry was cited by Keynes (1933) in an essay on the rapid protectionist trend towards economic nationalism and national self-sufficiency between the two world wars, the speed of which he thought could damage economic growth. Valéry and Keynes both essentially highlight the prevalence of politics as being inherently dominated by the now – a short-termism that might not mesh well with the longer time horizons of many environmental concerns and approaches, most notably that of sustainability, biodiversity loss or climate change. However, the relationship between humanity and resources ensures that politics, a term that covers the way that decisions are made in society, and political discourse more generally, is vital in determining environmental planning.

Taking into consideration democracy, a fundamental aspect of most political systems, further muddies the waters. In liberal democracies, periodic elections result in short-term electoral cycles, where those in government may have a mandate for only five years or so. Hard environmental choices that imply long-term change or threats to immediate growth do not fit well with brief, attention-driven policy windows. Beyond the temporal mismatch, the nature of party politics in most countries means that it is played out on populist grounds that can inhibit cross-party agreement. Yet if the long-term management of the environment is linked to different outcomes, behaviour or thinking, then understanding the political world is crucial, since it is concerned with reasoning, persuasion and, at the end of the process, legislation, policy and possible change. The fundamental tensions introduced in the previous chapter between authority and freedom – a recurring theme in environmental planning – are played out in the political sphere.

Environmental planning can be an intensely political activity, particularly when it aims at change. Whether this is by implementing new pollution control regulations or, more subtly, via the objectives of grassroots movements that argue for wider transformations, there are always political considerations concerning how resources are distributed, or how intervention occurs. The process of governance may be regarded as an intellectual or managerial tool to help navigate the world of politics and the conflicting opinions concerning the use of space or resources. The integrative nature of environmental planning means that it co-ordinates, consults, engages and assimilates knowledge from a variety of stakeholders. Agreements and consensus may be sought, which means that practitioners of environmental planning are also political actors. But while this expert arbitration and negotiation role is a core responsibility for environmental planners, theirs is just one of a number of voices. Therefore, this chapter on politics will also discuss other key players, most notably the private sector and the media.

The approach taken here will focus on the intersection between politics and the environment, rather than 'environmental politics'. This discussion is different from one pertaining to environmental or green politics per se, which tend to rest on two central beliefs: that there are limits to growth; and that the relationship between the human and non-human world is a non-instrumental one (Connelly and Smith, 2003). The use of 'politics' here refers not just to the activities of government, but also to a more inclusive definition that encompasses decision-making, resource distribution, relationships and interactions among a wide variety of groups, both formal and informal (Leftwich, 1983). This stance makes for a broader and less focused discussion, but is more appropriate to understanding environmental planning in theory and practice, which necessarily incorporates a diffuse range of stakeholders.

The broad scope of politics, from local community groups to global corporations, means that it is impossible to discuss all the players or, indeed, unpack every political system. While the discussion in this chapter is focused mainly on the liberal democracies that are commonplace in Europe, North America and Australasia, it will also be relevant for single-party regimes such as in China, as it is also concerned with ideologies, the market and the private sector. We shall first investigate the development of the environment within the political sphere, and explore the nuances of 'green politics'. The chapter will then build on this foundation by turning to the issue of differing political ideologies before examining two key stakeholders with regard to the environment and planning: the market and private sector, and the media.

Introducing environmental politics

'The politics of the Industrial Age, left, right and centre, is like a three-lane motorway, with different vehicles in different lanes, but *all* heading in the same direction. Greens feel that it is the very direction that is wrong, rather than the choice of any one lane in preference to the others. It is our perception that the motorway of industrialism inevitably leads to the abyss – hence our decision to get off it, and seek an entirely different direction.'

(Porritt, 1984: 43)

Jonathan Porritt, a former director of Friends of the Earth, used this analogy to highlight neatly the difference between mainstream political parties, who try to address environmental issues within conventional stances, and what we might term 'green politics', which advocates social justice between current and future generations, promotes environmental protection and eschews materialism. Or, to link with the ideas that will be discussed in the next chapter, 'greens' would argue that applying a biocentric outlook within an anthropocentric frame is an ineffective approach.

Chapter 2 showed that the environment has a long political history, yet the rise of environmental activism, advocacy and the formation of new political parties is a mid-to-late twentieth-century phenomenon. Long perceived as a 'single-issue' social movement, environmental activists often struggle for recognition in politics: environmental risks affect all people, so they are also theoretically addressed by mainstream political organizations. Therefore it is important to note that those espousing green politics are not only concerned with gaining formal representation, but also aim to influence the established political powers of the 'left' and 'right' to adopt more environmentally friendly positions.

Reformers motivated by improving social conditions and environmental health in the late nineteenth and early twentieth centuries provide our starting point. Their concerns were complemented by the simultaneous emergence of political movements with explicitly environmental concerns. At this time conservation was a key aim, as characterized by the Sierra Club, formed in the USA in 1892, or by writers such as Henry David Thoreau, who advocated a 'back-to-nature' way of life and a simpler existence that is familiar to many contemporary debates. Lowe and Goyder (1983) chart the episodic nature of environmental groups and their organization and expansion in fertile periods, such as in the late 1880s, and then occasionally lapsing into times with a relative lack of activity before coming to prominence again. Notably, the 1960s witnessed the environmental movement begin to branch out from a 'protect and preserve' perspective to incorporate a broader span of reactionary social concerns, from anti-war to nuclear energy to women's liberation. Organizations such as Greenpeace, the World Wildlife Fund and Friends of the Earth began to represent a new social movement that questioned the relationship between humanity and nature more fundamentally.

Dobson (2012) highlights how this flourishing political ideology was historically situated. It was a product of the rise in scientific knowledge, the means to communicate and form networks, and a reaction against the more visible excesses of capitalist society. Therefore, while environmental concern is in evidence throughout history, it took these wider developments to turn it into a distinct social and political movement. Tarrow (1994) further suggested that social movements and their support go through cycles. Anger and a sense of injustice are common catalysts in the birth of many movements. This may be critical to early momentum but can fade over time as movements enter the mainstream, the societal context changes, or longevity is undermined by a lack of institutional support. Equally, as will become apparent in the example of the West German Green Party described in Box 4.1 (p. 83), political opportunities can emerge and the group itself can change when some goals are achieved.

Blumer (1955: 199) defines social movements as: 'collective enterprises seeking to establish a new order of life. They have their inception in a condition of unrest, and derive their motive power on one hand from dissatisfaction with the current form of life, and on the other hand, from wishes and hopes for a new system of living'. Using this definition allows green politics to be situated within certain societal conditions: first, the ability to act collectively; and second, the need for a reaction against current practices. Any social movements can be analysed against these variables: on the level of change sought (that is, in individuals or society more generally) and the magnitude (that is, partial or total). For example, anti-capitalism groups advocate transformative societal changes while other organizations may focus on smaller-scale changes for individuals, such as encouraging recycling. Generally speaking, environmental politics discourses take two different paths. First, there is a deep-seated and quite radical attack on capitalism, materialism and current politics, such as highlighted by Porritt. Second, there is a more realistic and pragmatic approach focused on influencing within existing structures and managing current practices in a better way. Across the two, this covers a surprisingly broad range of viewpoints and questions. For example, does nature have intrinsic or instrumental value? And if so, what is valued by whom? Equally, to what extent should we compromise current growth for future well-being?

This diversity also explains the number of what may be loosely termed 'environmental organizations', from the more radical Earth First! to the very mainstream, and essentially extremely conservative, groups, such as the National Trust or the Council for the Protection of Rural England in the UK. Each group may try to influence in different ways: from ad hoc reactionary, direct action or by highly organized and well-funded lobby groups. In practice, green politics encompasses a broad church, from anarchists with alternative lifestyles to very traditional moderates who want to conserve existing green spaces in their locality. Like other societal groups, while members invest time, non-members may enjoy the fruits of any victories. This is known as the 'free-rider' phenomenon and is a common feature of environmental movements (Olson, 1965). There is evidence that membership of environmental organizations, particularly those connected with rural issues, is skewed towards the middle classes (Taylor, 2009). However, this is true for most voluntary organizations and does not necessarily mean that the environment is purely a concern for those sections of society.

Reflecting on what we know from the previous chapter concerning governance, it is therefore incorrect to label environmental groups as being only *one* actor. Indeed, there have been a number of occasions where issues have brought actors into opposition; nuclear energy and wind power being two of the most notable, where groups that are concerned with protecting landscapes may be in conflict with others advocating a retreat from fossil fuel use. Rather than viewing these groups as a distinct entity, it is helpful when examining environmental movements to view them as having a series of overlapping similarities. The philosopher Ludwig Wittgenstein (1953) refers to certain languages as sharing a 'family resemblance', in much the same way as different family members share some characteristics but not all, and this insight is applicable to environmental groups. This relates to the spectrum of environmental concern that will be outlined in the next chapter, and in particular the opposing viewpoints of light or dark green – they are members of the same 'family' but look slightly different. Linking to the issue of culture discussed in the previous chapter, social practices are also a key influence in your political outlook (Macnaghten and Urry, 1998). For example, if you are employed in a sector connected with the environment, tourism or agriculture, this will undoubtedly shape your stance in some way.

Even environmental organizations themselves can be inherently fractious. Grassroots activists within the same group may occupy differing positions; some may seek to challenge the entire institutional structure and hierarchy that those on another wing of the organization are happy to operate within. Arguing for environmental issues to receive a higher priority within politics, while simultaneously desiring entirely new political and economic systems, can expose deep ruptures within groups. Box 4.1 on 'the fundis and the realos' provides an example of this occurring in practice.

The environment has no voice so it needs advocates. Yet, as this illustration shows, people adopt contradictory positions across a spectrum and treat the environment differently depending on their worldview. Consequently, there is no single voice, rather there is a multitude that operates more like a cacophony than an orchestra. Instead of considering a social movement, such as Die Grünen, as a coherent 'group' it may be more accurate to think of it as a network that shares a degree of collective identity or a family similarity influenced by the flow and exchange of information through connections (Castells, 1996).

Environmental politics has developed almost beyond recognition since the 1960s. While some aspects remain unaltered – there are still 'fundis', for example, for whom environmentalism represents an argument against capitalism – in practice these radical voices are drowned out in mainstream politics by the very powerful 'realos', who embrace 'green business' sectors and prevailing economic agendas. Therefore this section also touches on the topic of political *ideologies* – a powerful aspect of politics as it permeates a host of fundamental issues that wield direct and indirect influence on the environment. It does not just affect 'environmental' views,

---

Box 4.1 The 'fundis' and the 'realos'

The diversity within environmental groups was brought into sharp focus from the 1980s onwards when the green movement started to form political parties and began to campaign in earnest for official representation. The West German experience is particularly illustrative here, as it represents a good case of this evolution from the politics of protest and conflict to one of mainstream influence, and how this may expose internal tensions. After forming in 1980, the Green Party (Die Grünen) quickly enjoyed success in the 1983 Bundestag elections and captured 28 seats. In 1985 it formed a coalition with the Socialist Democratic Party, and Joschka Fischer, a popular Green Party representative, became the Environment Minister.

While this may initially appear to be a political success, it does not tell the whole story. The whole concept of a coalition – working within the existing structures that serve to underpin structural problems – was anathema to some in the Green Party. Environmentalism had a strong counter-culture background that for some entailed an outright rejection of notions of left and right, and instead argued for a completely new relationship with the environment (Spretnak and Capra, 1984). Others wanted to modernize the party along more traditional lines, and thought that, by working within this realist framework they would be better able to achieve at least some of their goals. In Germany, these factions were christened the 'fundis' and the 'realos' – the fundamentalists and the realists.

While this internecine conflict was seen as damaging to the party, Doherty (1992) draws attention to how this might represent a maturing of the green political movement, comparing it to similar internal debates seen in socialist parties at the beginning of the twentieth century. For the Green Party, the discourse moved from an absolutist stance of 'right and wrong' or 'ethical and unethical', towards one of negotiation, concession and compromise – the basic staples of real world politics. Therefore, while green parties set out to change politics, politics can also change green parties.

---

but also any related stances regarding social change or the relationship between the state and the individual.

Environmental political ideologies

An ideology can be described as 'a more or less coherent set of ideas that provides the basis for organized political action, whether it is intended to preserve, modify or overthrow the existing system of power' (Heywood, 2003: 12). Ideologies are not fixed or static; they are often revised as society changes. Specific ideologies may not cohere with a particular political party, as there are many hues that colour beliefs across the political spectrum. In this vein, the political theorist, Andrew Dobson, who has written widely on citizenship, politics and the environment, marks out ecologism as a specific ideology, to be distinguished from environmentalism. He suggests that the former is more radical, wanting a new relationship with the natural world, whereas the latter is a reformist position that can be tagged on and subsumed under the different ideological positions. Dobson (2012: 201) considers ecologism as an ideology in a separate manner: 'because it has, first, a description of the political and social world – a pair of green spectacles – which helps us to find our way around it'.

Table 4.1 is intended to give readers an initial insight into some of the most relevant political beliefs they will encounter and is designed to help in relating politics to the environment. Any environmental intervention may be unpalatable to individuals of a particular political persuasion, and this table helps to explain why that may be the case. For example, suggesting government policy or legislation to change people's behaviour to a more 'sustainable' approach could be construed as an assault on individual rights to choose, as formulated in classical liberal perspectives. Similarly, calls for a move to increase energy efficiency may only be accepted when framed in terms of the economic growth and free market paradigm that resonates so strongly with neoliberals. Table 4.1 gives an overview of some, but not all, of the major ideologies that are linked to environment and planning. There are many more '–isms' than are laid out in this table and there are also some disagreements when representing ideologies in this user-friendly format. For example, in some renderings, feminism and ecologism are social movements that cut across the political boundaries of liberalism, socialism and conservatism. However, this section should give you a good foundation from which to explore further by linking political ideologies with some key thinkers before considering how this relates to different views regarding the relationship between the state, the individual and the environment.

Table 4.1 is designed to give readers a flavour of the major political ideologies and how they may take different stances towards the environment. From a theoretical perspective, readers will find it useful for their studies, and in particular when interpreting political

Table 4.1 *An overview of major political ideologies*

Political ideology/ disposition	Key thinkers	Relationship between the state and the individual	View of the environment
Neo-liberalism	Friedrich Hayek; Milton Friedman	Minimal state Human beings are rational and self-interested economic individuals	Rejects limits to growth. The free market determines worth
Traditional conservatism	Edmund Burke; Michael Oakeshott	Minimal intervention Focus on local scale, but nation state remains the primary site of identity Educated and trained elite need to govern paternalistically	Anthropocentric – humans are trustees or stewards of the environment. Intergenerational equity
Utilitarian liberalism	Jeremy Bentham; John Stuart Mill	Steady-state economics Rights-based language Tolerant of different ideas of the 'good life', including environmentalism	Anthropocentric; however some suggest that animals also have rights
Classic liberalism	John Locke; Robert Nozick	Minimal state Individuals have the right to accumulate as much land or property as they want	Nature only gains value when humans labour on it
Classic Marxism	Karl Marx	The state is a bourgeois instrument that oppresses the working classes Collectivist: giving primacy to the individual is dangerous as it pits them one against another	Belief in technical progress and mastery over nature 'Limits to growth' may be a means of maintaining the status quo
Revised Marxism	Neil Smith; David Harvey	Advocate a more co-operative system. The individual is best realized in mutual relation with others in a community	It is the capitalist exploitation of industry that causes ecological problems
Feminism	Val Plumwood; Judith Plant	The existing state is one that maintains patriarchal domination over women, who are subject to oppression	Anti-androcentric (male-centred) Ecofeminists tend to reject anthropocentric approaches
Ecologism	Andrew Dobson; Robyn Eckersley	Belief in the limits to material growth	Earth-centred (ecocentric) Nature has an intrinsic value

Source: Compiled from Dobson (2012), Dobson and Eckersley (2006) and Heywood (2003).

positions, but in practice it will soon become apparent that these ideologies are shared unequally. Anthropocentric views tend to dominate, as do those that reject limits to growth. While this is the prevailing view, it does not mean that it should not be interrogated. Regardless of the perceived different stances between political *ideologies*, as Porritt (1984) suggests, this may not translate into radically opposing stances between political *parties*. Consider the environmental views of the main political parties in various countries. While they may argue on how they manage a problem – that is, by high regulation or via market-based approaches – they may not address either the structural aspects causing the concern or the need to conform to norms of economic growth or technological solutions. Swyngedouw (2009) referred to an underlying consensus of this nature as 'post-politics', a political condition characterized by the absence of strong opposing forces. From this perspective, we are in a period of 'post-politics' in the sense that the hugely divisive ideological debates that characterized much of the twentieth century are a relic of a bygone era. Alternative approaches or radical institutional change that were such a feature of the politics of the past are now largely tangential to the policy discussion, with outcomes focused instead on allowing stakeholders to participate and agree technocratic managerial approaches within this mainstream frame. From this perspective, environmental concerns are frequently posited as an inevitable and unavoidable outcome of capitalism and its associated social and economic paradigms. This view privileges the capitalist ideology within which risks or impacts are seen as a part of modern society. However, approaching environmental planning in this techno-rational manner fails to recognize the critical importance of neoliberalism and global capitalism in driving contemporary urbanism, underpinning resource use or naturalizing crises (Evans, 2011).

Swyngedouw (2009: 609) argues that, within post-politics: 'disruption or dissent is reduced to debates over the institutional modalities of governing, the accountancy calculus of risk and the technologies of expert administration or management ... [it] annuls dissent from the consultative spaces of policymaking and evacuates the proper political from the public sphere'. This condition is connected to aspects of governmentality discussed in Chapter 3, where power is wielded to maintain the normal and marginalize opposing views. Given the perceived inability to debate and facilitate real change, or to express opposing views via traditional political avenues, such as the mainstream parties, it is little wonder that environmental concerns can often explode into a frustrated violence or dissension (Žižek, 1999). The anti-capitalist movements provide good examples of this occurring in practice.

Perhaps even more worryingly, some authors highlight how politics may not just be providing an absence of opposition, but can even act against the interests of the environment. Using a series of examples, from fishing to flooding, to the World Bank, Leal and Meiners (2002: x) offer words of caution against seeing government as a 'Saviour' by providing evidence of many public policies that harm the environment. They argue: 'dedicated environmentalists should not be so sanguine with "government solutions" for real problems'. Here, the issue is not 'government' as such, but rather the way that wider – and largely hidden – forces, such as those in the private sector, exert political influence and skew policies to outcomes that are more favourable for those particular actors.

The market and the private sector

The same issue of choice, or more specifically, the absence of radically different opposing political stances by the dominant political parties, was also raised by the influential US linguist and philosopher, Noam Chomsky. When asked in an interview whether he votes, Chomsky replied that he did, but without much enthusiasm given little variance among the policies on offer, stating: 'In the US, there is basically one party – the business party. It has two factions, called Democrats and Republicans, which are somewhat different but carry out variations on the same policies. By and large, I am opposed to those policies. As is most of the population' (*New Statesman*, 2010).

Here, Chomsky explicitly links business to politics, offering an insight into the causes of the post-political consensus; he underlines the influence of these significant yet less visible political actors who exert hidden power and often lack the transparency and democracy found in conventional political institutions. However, the private sector is not necessarily a murky, underhand or destructive operator when it comes to the environment, and to provide a more rounded understanding we shall also discuss the benefits of its involvement in environmental planning.

The market within which the private sector operates is essentially a means of exchanging goods and services, and, to a certain degree, it can be influenced by governments. The market plays a role in providing for the material requirements of society, though not always in a benign and neutral manner. For example, marketing and advertising are professions designed specifically to fuel desire for, or to generate increased consumption of, a product. The market is also a complex beast and can comprise public sector, private sector, new innovative hybrid partnerships, non-governmental organizations, charities or informal community groups – much more than a solitary political player, or one that can be depicted as simply 'good' or 'bad'. While it can be useful to introduce the subject in this manner, in reality, there is no single 'market' that exists independently of humans; there are a multiplicity of markets, each responding to our wants.

The private sector generally considers environmental problems as externalities, discussed in Chapter 8 with regard to environmental economics, which lends weight to the argument for state-level corrective action. Environmental pollution, for example, may be viewed as an adverse externality that could be managed by a 'polluter pays', cost–benefit analysis or compensatory approach. But this does not take into account issues such as criticality of assets, vital thresholds or nuances of carrying capacity, and instead is simply rooted in the language of economic trade-offs. While neoclassical economics may view the environment in a utilitarian manner as a supply of assets, this can be skewed beneficially by legislation, regulation or taxes. For example, sustainability can be viewed as a way to mitigate the inward-looking tendencies of the private sector and manage the environment better, extend resource use or compensate for losses. Furthermore, precautionary approaches or more regulation or procedures, such as environmental audits or environmental impact assessments (EIAs), can influence decision-making and enable the natural tendencies of the market to be tempered and environmental issues to be weighted more effectively.

Let us now explore a view that readers with a strong environmental persuasion might not feel instinctively comfortable about: growth can be very good for society. Socially and economically, the case is strong: capitalism creates jobs, wealth, raises standards of living, and provides many other intangible benefits. For example, preventing urban sprawl has become a perennial goal of the environmental movement. However, it should be noted that the actual area of land occupied by cities is surprisingly small considering that they account for over half of the world's population. The United Nations (2007) used satellite imagery to estimate that the total expanse of urban development (including green space as well as built-up areas) covers only 2.8 per cent of the Earth's land area. To put this in perspective, grouping every urbanite on Earth together in one place would occupy an area less than half the size of Australia. Therefore, the market doesn't just enable development; it also plays a role in conserving areas and promoting land efficiency by valuing it highly and protecting it via private ownership. As may be seen with regard to the example of 'the tragedy of the commons', described in Box 8.1 on page 180, putting land in the hands of private individuals or the private sector and monetizing it via a market may actually be a very good way to conserve it.

In addition, the word 'finite', taken as a given in much environmental discourse relating to the private sector, can be a powerful semantic that may never come to pass. There are always neo-Malthusian voices discussing population bombs (Ehrlich and Ehrlich, 1990) or resource peaks (Meadows *et al.*, 1972), but the market is an efficient mechanism to manage resources: scarcity raises commodity prices, which should depress demand. This basic fundamental of economics forms the basis of the perennial criticism of all resource 'limits' studies that may project demand and supplies and, by extension, predict simplistically that the world will run out of such and such a resource by 2050. Here, the market can prolong resource use, create the incentives for increased efficiency of production, encourage the search for new supplies, or drive innovation to design replacements. However, it can also be socially regressive, with a focus on cost which means that only the poor may be expected to change their behaviour as prices fluctuate.

Similarly, there are some dissenting opinions to the persuasive view that increasing numbers of people, as rational consumers of resources, will lead inexorably to an impending catastrophe (Ehrlich and Ehrlich, 1990). Simon (1980: 1434) argued that, while births are an initial drag on an economy, as people grow older, they become productive, which may be a benefit, heightening the possibility for innovation and diffusion of new knowledge. Or, as he phrased it: 'people bring not only mouths and hands into the world but also heads and brains'.

The private sector and the market, frequently the two-dimensional bête noire of the environment, are clearly more nuanced than they are often painted. While they do play a role in politics, and frequently with a view to reducing regulation or driving down costs, they can also price the environment in a way that protects some resources or helps to foster the ingenuity to develop alternatives.

The private sector can also encourage social changes that may, for example, reduce the need to travel, allow the rapid exchange of information or enable the establishment of new networks that can protect the environment. Since the market is essentially a mechanism of exchange and the private sector a way to provide goods and services, they do not operate in isolation; they are fundamental to the operation of societies and closely connected to the desires of people.

To better comprehend the relationship between politics, the private sector and the public, we need to turn our discussion towards a very influential, though sometimes unacknowledged, opinion-shaping force in society that mediates between key stakeholder groups. Since its inception, the news media has exerted a power over the public and politicians that extends far back from the present. Indeed, in a 1787 debate concerning the opening up of the House of Commons in Great Britain to press scrutiny, the MP and writer, Edmund Burke, perceptively identified the press as the 'fourth estate' – a newly recognizable, if much less visible, authority to sit alongside the three long-established 'estates' or broad social orders: the nobility, the clergy and commoners (Schultz, 1998: 49).

The media

Some may feel frustrated that environmental issues always seem to be poorly regarded in relation to short-term economic concerns, and perhaps think that this is because the case has not been made strongly enough, but in reality the problem is not so simply defined. After all, the environment is crucial not only to economic prosperity but also to human beings' entire future as a species. If an argument as fundamental as this does not work, then perhaps the problem is not with the case itself – rather, it is a result of the lenses through which it has to travel and the outlooks of those receiving it. Many of those who are in a position to influence environmental interventions have both significant bank balances and remarkably large economic and social incentives to maintain current practices. This point was notably made by the author, Upton Sinclair (1935: 109), who after an ill-fated attempt to gain political office with a radical agenda, explained the reason for his failure as: 'It is difficult to get a man to understand something, when his salary depends upon his not understanding it!'

Political responses may involve not just dismissing an argument, but also counter-attacking those who made it and misrepresenting the issue deliberately to create a political impasse. The merits of differing ideas are often played out in the media, which is frequently not a neutral observer where the environment is concerned, being influenced by a range of issues from prejudice and bias to populist angles and sensationalism. This section will now investigate in more depth how public opinion is formed, and the extent to which the media has a role in shaping this.

The way that people and professional stakeholders receive information and understand issues is critical to opinion-forming. Most people get their information from the media, which, in turn, holds a degree of power over politicians. While respected journalists and trusted news organizations, such as the British Broadcasting Corporation, have built their reputation on a pursuit of 'fairness' and balance, there are many more media outlets that have aims centred on financial or political objectives even though the general public may expect journalists to be largely impartial. There are newspapers, such as the UK's tabloid market, that have a well-earned reputation for bias. However, the way that TV media report environmental issues is also riven with inconsistencies and can create issues to gain the mandate for environmental planning, particularly in the way that their authority and gravity lends a degree of credibility and trustworthiness. Information is filtered through political, economic and journalistic practices, which influences content benignly and, more worryingly, will even deliberately sensationalize, misrepresent or recast environmental concerns to influence both the public and elected politicians, and to attract revenue-generating viewers (Bennett, 1996).

Just as the selective use of language can play a key role in influencing public opinion, images also shape debates and can be used to target particular groups of people. For example, the pictures selected to represent a story will influence the public in a certain manner. The devastated landscape of tree stumps from a newly logged area of rainforest; smoke from industrial-looking towers; and modern, almost futuristic, banks of solar panels are all images that are pervasive in the media when discussing environmental issues and, significantly, all of them can serve to mobilize, or even symbolize, entire agendas and generate public pressure for action (Beck, 2009).

Table 4.2 provides some examples of how common framing devices used to discuss climate change can influence different

Table 4.2 *Framing the issue of climate change: media image and audience addressed*

Framing device	Audience addressed
'Scientific uncertainty'	Those who resist change
'National security'	Those who resist change but have to act
'Polar bear'	Wildlife lovers
'Economic development'	Politicians and businesses
'Catastrophe'	Those who are worried about the future
'Justice and equity'	Those with strong ethical leanings

Source: Hulme (2009: 229).

sections of society. For example, emotive polar bear imagery can be used to appeal to wildlife lovers, while shifting from a 'scientific uncertainty' to a 'national security' frame will chime with people who may initially resist change but could be persuaded of a need to act. Equally, a focus only on 'catastrophe' will resonate strongly with those worried about possible future consequences, or engage people drawn to moving stories of personal loss. Yet, with all these approaches, while it may engage and influence one particular audience, other viewers may not respond in a positive fashion.

Images come replete with cultural meanings connected with the relationship between nature and humanity. These 'visual rhetorics' (Lester and Cottle, 2009) play an important role in raising awareness, expanding concerns beyond the local, influencing values and imbuing a sense of environmentalism, citizenship and responsibility (Dobson, 2003). They are therefore important in understanding the role of the public in environmental politics.

Perhaps more fundamentally, in a study of how the US mass media treats climate change, Boykov and Boykov (2007) argue that an adherence to journalistic norms, such as personalization, dramatization and novelty, can have a negative effect on the parallel occupational need for information, authority and balance. For example, the initial selection of topics to be covered is influenced by a variety of subjective factors, from the application of 'news values', particular editorial lines or even geographical proximity. Consequently, it can result in an amplification of risk, a focus on a singular dramatic event with a powerful story, or other mediated information that informs and shapes public-policy discourse (Nelkin, 1987). Rolling news channels also provide a further emphasis on fast-moving live events over other issues. The media even determines that most fundamental of issues: what is newsworthy.

The pursuit of 'objectivity', arguably a core journalistic value, has also led to a rise in environmental issues being discussed in adversarial ways with distorting effects. This is a frequent aspect of journalism where one expert is posited against another to debate an issue, with the journalist adopting the role of a seemingly unbiased 'mediator'. This duelling scenario, while appearing to fulfil the requirement for objectivity and reducing the need for journalists to rapidly acquire scientific knowledge, nevertheless presents problems. While a journalistic argument is essentially 'balanced' between two opposing views, this may not acknowledge the weight of scientific evidence in favour of one or the other. Providing equal airtime or column inches can suggest unfairly that both views have equivalent validity or support – whether they are scientific findings emerging from comprehensive empirical studies or individual value judgements. In practice, therefore, there is a paradox: the pursuit of journalistic balance may unwittingly perpetuate bias.

The different roles of journalists may also skew how information is presented. Lunney (2012) draws attention to an always lively, sometime caustic and frequently misinformed debate on climate change that occurs in the columns and letters pages of *The Sydney Morning Herald*. Here, scientists were accused of deliberate misrepresentation and falsifying data, with the entire peer-review process also being held up as flawed. Significantly, the research highlighted a distinction between journalists as science correspondents and those who may be opinion writers who often slavishly follow a more jaundiced editorial policy that can help to form popular opinion. In similar studies in the UK (Carvalho and Burgess, 2005) and Australia (McManus, 2000) it was highlighted that values and ideological cultures are critical in explaining how differing media outlets reinterpret scientific knowledge. Here, the desire to attract viewers and provide entertainment can help to frame environmental discourse in a more populist, antagonistic and superficial fashion.

As will be discussed in Chapter 6, scientists are frequently labelled as poor communicators when transported outside their preferred academic habitat (Hulme, 2009). They tend to use complicated terminology and are professionally trained to be cautious and caveated – traits that do not transfer easily into the media sphere with its opinionated analysts, desire for rapid explanations and a penchant for easy sound bites. Yet they are not entirely at fault; for example, many readers may find it surprising, given the rare and powerful scientific consensus on climate change, that press coverage may take a differing view. However, over a 15-year period in the USA, roughly equal attention was given to the opposing views on climate change that humans or natural fluctuations were responsible (Boykov and Boykov, 2004). Indeed, given how the media commonly treat the protagonists as 'equal' partners in debates and coverage, it is not unexpected that many opinion polls reveal a strong popular view that the science of climate change is 'not settled'.

The media decides what is newsworthy, what the facts are, and who are the relevant agents – potentially both transforming and excluding scientific 'news' (Carvalho, 2007). During the subsequent entrance of scientific findings into public policy discourse via the media, the information is reinterpreted, framed and disseminated, all of which can distort the intended message, partly because of the systemic problems of how journalism operates and partly as a result of the media sector more generally. The selection of the agents of authority, particularly within debate strategies, can also distort the degree of confidence in scientific findings.

The influence of the media in shaping environmental policies, or more simply creating what Kingdon (1995) referred to as the 'national mood', is a strong steer for politicians of all parties. While this may provide a critical factor in shaping the will to act, public opinion is fickle, easily influenced, and may not be a reliable barometer, particularly over the short term. This is a point reinforced by the philosopher Bertrand Russell (2006 [1930]: 92) who cautioned that 'One should respect public opinion in so far as is necessary to avoid starvation and to keep out of prison, but anything that goes beyond this is voluntary submission to an unnecessary tyranny.' Box 4.2 investigates the nuances of public opinion and politics further by providing a brief case study of climate change and US citizens.

Pointedly for environmental planning, given this brief exploration of the malleability and capricious nature of the influence of the media on public opinion, it is naïve to think that the education or awareness 'model' of scientific knowledge transfer, where behaviour or policy change is a simple matter of getting the message through, can succeed whatever the environmental concern. Knowledge is not a linear transmitter–receiver model, where active information producers influence the opinions of passive subordinates. Neither is it a 'canonical view' (Bucchi, 1998), a simple popularization of science with a view to informing the public: it is a harsh struggle for legitimacy and influence, with powerful and subjective actors. It is also not about 'facts' but rather 'truth claims', which are interpreted within an arena where values are opaque, and determined internally within media outlets. This is not just a matter of a simple, and more easily recognized, political bias based on ideology or ownership, but also a need to attract viewers and increase sales, such as by direct subscription or increased revenue from advertising. All of this can result in a lack of political pressure to act, influence the public or legitimize certain policy choices.

Conclusion

Otto von Bismarck (1815–98), the first chancellor of Germany, perceptively depicted politics as the 'art of the possible', and if this is the case it may help to explain the failure to address many environmental issues in liberal democracies. Radical alteration to the status quo would bring unacceptable changes to certain powerful groups, and the nature of political discourse in many countries tends to privilege mainstream views and pro-economic growth positions. Given the importance of the business sector and the nature of political funding, parties, and even some politicians, can also be greatly influenced by vested interests. This may instinctively cause concern, but a counter-argument would say that these leaders are merely giving us *exactly* what the majority of society wants. Politicians are ever aware of the need to be popular.

Essentially, politics is about the normative: what *should* happen. And when we accept this basic foundation it is clear that, no matter what occurs or how elegant a solution is applied, some people will not be happy. Consequently, it links to the role of governance and use of power explained in Chapter 3, both with regard to the ability to influence decisions themselves, and those actors who are involved in decision-making. Environmental concerns are also connected with time, an issue particularly relevant to the contemporary nature of politics. Forthcoming problems need to be balanced against current well-being; after all, future generations are not current voters, a factor of which those advocating sustainability or climate change initiatives are all too aware.

The twentieth century has witnessed a political transition from the conservation of nature as an entity almost separate from society,

Box 4.2 Climate change and public opinion in the USA

Public concern and political stances regarding climate change in the US have fluctuated significantly. Brulle *et al.* (2012) investigated the reasons for the changes in a recurring Gallup poll that asked how many people worry 'a great deal' about climate change. The responses rose from 26 per cent in 2004 to 41 per cent in 2007 and then dropped back to 28 per cent by 2010, seemingly in defiance of advances in awareness, education or scientific consensus. They highlighted five major influences on public opinion on this issue: extreme weather events; public access to scientific information; media coverage; cues from elite groups; and the success of advocacy organizations. McCright and Dunlap (2011) conducted similar research investigating how political persuasions in the USA may affect the view of climate change. They discovered that liberals and Democrats are more likely to hold beliefs consistent with the scientific consensus than are conservatives or Republicans. Furthermore, this divide has grown substantially since the early 2000s, perhaps reflecting the markedly opposed stances of the political leaders during this time.

A separate study widened the US political landscape to include respondents who identified themselves with the strongly right-wing Tea Party. It found that 53 per cent of 'tea partiers' do not believe in global warming, in comparison to only 8 per cent of the more left-wing Democrats. It also discovered that 30 per cent of Tea Party supporters considered themselves to be 'very well-informed', with Democrats, Independents and Republicans polling much lower at between 8 per cent and 10 per cent when asked the same question. Interestingly, the respondents were also asked 'How much more information do you need to hold a firm opinion on global warming?' Again, Democrats, Independents and Republicans replied at comparable levels of between 17 per cent and 22 per cent. Yet Tea Party supporters considered their mind to be already firmly made up with a huge 52 per cent (Leiserowitz *et al.*, 2011).

The views of the public do not just differ with regard to their political allegiance, however. Donner and McDaniels (2013) further examined how opinions on climate change varied in the USA between 1990 and 2012, and then compared this to national

→

→

temperature fluctuations. They discovered that climate variability could affect public opinion because concern strengthened alongside increases in temperature and lessened when extremes did not occur. In this study, differences between those who identified with mainstream, traditional political parties did not differ too much. However, there was a marked change between these people and those supporters who identified themselves with the most right-wing party. These respondents tended to hold the most negative opinions, be firmest in their stance and, significantly for those who think that environmental planning is merely a matter of making sure the message is transmitted effectively to the public, do not require any more information. In other words, there are people who feel they have made up their minds and are not receptive to further information.

This difference may be better understood by considering Table 4.1 and the potential policy ramifications in accepting that climate change is a serious concern. And it is this aspect that is perhaps the most important point in understanding the reasons for these disagreements. If climate change is as clear a danger as the science suggests, there would be a need for stronger government intervention, something that is at the core of differences in the political worldviews of parties. On a national basis this would probably entail measures aimed at reducing CO_2 emissions and preparing society for any impacts. These would generally involve an increase in costs for industry and businesses alongside measures designed to reduce the personal freedom to consume carbon, such as by tightening environmental regulations or raising taxes on fuel. From an international perspective there would be a requirement for global agreements, perhaps reducing global free trade or putting taxes on imports of certain goods.

Whichever way you look at the issue, believing that there is a need to act on climate change pushes the debate towards adopting measures that are essentially the opposite of what the political right has championed for decades: free trade, low taxes, low regulation, personal freedom and small government. Therefore some voters will instinctively reject, or be sceptical of, environmental concerns because of their worldviews and a desire to avoid any possible changes that this threat will demand of their country and behaviour.

towards the view that societies in general need to be greener (Dobson, 2012). This could be viewed as a positive process that helps to internalize the environment within our cultures and behaviour. The scope of influence has also expanded, and environmental issues now span what are termed both high and low politics. Where the former concerns elite-level inter-state concerns such as international agreements, sovereignty or security, and the latter pertains to day-to-day issues such as policy implementation or public administration. Sustainability, for example, provides an approach that advocates weaving the two aspects together. Environmental political discourse has also developed, and alongside the apocalyptic narratives of the mid-twentieth century there has been a gradual softening, with the optimism of ecological modernization and certain interpretations of sustainability being markedly more conciliatory, partnership oriented and, significantly, more palatable to business and public audiences.

The politicization of the environment means is it inevitable that it will be affected by the distorting lens of political ideology, short-term strategic value and the media. Despite the popular view that those concerned with the environment are a single actor, there is a range of 'green politics' with a diverse range of political opinions, and with internal and sectoral disagreement apparent in these groups. Considering the range of stances, from radical direct action to middle-class preservation agendas, it is perhaps surprising that this plurality does not have a higher profile. Indeed, the whole ethos and meaning of 'conservation' is a resistance to change, which is anathema to many in the 'environmental movement'. Further, preserving the countryside by resisting modifications to land may privilege elite interests and those who have benefited from the current distribution. We shall discuss issues connected with this further in Chapter 10 on 'justice'.

In addition to contrasting worldviews, the logics that determine political positions are also different. For example, when considering fossil fuels and CO_2 emissions, a 'policy wonk' working in government may assess these by considering how efficient production may be with regard to tonnes of carbon per unit of energy, while an activist is looking for an opportunity to heighten awareness, influence the news cycle or to use an extreme case to symbolize what is going wrong. Bad news is ever newsworthy, and news influences politics. Both interpretations are relevant, but science, statistics and 'facts' can be used appropriated and selectively by political actors and the media to support multiple agendas. In the world of politics, where worldviews are habitually firm and u-turns taken to be a sign of weakness, they may also be used for 'confirmation bias' – the tendency for people to seek evidence that reinforces existing viewpoints while paying less attention to aspects that do not.

Now that we have a more solid appreciation of issues connected to governance and politics, the three chapters that follow develop the discussion to consider how other key factors also frame the nature of environmental planning, from the use of concepts, to the nature of science, and to the ability of policy to take remedial steps.

Chapter 5

Framing Concepts

'The sustainable city needs to be treated as an open or empty
concept which is filled by sets of competing claims about what
the sustainable city might become.'

(Guy and Marvin, 1999: 273)

Concepts are not neutral devices. They hold power by framing
debates and have inherent logics that steer intervention down
certain pathways. And, as the quotation above highlights, readers
should be aware of the power inherent in any direction of travel
and the relationship to the political arena. While there may be a
tendency within environmental planning to focus on the specifics
of a policy, or to monitor the implementation of any law, taking a
step back from procedural or regulatory perspectives to consider
the concepts in play can encourage some very interesting discussions – and ones that can lend a real depth to analysis. Indeed, the
defining of any environmental issue or argument, that most basic
activity that is frequently passed over in favour of more substantial matters, is enormously powerful. It possesses the potential to
affect a host of factors that can subsequently frame the debate:
from who should be involved in discussions, to what priority
should be afforded to the issue, to shaping any future strategy for
intervention.

The term 'frame' is an incredibly useful one for environmental
planning and is directly related to the influence that concepts hold.
It stems from the work of Goffman (1974) and argues that there
are cognitive structures that inform how we perceive the world.
These may occur unconsciously, or be deliberately constructed, but
simply put, they provide a representation of reality informed by
our experiences. As they can promote certain viewpoints, arguments, problems or solutions over others they attribute meaning,
which can be very influential. To explain this notion more clearly,
Entman (2004) uses the example of President George W. Bush's
speech after the 9/11 attacks in which he repeatedly used words

such as 'terror', 'war', 'good' and 'evil', and by doing so framed the narrative in an emotive way. This had the effect of uniting the country behind the government interpretation of events and effectively served to exclude other explanations. In retrospect, the choice of words in this initial speech had a major influence over how the event was understood by citizens, and set the foundation for future political response. The following illustration highlights this aspect further.

In 1974, the geographer David Harvey wrote an influential paper entitled 'Population, Resources, and the Ideology of Science', exploring how powerful elites manipulate definitions and concepts for their own ends. It also highlighted the subject and power of framing, and argued that this ability should not be conceded unknowingly. Harvey used the case of the 1972 Stockholm Conference on the Human Environment, which paved the way for subsequent international sustainability conferences, where the Chinese delegation disputed that there was any scarcity of resources, and even claimed that it was meaningless to use such terminology. Many readers may find this position strange, as the term 'scarcity' might appear uncontroversial and even one of the fundamental aspects of the environment and sustainability fields. Yet the term is defined both socially and culturally. Some countries have an abundance of a particular resource while others do not, and some societies may value something that others do not. Further, demand for various resources changes temporally and spatially and can be boosted artificially. Scarcity is therefore connected with culture, human activity and the ways that societies are organized, and is even pivotal to the success of capitalism with its fundamental supply and demand rationality. Therefore, while it may undeniably be experienced, it is neither automatically a 'problem' nor 'suffered' equally. Harvey (1974: 274) further linked the use of definitions in this example with power and geopolitical relations, arguing:

> If an existing social order, an elite group of some sort, is under threat and is fighting to preserve its dominant position in society, then the overpopulation and shortage of resources arguments can be used as powerful ideological levers to persuade people into acceptance of the status quo and of authoritarian measures to maintain it.

Box 5.1 provides more depth on this key environmental concept.

Box 5.1 Limits and scarcity

'Many persons perhaps entertain a vague notion that some day our coal seams will be found emptied to the bottom, and swept clean like a coal-cellar. Our fires and furnaces, they think, will then be suddenly extinguished, and cold and darkness will be left to reign over a depopulated country. It is almost needless to say, however, that our mines are literally inexhaustible. We cannot get to the bottom of them; and though we may some day have to pay dear for fuel, it will never be positively wanting.'

(Jevons, 1866: 2)

William Stanley Jevons (1835–82), a Victorian economist, addressed the issue of limited coal resources in his 1866 book *The Coal Question*. His main concern was economic, and in particular regarding the influences and advantages that possession of this resource brought to Britain, but his work has since gained a wider significance on resources and their use more generally. The intensive resource use Britain had enjoyed helped it to attain its economic supremacy, but coal was finite and demand was growing. While supply and demand economics would prolong supplies, he argued that there would eventually be an impact on prosperity as scarcity and the costs of extracting coal from ever-deeper mines took hold. In doing so he touched on later narratives connected with limits, from sustainability, to peak oil, to overpopulation.

As a result of his study, a so-called 'coal panic' was discussed and a Royal Commission on Coal Supplies was appointed between 1866 and 1871 to investigate the issue (Bradley, 2009). Significantly for environmental concern, his work also identified what has subsequently become known as 'the Jevons paradox': a situation where improving efficiency, such as by new technological innovation, typically has the effect of reducing costs and, consequently, these measures may lead to an increase in use. For example, energy efficiency is held as a core strategy to limit carbon emissions, but if it leads to a reduction in energy bills it may provide an incentive to consume more energy and be self-defeating.

Perhaps the best known exponent of a 'limits' approach is that provided by Malthus (1766–1864); indeed, it is the fate of all such discussions to be labelled typically 'neo-Malthusian'. In his famous work *An Essay on the Principle of Population*, Malthus adopted a simple, but powerful, stance that has a lingering relevance, stating, 'the power of population is indefinitely greater than the power in the

→

→

earth to produce subsistence for man' (Malthus, 1993 (1798): 13). His argument that human populations will eventually outstrip resources was based on a compelling demographic and ecological mathematical premise: if unchecked, population rises geometrically (2, 4, 8, 16), whereas subsistence only increases arithmetically (1, 2, 3, 4). Therefore, over time, we shall run out of food, and when that happens, famine, disease and war will inevitably restore the balance. Malthus adopted a global perspective in linking the capacity of social, economic and environmental systems, and challenged a simple reliance on science and technology (Malthus, 1798), which ran counter to the notions of inevitable, incremental progress that were popular in his time.

The fingerprints of Malthus rest heavily on Western environmental thought. Resources are clearly critical to prosperity, and recurring themes around limits, closed systems and resource frontiers can provide a compelling inevitability. These declensionist narratives, detailing a pessimistic, unwavering decline, are commonly used in debates centred on population behaviour or resources, but can frequently descend into environmental catastrophism that can divide and frame the debate in an extreme manner that may inhibit consensus building. It is also difficult to be certain about the inevitability and rate of resource consumption, as there is uncertainty over both supply and demand. For example, regulations, taxes, policy or best practice can all influence resource use, while the entire sustainability movement exerts a similar influence by distorting market norms.

To understand how these concepts of scarcity and limits might impact on environmental planning it is useful to consider who might use them, and for what purposes. They have tended to be adopted by those seeking to alter norms of resource use and distribution, whether to make them conform to their moral worldview or to preserve power. For example, limits narratives have been seized upon by a host of environmental thinkers and groups in order to elicit *change*. Indeed, Harvey argued against neo-Malthusian thinking, stating that it was not a rational logic, but rather an ideology. Linking population 'explosion' discussions to the works of Marx, he suggested that the ruling ideas of the time are the ideas of the ruling classes. He stated: 'whenever a theory of overpopulation seizes hold in a society dominated by an elite, then the non-elite invariably experience some form of political, economic, and social repression' (Harvey, 1974: 273). This also provides an example of how critical thinking can challenge received wisdom.

If you have viewed the concept of scarcity as an unchallenged cornerstone of the environmental movement, this brief introduction may well have softened this belief somewhat. It may appear to have a neutral, even commonsense, logic, but if you accept scarcity as a frame of reference then it leads rationally to certain policy responses – perhaps those based on conservation and management that may be favoured by some powerful actors. Equally, it may link to international co-operation, with market or policy mechanisms used as a means of influencing the 'price' of resources or to open new economic markets, such as occurred with offsetting or carbon trading. To deepen understanding of the power of definitions, and how even seemingly benign concepts can be challenged, readers may wish to consider a counter-argument – that scarcity is a tool that serves the Western elites, who have already used resources in gaining advancement and now wish to limit the ability of countries with vast supplies to progress as economic competitors. What is undoubted is this: accepting the notion of scarcity as a framing device will benefit some countries, sectors or interests more than others. Therefore, concepts have the power to frame debates, generate inherent logical arguments and engender certain desirable outcomes, and, as such, we need to know more about how and why they emerge as well as where they may lead.

This chapter discusses selected concepts that are commonly used in environmental planning. While many of these concepts may be viewed as impartial, interchangeable or uncontroversial, they represent differing ideas and approaches that have consequences for the way that problems are subsequently considered and addressed. We shall explore initially how people's worldviews may frame their interpretation of concepts before examining three key environmental planning concepts in more detail: sustainability, risk and resilience. This material can be applied in any essay or coursework relating to the environment; an engagement with conceptual issues can help to demonstrate a more sophisticated appreciation of the complexities of environmental planning. In addition to the possibility of gaining a higher grade, there is a more ambitious hope: that the new insights will encourage a greater appreciation of the subject.

The spectrum of environmental concern

The Sierra Club is a well-respected US grassroots environmental organization founded in 1892. Since that time it has campaigned successfully to protect wilderness areas, promote the responsible use of resources, and educate people on environmental issues. It also states that in its mission it will use: 'all lawful means to carry out these objectives' (Sierra Club, 2012: 1). However, this strategy of exerting policy influence was deemed to be too mainstream for some as it was not effective in challenging why actions damage the environment. Earth First! was founded in 1980 as a result of a simmering dissatisfaction with the conventional approach of groups such as the Sierra Club, and instead took a very different stance, advocating direct action, civil disobedience and sabotage as a means of forcing systemic change. A co-founder of this group argued that its major accomplishment was to 'expand the environmental spectrum to where the Sierra Club and other groups are perceived as moderates' (Foreman, 1991: 139). These groups could both be defined as 'green', but clearly one was more radical and anarchist than the other. By extension, it is incorrect to picture the environmental view as something singular or easy to predict; the reality is more complex – and more interesting – than that. This example is useful in illustrating how individual worldviews differ, and even how those who may be seen to be on the same political 'side' can perceive environmental issues very differently.

Before we delve too deeply into individual concepts, it is worth taking a little time to understand the nature of the varying perspectives of environmental concern, because these influence how environmental concepts are understood, and how this may be an individual matter. We have already seen that there are differing visions of why the environment should be protected – ranging from a narrow, short-term utilitarianism based on resources, to a broader repositioning of the environment as the main, overriding priority. It is useful to imagine this situation as two diametrically opposing viewpoints, each occupying one end of a spectrum, and with a gradual softening and shift in opinion as you travel from one end of the continuum to the other. An appreciation of this notional spectrum is not designed to consign people to holding particular entrenched viewpoints. Rather, it should illustrate the multiple shades of grey, or more aptly, 'green', that can influence how environmental issues are interpreted. What may appear superficially to be opposing moral worldviews that can never be reconciled are revealed to be deeply nuanced and varied.

The politicization of the environment during the second half of the twentieth century helped to throw these varying positions into sharp focus. During the 1960s and 1970s, when many of the problems affecting the planet started to receive increased attention, there was a view that the type of environmentalism commonplace at the time was not challenging enough, as it essentially advocated a reformist, state-centred approach. By arguing for a continuation of the same institutions and values, it perpetuated a mainstream strategy, but one just a little 'greener' where, for example, policies may be designed to mitigate impacts but the underlying practices may be largely unaltered. Alternatively, some argued that what was needed was a more radical agenda, which demanded that institutions and social policies become more ecologically focused. To depict the differences between positions, Arne Næss, a Norwegian environmental philosopher, coined the terms 'shallow' and 'deep' ecology to illustrate the emerging spectrum of green thought. The former took the view that environmental problems could be solved within existing society, while the latter desired to ask deeper questions as to what it is within societies that causes and underpins these issues (Sessions, 1995). This shallow/deep terminology depicting positions of environmental concern has subsequently been employed in a similar vein elsewhere: for example, in sustainability literature it is commonplace to hear of weak/strong or light/dark interpretations that occupy opposing elements of a notional continuum. Regardless of the dichotomies used, or the concept to which it is applied, the argument is largely a similar one.

It is helpful to highlight the nature of these differences with an example. A conventional environmental planning debate could fall between two competing viewpoints, the 'technocentric' and the 'ecocentric', a concept identified by O' Riordan (1976). The two different approaches help to depict divergent strategies to address environmental planning issues, with each stance stemming from its own economic, political and philosophical outlook – though at its basic level the debate can be reduced to a clash between technology and nature (Castells, 1978). It should be emphasized that despite each theoretical standpoint focusing on the relationship between humanity and nature, each individual belief may be found wanting from the point of view of providing an agreed basis for green politics within contemporary societies (Barry, 1999). Table 5.1 emphasizes the major differences between these competing viewpoints and gives an idea of how the spectrum of environmental concern may reveal widely different interpretations of any perceived problem.

The technocentric approach advocates that environmental protection can be incorporated into the existing political and economic institutions of modern society, and crucially that this

Table 5.1 *Technocentric and ecocentric approaches to environmentalism*

Ecocentrists	Technocentrists
• General lack of faith in large-scale modern technology, a reliance on experts, a lack of democratic accountability and authoritarian government	• Belief in continuing economic growth and resource exploitation with various regulatory mechanisms to mitigate the most adverse consequences
• Critical of capitalism's accumulation of material wealth and growth for its own sake	• Hold that politics, science or technology will find a solution to contemporary problems
• Nature is inherently important to the full realization of human beings	• Accept wider discussion with those who are affected adversely. Typically through the use of 'appraisal' techniques
• Community identity and local scales are emphasized in the aspects of human work, home and leisure	• In matters of economic growth, public health and safety, the views of scientific and technical experts are privileged
• Hold that morality is determined by ecological and natural laws	• Give support to effective environmental management agencies
• Human activities of work and leisure should be integrated to enable individual and community improvement	• Economic growth is the legitimate goal of all policies
• Endangered species and unique landscapes have a right to remain undisturbed by human intervention	• Economic growth leads to sufficient resources that will trickle down and provide the will to overcome any weaknesses
• Highlight citizen participation in community affairs and the rights of minorities	• Arguments for wider citizen participation in policy are viewed with scepticism

Source: Adapted from O'Riordan (2000).

should be achieved without threatening economic growth, material prosperity or liberal democracy (Garner, 2000). The overall view is human-centred and suggests that the goals of economic growth and environmental protection are not necessarily irreconcilable; therefore, the notion that there may be environmental limits is rejected. The onus is put on science and technology to solve problems as and when they appear, without altering the roles or values of our existing institutions. A good example of a technocentric solution would be a catalytic converter; a device that came to be fitted as standard in cars to reduce air pollution. This is technology that has developed in direct response to a recognized problem and one that necessitates no behavioural change or threat to growth. Within the technocentric category, differences may also be apparent; for example, some are prepared to make some concessions to the environment without altering the existing political and social order, while others believe that science, technology and human ingenuity can overcome any problem presented to them (Dryzek, 1997).

On the other end of the spectrum, an ecocentric approach desires to change the fundamental economic, social and political institutions and values. Otherwise, it is argued that established power relations will continue to perpetuate inequality between both the actors involved in the environmental planning process and the weighting afforded to environmental objectives. This view suggests that that there is a limited capacity of ecological systems to absorb the effects of economic activity without feeding back impacts that are harmful to humans (O'Connor, 1974) and that a society adopting a technocentric approach will eventually suffer environmental catastrophe. The ecocentric outlook argues that there must be a limit to economic growth, dependent on factors such as population and resources; as such, its intellectual roots can be traced back to the work of Malthus.

Differences are also in evidence as one progresses along the spectrum – deep environmentalists take the view that other life forms have the same right to exist as humans and believe that there ought to be a prima facie disposition in favour of the non-interference with nature by humans. This view advocates a shift in the onus of persuasion from those who want to preserve to those who wish to destroy (Dobson, 2012). Alternatively, others may take ecological relationships as a guide to a more socially compatible economy, and view economic and cultural diversity as the cornerstone of local well-being (O'Riordan, 1995).

This spectrum of environmental concern does not just include technocentric or ecocentric views; it could be used to understand how many environmental issues and concepts may be interpreted differently. For example, market-based versus non-market-based is another similar spectrum, within which strategies may differ from the alternative pricing of goods to their outright banning. Similarly, anthropocentricism versus biocentricism are typically placed as diametrically opposed outlooks. The former adopts a human-centred perspective that accords values and rights to nature but believes that nature is there to serve human needs. It contrasts with a biocentric position, which considers all life to have equal value, with humanity not being superior to other life forms. Finally, resourcism versus preservationist stances diverge between a belief that resources are there to be exploited by humans to a view that the natural world has value in itself, not just what humans attach to it. The key issue here is not the specific terminology or concepts, but rather that there is a divergence of views that can be pictured as a spectrum from one extreme position to the other.

While it can be useful to depict positions within this conceptual frame, there are some voices of caution. Garner (2000) criticized the compartmentalization of any two approaches and states that it is perfectly possible to occupy positions within multiple ideologies. For example, an acceptance of the limits to growth does not prevent the same person adopting an anthropocentric ethic. Barry (1999) also described the problems of dialectical thinking – the use of polar opposites – as being oversimplistic and potentially unhelpful. However, in the context of this chapter these disparate philosophies are useful mechanisms for recognizing the complex milieu in which environmental planning operates, and why concepts may be deemed to be 'empty', waiting to be filled by competing claims (Guy and Marvin, 1999).

It is important to note that the extreme divergent ideologies outlined here to display difference are not the only approaches to environmentalism, as there are any number of positions in between that are less polarized. In effect, people may occupy any point on a notional spectrum of environmental concern, and while there could be agreement on the gravity and urgency of a problem, the desired solution may be wildly different. For example, the pressure group Earth First! argue for biospherical egalitarianism, a position that some will find extreme, which maintains that humans are deemed to be on a par with all other organisms, from animals to viruses. More mainstream groups, such as Friends of the Earth, are concerned with fighting pollution and resource depletion, but are more human-focused. The following section draws on these understandings in order to unpack what has become one of the most disputed contemporary environmental concepts: sustainability.

Sustainability

Since its initial emergence during the late twentieth century, sustainability has become a cornerstone of environmental planning and represents how green politics has entered the mainstream. It is commonly defined as: 'development that meets the needs of the present without compromising the ability of future generations to meet their own needs' (World Commission for Environment and Development (WCED), 1987: 43). I have started this section deliberately with this formal understanding of the concept as detailed within the report entitled *Our Common Future* report (frequently referred to as the Brundtland Report) for a number of reasons. First, to keep this definition in mind as we progress through the discussion in order to consider how it may subsequently have been adapted and interpreted. Second, as we begin to scope the initial aims and objectives of sustainable development to reflect on how *radical* it was at the time – a factor that may be hard to reconcile with its seemingly uncontroversial presence within the current policy arena. But in order to put the idea into context we shall start a little earlier than 1987 to chart how the concept gradually emerged, and to investigate its stark differences from conservation.

Sustainability may be introduced initially as an attempt to balance the need to protect the environment *and* to enable economic and social development. Given this, one might expect that some of the principles underpinning the concept may have prefaced its translation into the public policy lexicon. The first recorded use of the term 'sustainability' (*Nachhaltigkeit* in German) was reputed to be in 1713, in the book *Sylvicultura Oeconomica* written by German scientist Hans Carl von Carlowitz (1645–1714), who was in charge of mining for the Saxon court in Freiberg. Because of concerns regarding the scarcity of timber for mining, he developed new practices to ensure the continued availability of supplies, advocating that the amount of wood cut down should be considered alongside the reforestation of other areas (Schmithüsen 2013). Though not employing the term specifically, we can find earlier related historical examples. In the fourteenth century, German kings Albert I and Henry VII ordered that some formerly forested agricultural lands be returned to forest. Though this protected the environment and sustained resources, the strategy primarily emerged from the need to protect valuable hunting grounds (Glacken, 1967).

These attempts to balance environmental, social and economic needs may fit in with the reasonable-sounding definition at the opening of this section and appear to have anticipated the twentieth-century version of sustainability by some centuries. From this perspective, sustainability may not be too different from any economically-driven environmental protection strategy since time immemorial. Indeed, without a firm grasp of what the concept stands for, sustainability can be easy to conflate with conservation practices such as these. Though the examples do not mirror the more modern concept, they serve to highlight the importance of understanding exactly what sustainability means. Ascertaining how it diverges from more traditional approaches to environmental management, such as conservation, is important in order to grasp when 'greenwashing' or other misleading policies are pursued. The resourcist examples given in the previous paragraph are used here to emphasize that environmental protection may not necessarily emerge from the most altruistic of motives. It also stresses that a policy to 'sustain' does not necessarily make something 'sustainable'. The key to understanding sustainability, its rapid trajectory and the potential impact on practice is based in its stark differences from more conventional environmental management.

Sustainability in its more contemporary incarnation is a product of a variety of international meetings that established environmental issues firmly on the world stage. Beginning with the first UN conference on the Human Environment in Stockholm in 1972, the UN established the World Commission on Environment and Development in 1983 in response to growing concerns about deteriorating human and natural environments and the consequences of this. It was chaired by Norway's former prime minister, Gro Harlem Brundtland, and was notable because it engaged actively with the *global* nature of causes and solutions. The final report in 1987 provided the cornerstone of how we understand sustainable development. Its message of marrying economic growth and social progress more effectively with the environment presented a more palatable alternative to the radical opposition of environmental politics of previous decades and created a great deal of political momentum.

One example is the 1992 Rio Earth Summit, which was attended by 178 world leaders and produced 'Agenda 21', a declaration that promoted sustainable development via more integrated economic, environmental and social decision-making. This is a voluntary UN resolution designed to pursue sustainability objectives across all scales, particularly at the municipal level, where it became known as Local Agenda 21 (LA21). Rather than using top-down inflexible mandates it was advocated that local strategies should be developed in close conjunction with citizens as an effective means by which the core sustainability notion of 'think global, act local' can be pursued. Its impact and implementation varied spatially, with, for example, European communities tending to engage strongly with the initiative, while areas in Asia and North America have been less active (Smardon, 2008). Yet even in well resourced nations the progress has been problematic and affected by aspects such as political, institutional and cultural nuances (Lafferty and Eckerberg, 2009). LA21 has also been subject to resistance, particularly in the USA. Here elements of the Republican Party have argued that it erodes national sovereignty and threatens aspects of the American way of life, such as individual rights, car ownership and living in suburbs (Kaufman and Zernike, 2012).

Regardless of this local initiative, at its heart sustainable development is a call for action on a planetary scale. The Brundtland Report powerfully concludes:

> As the century began, neither human numbers nor technology had the power to radically alter planetary systems. As the century closes, not only do vastly increased human numbers and their activities have that power, but major, unintended changes are occurring in the atmosphere, in soils, in waters, among plants and animals, and in the relationships among all these. The rate of change is outstripping the ability of scientific disciplines and our current capabilities to assess and advise. It is frustrating the attempts of political and economic institutions, which evolved in a different, more fragmented world, to adapt and cope. (World Commission for Environment and Development, 1987: 343)

Take a moment to reflect on this paragraph and its key messages. It explicitly identifies not only that humans are damaging the planet, but also that our current norms of science, governance and management are inadequate to prevent this decline. Crucially, this was not a lone voice or pressure group but a consensus political view on an international scale that advocated a huge transformation in the relationship of humans to the environment across the globe. It regarded the next few decades as being crucial and spoke of a need to break out from old approaches to development and environmental protection by adopting new values and behavioural change. The text also introduced many innovative ideas, such as the notion of intergenerational equity and a recognition that the world needs to operate together with institutions and economic systems adapted to facilitate this new approach.

From this perspective, the lines between sustainability and previous conservation or management strategies are much easier to identify. Reflecting on the Brundtland Report we can appreciate just how profound a shift it advocated. It did not just want to protect the environment, it wanted to protect people as well, even those on the other side of the world or those not yet born. It also desired to change the institutions, politics and values that perpetuate environmental problems. In this respect it could be viewed as advocating as radical an agenda as some of the more extreme pressure groups.

To try to capture sustainability in a simple form, scholars have identified three encompassing pillars: environmental, social and economic; or alternatively, the three 'Es': economy, equity and environment. Both descriptions seek to explain the need to integrate multiple dimensions in order to achieve a more sustainable future. The concept also has spatial and temporal implications, with human concerns directed across a wider geography and a longer time span than the norm. Figure 5.1 demonstrates a notional representation of how this 'gravity of attention' may look in practice. Every possible concern can be located at some point within the

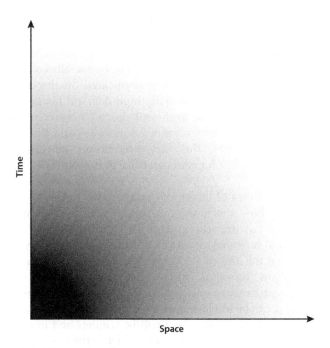

Figure 5.1 *The gravity of attention*

graph, but most people's focus is usually drawn towards the darker shaded areas representing the natural allure of the immediate, both in terms of time and space. Sustainability argues for something different; a long timespan encompassing a global perspective, which is one reason why it is both innovative and challenging to implement.

Looking back to the definition of sustainable development, it is helpful to start unpacking this by analysing its two key related concepts: *needs* and *limitations*. The former concerns critical thinking about what is essential and for whom, and, as with scarcity, we shall see it is not a simple issue. In 1943, a classic paper by the psychologist Abraham Maslow argued that there was a 'hierarchy' of human needs with basic ones, such as food and water, at the bottom of a pyramid and then four other progressively higher tiers – safety, belonging, esteem and self-actualization – that can be engaged with as each level is secured. So, from this perspective, people's needs, and therefore resource requirements, can be relative to their affluence or security.

Herbert Marcuse (1898–1979) further highlighted the difference between what he called 'real' and 'false' needs – or more simply what people really need and what they desire, where the latter may be fuelled by the mechanisms of the consumerist capitalist society. This complicates matters even more. From this position, 'needs' are not necessarily firm requirements – they can be socially constructed and the success of many societies is predicated on the economic benefits of maintaining an artificially high demand for goods and services. But if you distil the argument down to *essential* needs – that is, those you need for continued survival – and discard any relative, cultural desires, this may present an unrealistic and unworkable approach, a hairshirt sacrifice that politicians dare not enforce.

The second concept of limitations is connected to this and relates to determining how much we can use. Again, this is subject to debate: how exactly are scarcity and the nature of resources to be understood, and how may resources be distributed equitably? There is no doubt that the idea of a concept that links the natural environment with how economic and social development consumes resources is a progressive one, but it also raises very difficult questions of how it can be implemented in practice. If resources are to be accessed and used differently there will be winners and losers, from individuals to companies to nation states. Hence there is a real possibility for resistance and conflict to become apparent. The tensions between the triple aims of sustainability, combined with the short-term economic and social implications of any change in development norms, also neatly illustrates why sustainability is contested: we have a concept with inherent wriggle room and a desire by some to maintain current practices.

One strategy to help deliver sustainable development has been to translate its principles into a number of performance indicators. These are targets used to communicate, measure and monitor progress from the local to the international scale. However, as will be discussed in Chapter 8, the use of indicators can lead policy down prescribed pathways related to the availability of data or to established political priorities. This can also change the meaning of sustainability, away from its initial emphasis and to an alternative relationship between the environment and development, or an engagement with inter- and intragenerational equity, or even a reconfiguration of institutions and governance, and instead serve to maintain a business-as-usual approach. Consider the following iteration of the UK government's Sustainable Development Strategy. It proposed to reach its aims: 'through a sustainable, innovative and productive economy that delivers high levels of employment; and a just society that promotes social inclusion, sustainable communities and personal wellbeing' (HM Government, 2005: 16). If you compare this to the message in the Brundtland Report it is increasingly clear how sustainable development can be co-opted and manipulated to deliver political outcomes, such as high levels of employment, and be written in such a vague manner that can challenge interpretation and delivery. It also neatly illustrates the differences between 'strong' and 'weak' sustainability, as discussed in the previous section.

Despite its radical roots and transformative agenda, sustainability is commonly appropriated as a vehicle for the continued delivery of the status quo, with the main institutions underpinning economic development largely unchanged. Indeed, the concept is routinely appropriated and prefixed to a host of aims, some of which may appear contradictory. A useful exercise to begin analysing the uses of sustainability is to compare the meaning to a conservation agenda and consider these two questions: What are the differences in emphasis? And how may this lead to varying outcomes? Critical thinking is needed to ensure that a concept designed, in part at least, to promote a better use of environmental resources over longer time periods is not used to justify the opposite.

Sustainability as a framing concept exploded on to the world stage during the latter period of the twentieth century. While still relevant, its importance has arguably waned within environmental planning in recent years, particularly as a result of the perceived inability to achieve its aims in practice. The difficulty in describing what a sustainable result might look like raises concerns regarding whether it should be viewed as relating to outcomes or more as a *process* – a way of thinking used to guide decisions that may possess almost moralistic values. Consequently, while it may have the ability to educate and build consensus, attention has turned to alternative concepts, such as risk, that help us to understand the dynamic relationship between humanity and nature.

Risk

Modern society, and in particular institutions of governance and public administration, is said to be characterized by concerns about risk (Beck, 1992; Giddens, 1991). Risk is viewed as being ubiquitous, with hazard awareness a common feature of everyday life and the environment is increasingly seen through the prism of risk management rather than the traditional logics of resource scarcity or conservation. Observers of the 'risk society' (Beck, 1992) argue that threats emerge from the inherent nature of society, which has the added incongruity that technologically advanced cities and increasingly knowledgeable populations are in fact rendered more vulnerable by the very same catalysts of modernity. Science, technology and the highly networked and globalized nature of contemporary society foster new risks; for example, rendering people vulnerable to events that may occur on the other side of the world. In consequence, society has become much less likely to accept mere fate as a primary explanatory factor in understanding the perils that afflict human society. Rather, we now demand explanations, mechanisms to manage risk, and financial compensation (Mythen, 2004), with sectors and industries, from bespoke security solutions to hazard mapping information, established to service the risk society. From this perspective the boundaries between 'natural' and manufactured risks are blurred, with nature and society increasing enmeshed (Beck, 2009).

An awareness of differing risks is part of life, but with regard to environmental planning it is closely related to the possibility of future events, such as the long-term stress of climate change or the rapid impact of a natural hazard. A risk-based approach can help to mitigate the potential impact of any change to environmental, social or economic systems. As Douglas and Wildavsky (1983: 1) put it: 'can we know the risks we face, now or in the future? No, we cannot; but yes, we must act as if we do'. Though the concept is mainly anthropocentric it can help to deliver proactive environmental planning, and the probabilistic approach meshes well with decision-making norms, which like to prioritize the efficient use of time and money. It also has an emerging role within environmental planning. For example, the UN-Habitat (2007: 205) division specifically identifies the need to change the perception of planning as being predominately about facilitating growth and development, highlighting its wider potential to manage risk, and stating that 'Land-use planning is perhaps the most fundamental tool for mainstreaming disaster risk reduction into urban development processes.' This section will help to clarify the origin and development of the concept of risk, introduce some of the ways by which risk management strategies can relate to environmental planning, and draw attention to some of its flaws.

The transition from a view that future events were, at least in part, reliant on fate, celestial providence, or the support of Lady Luck, to a more quantitative basis for understanding risks has occurred in small, incremental stages over the past few hundred years. Considering risk from a more technical perspective had its foundation in the maritime ventures of the sixteenth and seventeenth centuries and was related to providing financial compensation for the impact of acts of nature that could be deemed to be outside of human responsibility (Lupton, 1999). The mathematicians, Blaise Pascal and Pierre de Fermat, provided a further development by solving the Pacioli Puzzle, a probability problem set two centuries earlier by a Franciscan monk. The dilemma concerned how to split the remaining pot of a gambling game that ends prematurely. If a 'best out of five' dice game between two people ends after three rounds, how should the money be distributed fairly? One player had to be ahead, so a 50/50 split seemed unfair. During an exchange of letters, the mathematicians plotted the differing trajectories the game could follow and determined that that the gambler ahead by two games to one would win for three-quarters of the time so he was entitled to 75 per cent of the pot if the game ended at this early point. In essence, they provided the foundation for the theory of probability and the forecasting of future events.

The development of the understanding of risk and future possibilities increased further in the following centuries through Jacob Bernoulli's (1713) 'Law of Large Numbers' and Abraham de Moivre's (1718) 'The Doctrine of Chances' both of which started to develop an understanding of statistics and larger datasets. Risk was gradually moving from being something related to divine providence, or an accident of chance, to an understanding that some occurrences can be quantified and therefore anticipated. The improvements also provided the basis for a transition from the basic estimation of probability to the related fields of sampling and distribution, both of which enabled more uncertain outcomes to be estimated. For example, the collection of historic data within actuarial tables enables life insurance to be taken out; no one knows how long a person will live, but with a large store of data on how long people live and a knowledge of lifestyles and so on, an estimate could be provided. While it may not be 100 per cent accurate in any single case, when the cases are considered from a larger sample of society this is evened out.

The scientization of risk and its associated concepts essentially gathered pace in line with advances in mathematics and probability. In the early twentieth century an economist, Frank Knight, provided an important breakthrough when he drew a distinction between 'risk' and 'uncertainty' within any event, suggesting that risk is when there is a known chance, and uncertainty is when the odds of the occurrence are unknown (Knight, 1921). This aspect of risk is useful to reconsider as it highlights the difficulty in assigning clear values to complex and sometimes relative issues, and from there to related concerns, such as how to consider what is unknown within decisions. This has been attempted, for example, in environmental planning, by the creation of climate change scenarios, following the precautionary principle or by investing in increasing the knowledge base. However, relying on science and technology as tools to manage the concept of risk may not be straightforward. In practice, advances have the potential to create newer risks as society progresses, such as a flood defence system failing, or a nuclear explosion. At the same time, the knowledge generated also reveals more ignorance as gaps in understanding become apparent. Perhaps incongruously, it follows that the understanding of risks may become *more* uncertain as knowledge increases. To understand this tricky idea, consider the feeling you get from reading an academic textbook: the more you discover, the more you are exposed to new areas you might not comprehend fully at that moment.

In general, the contemporary understanding of risk has been influenced heavily by its development via the insurance and legal industries, who employ statistics and probability to prescribe financial compensation for future undesirable events. Essentially, this enabled risk to be monetized, whether by recompense for a detrimental event or as a means to relate risk to cost–benefit decisions, such as the provision of new flood defences. Further, the phrase 'Act of God' was developed by these professions as a useful and durable tool for referring to natural events that cannot reasonably be foreseen and therefore for which no one can be held liable. The origin of this phrase relating to unknown factors affecting the potential losses of maritime ventures also reveals much about the subsequent management of risk. It suggests that some risks are normalized in our everyday life – they cannot be avoided, so we just have to accept them and perhaps take out insurance. This economic, quantitative approach also raises questions of equity and justice – it is fine for those who can afford to partake, but what of those individuals, or even countries, who cannot?

Furthermore, the term Act of God in risk management has helped to shift perceptions of accountability from people, governments or economic systems towards nature. While it may be understandable that society used to view extreme events as a punishment from God for various actions of impiety, modern knowledge should make this axiom redundant. Hurricane Katrina emphasized forcefully that the effect of a severe storm of natural origin was a disaster caused by essentially very human mistakes: from the location, design and construction of parts of the city; to the selection, quality and maintenance of protective levees; to a lack of preparedness and subsequent implementation of a disaster response strategy. The terminology is actually incredibly unhelpful as it is a legacy of outdated thought and deliberately blurs the causal link between human activities and natural hazards, and provides a barrier to pursuing effective managerial responses.

The acknowledgement that risk is connected to our perceptions and constrained by information in turn forms the basis of the more contemporary standpoint that risk is socially and culturally constructed. Beck (1992: 99) argues that risk has become shaped by statistics and the expansion of the insurance industry, and he referred to: 'systematically caused, statistically describable and, in this sense, "predictable" types of events, which can therefore also be subjected to supra-individual and political rules of recognition, compensation and avoidance'. Douglas (1992: 58) further highlighted how different professions may interpret risk differently within decision-making, arguing that: 'when faced with estimating probability and credibility, they come already primed with culturally learned assumptions and weightings ... they have set up their institutions as decision processors, which shut out some options and put others in favourable light'. Therefore, the way that risk is conveyed in environmental planning may not reflect either its complex conceptual nature or the ambiguity in its evaluation. The simplistic language of risk calculation as a line on a map or a percentage chance may falsely reduce uncertainty to a comforting illusion of deterministic, probabilistic processes within which the inherent gravitas of scientific calculations can attach a misleading confidence to what may be very tentative outcomes. This was a point recognized by Wynne (2009: 308), who argued that the current methodology for managing risk is erroneous and 'the dominant risk science approach is more than a method; it is a misbegotten culture which inadvertently but actively conceals that ignorance'. In short, the way we frame and interpret the concept of risk shapes our understanding and responses.

The example of flooding can serve to highlight the importance of this discussion for environmental planning. After a spate of damaging flood events across Europe from the end of the twentieth century onwards there was a desire for more information regarding exposure to this risk. To this end, the European Union Floods Directive (European Commission, 2007) required Member States to map the extent of flooding and ascertain how many assets were at risk. This information could then be used for a host of managerial measures, not least environmental planning. Yet, while information on risk is valuable, it may also be very uncertain and should be treated with caution in decision-making. With regard to England, tracing how information on risk changed dramatically within a 10-year period is particularly illustrative.

In the aftermath of the year 2000 floods, the very precise figure of 1,724,225 properties being at risk of fluvial, tidal and coastal flooding was given, the first real national indication of exposure. At this time there was no indication of flooding appearing outside these traditional areas. In the wake of continued flooding, however, exposure to surface water (incorporating urban runoff and local drainage failure) was newly included in 2004. It was projected that 80,000 properties were at risk from this source. In the same year, around 1,100,000 properties were identified as being at risk from groundwater flooding, 112,855 of which were also at risk from conventional flood sources. However, in the summer of 2007, floods inundated whole areas that were previously deemed not to be 'at risk' and seriously undermined the effectiveness of this approach. The subsequent review of this catastrophe demonstrated that the errors were not just minor aspects, such as an inaccurate distinction between medium- or high-risk areas, or a slight miscalculation of floodplain boundaries, rather it was a complete failure to realize that serious national flooding could come from multiple sources, in particular from surface water and inadequate drainage (Pitt, 2008). Again, the overall figure was revised upwards, but this time in a dramatic fashion. The figure of 80,000 properties projected to be at risk from surface water flooding was scaled up to 3.8 million, making this hitherto largely unrecognized source the greatest flood risk (White, 2013).

Table 5.2 captures the developing knowledge on risk to provide an accessible overview of how quickly information has changed, concerning both the estimated number of properties at risk of flooding and from which source. While the definition of risk can vary over time between documents, the table is useful as a didactic device; not necessarily with regard to attaching a firm significance to the number of properties, but rather as a demonstration of the way that a firm reliance on quantification as means of risk management can be flawed.

The clearest message from the changing evidence base since the year 2000 concerns the value of critically approaching what may

Table 5.2 *The changing knowledge of the sources of flood exposure in England between 2001 and 2011*

| Year | Estimated properties at risk by source | | | | |
	Rivers and sea	Surface water	Ground-water	Reservoir failure	Total
2001	1,724,225	0	0	0	1,724,225
2004	1,740,000	80,000	1,700,000	0	3,420,000[1]
2009	2,400,000	3,800,000	1,700,000	0	6,800,000[1,2]
2011	2,400,000	3,800,000	1,700,0001	1,100,000	7,900,000[1,2]

Notes: [1] 112,855 properties are at risk from both rivers and the sea, and groundwater flooding; [2] 1,000,000 properties are at risk rom both rivers and the sea, and surface water flooding.

Sources: National Audit Office (2001); Evans *et al.* (2004); Jacobs Engineering UK (2004); Environment Agency (2009; 2011).

Box 5.2 Risk management and communication

In 2010, Eyjafjallaokull, a volcano in Iceland, erupted and spewed out plumes of volcanic ash several kilometres into the atmosphere. There were concerns that the ash would damage aircraft engines, and as a result, air space was closed in parts of northern Europe for six days between the 15 and 21 April 2010. Millions of passengers were stranded or had to alter their travel plans and it was estimated by the International Air Transport Association (IATA) (2010) that the airline industry alone lost US$1.7bn over this very short period, with many more losses estimated for business and related activities. The airspace reopened, partly as a result of pressure from passenger and airline groups, but also because of the ongoing economic and social implications. The blanket ban was deemed to be a blunt instrument to manage such a dynamic risk, and after comparing the results of theoretical models with those of test flights, new data allowed a more sophisticated view of the threat of volcanic ash. Given the fear of the effect and movement of the ash cloud, particularly among the public, however, flight safety remained a source of major concern. It was therefore a surprise when, on the very day the airspace was reopened, the front page of the UK newspaper, the *Daily Star*, carried a photograph depicting a jumbo jet with its engines aflame looking as though it was on the verge of crashing. This was accompanied by a sensationalist headline: 'Terror as Plane Hits Ash Cloud'.

But what was the real story here? Most people reading the headline and viewing the associated images, particularly given their

→

ostensibly appear to be very accurate scientific datasets in environmental planning. With regard to flooding, the data appears to be particularly subject to rapid and fundamental change, and raises questions as to the extent to which it can be distilled to a probabilistic figure or a clear spatial delineation between 'safe' areas and those 'at risk'. This is partly related to the dynamism of the system within which the knowledge is constructed, where climate change exerts an unknowable forcing effect. Equally, where planning and policy interventions occur they may also serve to drive risk. For example, flood defences also increase exposure via the 'escalator effect' (Parker, 1995) or 'safe development paradox' (Burby, 2006), whereby they subsequently make the land behind them appear safe and attractive for development. Furthermore, the general increase in urbanization within a catchment will increase surface water runoff in ways that

→

front-page prominence, would think that the decision to reopen the airspace had resulted in immediate disaster. Had a plane crashed on the very first morning that flights had resumed after restrictions were relaxed? In reality the story depicted an image from a TV documentary from 1982 that had reconstructed a historical incident. The paper was subsequently removed from shelves at a number of UK airports, with Gatwick airport's director of communications, saying 'We thought it was inappropriate at this point in time after six days of disruption and as people were anxious to get to their holiday destination or to return home to have these sort of computer-generated images on the front page' (Plunkett, 2010). After a number of people contacted the Press Complaints Commission to object, the *Daily Star* was forced to clarify the story.

Considering the discussion so far in this chapter, let us take a moment to reflect on the way risk is framed, managed and communicated. Beck (2009) suggests that the catastrophic images frequently used to discuss environmental concerns, such as those linked to climate change, shape general interpretation and provide pressure for action. Yet, as this case demonstrates, this approach can also misrepresent fears, particularly if the nature of the coverage is melodramatic, which can reduce credibility, or the impacts seem so severe and imbue the public with such a sense of powerlessness that it inhibits action, such as can occur with climate change (Hulme, 2009). Therefore, the media has a crucial role in portraying risk and uncertainties as it can greatly influence the political discourse around intervention.

challenge accurate quantification (White and Howe, 2004; White, 2008). As Adams (1995: 29) puts it: 'risk is constantly in motion'.

Given the instability in applying this concept, it is important that ideas such as these are subject to deep consideration in order to be effective. Though risk-based approaches are becoming enshrined in policy, they are usually applied and interpreted in a narrow and procedural manner, perhaps reflecting both the inchoate field and the nature of environmental planning. However, we can see that risk management is anthropocentric, statistically focused and open to interpretation – it holds different meanings for different people dependent on a range of factors – from which factors were included in the calculation, to a person's culture or profession. Box 5.2 discusses risk management and how it may be communicated in more detail.

Viewing the environment in a risk-based manner does fit with modern ways of managing nature as a hazard (for example, flooding, earthquakes and so on) as well as having synergies with the use of evidence, quantification and approaches such as the precautionary principle or cost–benefit analysis. In practice, managing an actual or perceived risk is a common rationale for action in much of environmental planning and will be represented in claims and counter-claims concerning a wide range of concerns, from the possible loss of a treasured space or species to managing acceptable levels of pollution or noise, or the financial impact on industry. Yet, as we have seen, risk as a concept is contested and influenced by competing agendas, all of which are designed to influence perception and priorities, and shape debates.

Bringing the environment within a security discourse based around the risk to lives or livelihoods also influences the nature and rationale of intervention. The media is inevitably drawn to being a willing partner in this reframing, but the construction of environmental issues within this medium means that there is a cacophony of views and voices, all vying for attention and many of which present conflicting evidence. Essentially this has moved seemingly neutral or 'empty' concepts towards new political spaces that are the hallmarks of contemporary environmental discourse. Here, actors and agencies such as the media, think-tanks, scientists and the public sector conclude, compete and negotiate. Clearly, the problems for those concerned with environmental planning are not only in determining how risk can influence decision-making, but also in establishing a strong mandate for environmental planning intervention, particularly where significant concerns may be expensive or require substantial changes to the status quo.

When predicting a coin toss or throw of the dice, the probabilities are clear and set; with regard to environmental or social risks, however, this simply does not apply and we need to make decisions in an uncertain world. To integrate risk and related concepts successfully within decision-making processes, there is a need to provide a degree of conceptual clarity since the way a topic is defined can have significant repercussions for policy and its subsequent interpretation within environmental planning decisions. For example, it has implications for the way that risks are weighted in order to assign priorities for action – the probability and impacts of any occurrence are an inevitable factor in decisions when there is competition for resources. Equally, it can affect the final allocation of responsibility or accountability – is it the nation state, private sector, local authority or the individual who needs to act? Cultural factors also come into play that skew risk both spatially and temporally. For example, if there is a flood in the UK, financial compensation is usually a matter between homeowners and their insurers. In the Netherlands, the state simply pays compensation and there is no private sector involvement. As a result, people in the two countries view this particular risk differently.

Reflecting on the role of humanity in influencing and accepting various risks, it is clear that understanding and defining the concept is related to power and culture, such as by the dominant methodology used in making decisions. Moreover, while institutions or agencies may have key roles as risk managers, some inter-related, complex and expensive risks are leading to governments adopting a view that the public will need to take more responsibility regarding determining their own exposure and adapting as necessary (White and O'Hare, 2014). In turn, this greatly increases the number of stakeholders who can influence the concept within environmental planning. It also suggests that the need to act when information may be incomplete or uncertain will be important. This is linked to notion of 'resilience' and, as will be seen in the next section, resilience is a similarly slippery concept to sustainability and risk.

Resilience

On 12 February 2002, the former US Secretary of Defense, Donald Rumsfeld, made this statement at a news briefing:

> as we know, there are known knowns; there are things we know we know. We also know there are known unknowns; that is to say we know there are some things we do not know. But there are also unknown unknowns, the ones we don't know we don't know. (US Department of Defense, 2002)

Deeply hidden in this much-mocked opaque assertion is a surprisingly useful concept: we live in an intensely complex, interconnected and uncertain world, and consequently we should recognize that our knowledge is incomplete. To manage risks effectively we need to recognize that not all threats can be either measured or even foreseen. 'Unknown unknowns' appears to be a paradoxical phrase, but its message can provide a useful basis for understanding unusual, unpredictable events and the consequent need for inbuilt 'resilience' within environmental planning.

Superficially, 'resilience' is undoubtedly an agreeable 'motherhood and apple pie' notion (so-called because no one would disagree with them). To argue that society, the economy, cities or infrastructure should be *less* resilient is illogical, akin to a contemporary planner suggesting that development should be 'unsustainable' or a politician arguing against 'progress'. This servile acceptability has proved to be instrumental to its rapid incorporation into the contemporary lexicon of academics and policymakers; resilience instinctively appears incontestable, portraying a desirable, aspirational goal relevant to practically any given issue. Like sustainability, the development of the concept has also given resilience multiple meanings, thus providing considerable scope for interpretation (Brand and Jax, 2007) and widening its potential application. This pliable, optimistic character has aided its transferability, particularly within politics and environmental planning, where the concept has rapidly gained currency in recent years. However, this lack of normative contention should not simply allow the concept to be unpacked uncritically, promoted automatically or employed unthinkingly – bear this in mind when considering how resilience may lead to particular environmental planning approaches and outcomes.

To appreciate the intricacies of resilience, attention should first turn to the concept's germination. The term's origins can be traced to ecology and natural science (Walker and Cooper, 2011), but resilience has since been adopted to serve a multitude of disciplines, from psychology and psychiatry (Kaplan, 1999) to social and community development (Adger, 2000), to engineering and design (Bosher, 2008), and to flooding and drought (White, 2010). In a seminal 1973 paper, Holling (1973) distinguished between two notions of resilience. The first was 'engineering resilience', developed from economics, mathematics and physics, which referred to the ability of an ecosystem to return to stability or equilibrium after a disturbance. Though useful within certain circumstances, it was when this relatively stable definition of resilience was reconfigured to be relevant to more dynamic circumstances that its influence expanded. Holling further argued that there could also be an 'ecological resilience' concerning the ability to absorb shocks: 'and still persist' (1973: 17). He states that these are essentially two contrasting aspects of 'stability', with engineering resilience being concerned with maintaining *efficiency* of function while ecological resilience relates to maintaining the *existence* of function (Holling, 1996: 33). This latter aspect encompassed the more evolutionary notion of the need to adapt to changing normalities, emphasizing the heterogeneous links between social and ecological systems. It also had the effect of tempering the static, almost technical, focus of resilience with a new social consideration connected with facilitating the ability to 'cope'. This development helped to transform the concept into one with wider desirability. The more holistic, precautionary interpretation focused on engendering system enhancement has helped to promote its application within environmental planning, with integrative properties that potentially connect ecological, physical and social systems proving attractive (Godschalk, 2003).

From relatively discrete beginnings, resilience now has potentially profound implications for environmental planning. However, in practice, resilience has been discussed most commonly as a framing concept to build capacity to manage specific uncertain risks, such as climate change, terrorism, flooding, or economic and regional decline. In addition to simply recovering from a disaster or adapting to changing normalities, resilience can also have a strong human element, which focuses on the nature of institutions and the ability of a society to meet the multifaceted challenges of the future. This may link to more intangible social and cultural aspects. For example, resilience to a threat can be increased by poverty reduction, more effective decision-making or behavioural change.

A wide range of contemporary risks threaten not just the ability of states to demonstrate control and governability, but also of markets to operate, for capital to be efficiently accumulated and for societies to lend legitimacy to these ensembles. In short, 'shocks' or uncertainty highlight societal vulnerability, and resilience strategies demonstrate that a degree of control and order can still be marshalled. Significantly, therefore, resilience may also be described as a mechanism to promote political *confidence* as well as practical *outcomes*. It has become a 'useful but unspecified metaphor among policymakers in the context of uncertain and disruptive change' (Pike *et al.*, 2010: 61). This does not necessarily advocate an avoidance of the risk, perhaps by changing the economic or social practices that may create it, rather the concept may be used to argue for a need to cope better with the impacts.

Resilience is also a 'fuzzy' concept; appearing to be action-oriented and aspirational without being tied to particular approaches or outcomes. In theory, it may have synergies with technocentric interpretations, such as the construction of earthquake-resilient buildings, as well as ecocentric ones that promote policies to limit CO_2 emissions driving climatic change. Therefore, it may also be conservative in that it could serve to embed or monetize risk exposure, or radical by advocating systemic societal change to a new normality. However, though widely presented as a possible paradigm shift with significant socio-cultural implications, in practice resilience in environmental planning has tended to be characterized by a simple return to normality that is more analogous with planning norms, engineered responses, dominant interests and techno-rational measures centred on reactive measures on the building scale (White and O'Hare, 2014). While the concept offers huge potential within environmental planning, such as with regard to community empowerment or as a means to adapt to uncertain events, again, we see the difficulties in moving a concept from rhetoric to reality, such as resilience from what, and for whom?

In much the same way that sustainable development similarly captured the zeitgeist of the late twentieth century; resilience may be the perfect symbol for the beginning of the twenty-first: a conveniently nebulous concept incorporating shifting notions of risk and responsibility bounded by a reconstituted governance framework; all of which can engender confidence and potentially facilitate the transfer of costs away from the state to the private sector and communities (O'Hare and White, 2013). While resilience does offer easy potential as a means of managing specific risks, such as by changing building materials or thinking about the location of development, it is much more difficult to translate into practice when considered from a socio-cultural perspective. We may be able to design and implement a resilient building, but compare that to the difficulty in merging social and environmental systems, or even creating a resilient society. However, it does appear to offer a useful concept for considering how to deal with the manifold unpredictable events that are such a feature of modernity. Adapting to become more able to cope with changing environmental, social or economic risks is a valuable characteristic in a world of complex problems that are hard for the scientific community to manage.

Conclusion

This chapter has been designed to highlight the power of concepts in environmental planning: from their initial selection to how they are defined and operationalized. Concepts such as sustainability, risk and resilience will continue to permeate environmental planning and academic discourse as they are perceived to offer a useful framework to better understand and address environmental change. Perhaps more interestingly, concepts also allow us to pose alternative questions and perceive issues differently, or in the evocative words of Marcel Proust (1871–1922) from his novel *In Search of Lost Time* (1992: 343) 'to possess other eyes'. Methodologies to facilitate more effective decisions are crucial. In practice, our ability to conduct environmental planning effectively will be shaped significantly by the way in which environmental managers, built environment professionals and those in related professions frame and interpret concepts, and use them to inform responses.

Considering the widespread use of concepts such as these one might be forgiven for assuming that there would be a consensus on their meaning usage. As readers will now appreciate, the terms are used liberally and occasionally confusingly, and in some quarters they almost seem to have been designed specifically to be pliable and vague. This is best demonstrated by considering the wide and varied interpretation of sustainability, which has been employed in unforeseen and often contradictory directions. Indeed, some observers even indicate that it is this lack of specificity that may have contributed to the growing popularity of terms such as 'sustainability' or 'resilience' in the social sciences (Klein *et al.*, 2004) and policy (White and O'Hare, 2014). While such a characteristic may proffer a valuable rhetorical commodity for politicians, it is less useful for those concerned with environmental planning practice.

This chapter was designed to emphasize that, just as urban areas exhibit a dazzling array of forms and are under a set of differing pressures, designing transferable and effective environmental planning measures is similarly difficult. Concepts are not fixed artefacts; they are contested assemblages that may change over time and space. To confuse matters even more, there are differing concepts, each of which possesses multiple pathways, logics and measures. While sustainable development has been useful as a tool to amplify environmental consciousness, and risk and resilience have demonstrated potential in addressing specific, but uncertain, threats, this pliability needs to be recognized and addressed to contribute towards environmental planning. Acknowledging this conceptual fuzziness is important, as the way that problems are framed leads to differing responses so there can be significant scope for interpretation and disagreement.

The multiple environmental worldviews discussed earlier provide an insight into how concepts can be subject to dispute, from their simple definition, to their appropriation and eventual translation into policy. And when one considers that there are a variety of framing concepts, each subject to similar pressures, and each with the ability to shape responses and outcomes, one can start to appreciate how the selection of a concept with the ability to frame a debate is not an inconsequential step. In addition, not only might these concepts be interpreted differently, but the concepts themselves may be in opposition. So selecting an approach that has more of an emphasis on sustainability will have differing implications for environmental planning than one based on resilience.

Having explored often-used concepts, it is important to iterate that difference does not render them entirely unhelpful. The strengths of these concepts are that they may aid understanding and supply a distinct view of how intervention should occur. Sometimes they can even link environmental, social and economic goals, and when this happens real progress can be made. Significantly, as they can be used at the very start of environmental planning, they also have the power to shape scientific endeavour, an issue to which we now turn.

Chapter 6

The Role of Science

> 'In wishing to bring a modicum of natural science to the planning process, I am, like most other planners, seriously hampered by ignorance of the subject.'
>
> (McHarg, 1969: 47)

Science is traditionally regarded as an essential component in enabling effective environmental planning. Yet the integration of science into the practice of environmental planning is far from smooth or unproblematic. This can often be conceived as ignorance on the part of planners; the pioneering landscape architect, Ian McHarg, observed as much in the opening quote above. However, the way that science is conducted and compiled can also play a role in enabling or inhibiting its translation into the arenas of policy and practice. This chapter will investigate these issues and show that 'science' cannot be brought straightforwardly to the planning process, since science and planning constitute different types of knowledge about the world – both equally valid – that need to be acknowledged and integrated. This chapter is positioned within an interdisciplinary perspective that aims to highlight the importance of scientific literacy – the knowledge of science as a *process* to inform environmental planning. By understanding how 'science' works, particularly its methods and limitations, among other factors we can shed light on why some problems are solved instead of others, or how data can struggle to prove causal effects. What is particularly illuminating to understand is how the scientific approach is inherently riddled with *doubt*, a factor that may be anathema to politicians or decision-makers whose culture is based on certainty. If we hold that science is one of the fundamental building blocks of environmental planning, these issues need to be engaged with actively if we are to make intelligent and sensitive environmental interventions.

This chapter develops the conceptual discussion in Chapter 5 by examining, in a similar fashion, key factors linking science and environmental planning. We begin by looking briefly at how science operates and by doing so we can begin to challenge initial perceptions that might be held. First, we investigate how scientific knowledge can either be regarded as developing cumulatively by building incrementally on previous data, or by a more circular route punctuated by irregular periods of revolution. Second, we shall address the question of whether science can be entirely objective, and examine the difference between facts and values. We then investigate the issue of doubt and certainty before looking at the role of the expert and expert knowledge. Taken together, these debates represent major communication problems between science and environmental planning. The final section explores the science–policy interface to help to understand the practical complexities of transferring scientific data and findings into the policy sphere. While of value in itself, this chapter also provides a logical bridge from the earlier conceptual material to the more practical world of policy that is covered in the next chapter.

Accumulation and revolution

To understand the role of science in environmental planning it is, first, helpful to be aware of how it works and how it may be subject to change. We discussed in Chapter 2 how science can be viewed as an incremental activity that develops by building on the achievements of successive scientists. In this rendering, science then becomes a problem-solving activity that searches for answers to questions or provides the evidence to act. Therefore, over time, science may be seen to provide a rising degree of confidence for policy-makers as new data is discovered and analysed. Although simplified, it is this view of science with which you are probably most familiar.

This view was challenged fundamentally in Thomas Kuhn's seminal text *The Structure of Scientific Revolutions*. Here, Kuhn (1962: 10) defined 'normal science' in exactly this intuitive sense: one that progresses logically based on accepted fundamentals, stating: ' "Normal science" means research firmly based upon one or more past scientific achievements, achievements that some particular scientific community acknowledges for a time as supplying the foundation for its further practice.' However, Kuhn had another purpose in pointing out this definition of 'normal' science. He wanted to show that the development of scientific knowledge does not necessarily occur only along this smooth, linear path: science actually depends on intermittent, turbulent periods of revolution that shake long-held convictions. In recognizing the unsettled nature of science, those concerned with environmental planning can better appreciate its limits and comprehend why some problems may subsequently challenge intervention.

While there may be innumerable small additions to knowledge created in many different disciplines, occasionally there will be a significant shift with widespread ramifications. Darwin's work on evolution is a germane example. When visiting the Galapagos Islands he collected evidence that did not fit with established views and necessitated the development of a new hypothesis to better explain what he had discovered. Kuhn (1962) used this example to draw attention to the disparities between the way that science is perceived and how it actually operates, and in doing so identified three chronological phases to scientific knowledge. The first stage in the process can be characterized as an initial *pre-paradigm phase*, where there is no consensus over an accepted theory. As inquisitiveness grows, science advances until any one of a number of competing theories eventually becomes accepted by the community. At this point, a period of *normal science* begins, which allows problems to be addressed in the context of this dominant paradigm. This phase lasts until data starts to reveal anomalies that cannot be resolved within the existing frameworks. Where weaknesses persist, the final phase, *revolutionary science*, begins, in which existing assumptions and frameworks are re-examined and new theories may be developed. Eventually, a new paradigm is accepted that better fits the evidence – what Kuhn termed a 'paradigmatic shift' – and the process continues. In this rendering science becomes a cyclical, revolutionary process that does not occur within a determinate time. Box 6.1 highlights how this has occurred in practice.

In retrospect, the impact and legacy of Kuhn's influential work could be seen as proof of his own argument: the accepted paradigm of gradual, continuous accumulation was challenged, and the new understanding based on cycles of stability and revolution that better fits the evidence gradually became normalized. From an environmental planning perspective, similar periods of normality punctuated by occasional 'paradigm' shifts can be observed that affected the development of the discipline, from the birth of central state control around the start of the twentieth century, or the move from quantitative evidence bases to the emergence of discursive

Box 6.1   The Copernicus Revolution

The gradual realization that the Earth revolved around the sun and not vice versa, known as the Copernicus Revolution in honour of the main protagonist, is an example of a scientific paradigm shift. Throughout human history there had been a strong belief that the Earth was at the centre of the solar system, an opinion based on how celestial bodies appeared to orbit in a predictable fashion around our planet each day, and that in comparison to this dynamism the Earth appeared to be unmoving – a central pivot around which all others shifted. This view is commonly called the geocentric model, or the Ptolemaic system, after the work of the Greek astronomer, Ptolemy.

As advances were made in fields such as technology, mathematics and astronomy, eventually new ways of viewing the heavens were developed, and alternative theories to explain observations on planetary motion were mooted. The long-held view was challenged by increasingly precise observations connected with the movement of planets that did not fit with this established paradigm. In the mid-sixteenth century, Nicolaus Copernicus (1473–1543) published *On the Revolutions of the Heavenly Spheres* (1995 [1543]), a work that would not alter perceptions immediately, but would set in train an alternative hypothesis that would be tested and improved over the next few centuries by other luminaries such as Johannes Kepler,

→

methods in the latter part of the same century. Even in this brief section readers should be able to grasp that science is a much less stable and incremental activity than might have been supposed. Yet this is not the only route into questioning science: there is also an issue over how *objective* it might be – we shall turn to this query next.

Objective and subjective

It is easy to picture a stereotypical scientist as someone wearing a white laboratory coat, perhaps with a multitude of coloured pens in their top pocket, conducting experiments in a neutral manner in a quest to discover 'the truth'. This is the archetypal view of the *objective* scientist. Objectivity has often been seen as a basis of the hard sciences: typified as a neutral observer, free from political or

Galileo Galilei and Isaac Newton until it became broadly accepted. The book argued for a radical shift by presenting a heliocentric view of the universe, or, more plainly, one where all the planets moved around the sun, which appeared to answer the observed anomalies in a more effective manner.

It can be tempting to view this development as a straightforward transfer of centrality from one celestial body to another, yet this belies the impact that such a shift brings. As Kuhn (1957: 94) put it:

> To describe the innovation initiated by Copernicus as the simple interchange of the position of the earth and sun is to make a molehill out of a promontory in the development of human thought. If Copernicus' proposal had had no consequences outside astronomy, it would have been neither so long delayed nor so strenuously resisted.

For example, it challenged powerful worldviews of the time from the influential role of astrology, which was a tool of decision-making for kings, to the view that the Earth, and by extension humanity, holds a special position as the pivot around which everything revolves. More broadly, the intellectual advances and changes in thought also helped to support the burgeoning Scientific Revolution.

social sensibilities. This contrasts with *subjective* approaches, which are more commonly seen to be rooted in appeals to emotion or bias, or governed by self-interested concerns. However, the philosopher Michael Polanyi (1958: 18) asserts that 'complete objectivity as usually attributed to the exact sciences is a delusion and is in fact a false ideal'. He holds that everyone – be they scientist, architect or builder – is inherently limited and influenced by their way of life. While the scientific method and other accepted processes for conducting scientific research mean that the results can be deemed rigorous and sound, they may not be as detached or unbiased as one might initially imagine. This is because science not only operates within society, but is also inextricably intertwined with it. What we know to be scientific 'fact' is itself a social construct: the language that scientists use aims to be technical.

Let us begin our discussion by considering how and why environmental problems receive attention. While there is always a role for independent researchers, it is typically governments or similar agencies that play a key role in funding scientific endeavour, directly by grants or by a more general influence over the directions that academia or research institutions take. The media also play a role in highlighting particular issues and influencing popular opinion. Furthermore, scientists are encouraged to feed the results of their research back into society in order to engender a positive impact, perhaps by affecting policy or practice. Indeed, it is now a general requirement for scientists to consider public engagement and other 'impact' strategies to communicate their findings effectively to the wider stakeholders. This relationship ensures that science is not a passive, detached observer, but rather an active, and occasionally flawed, participant.

Research does not, and cannot, take place in a philosophical vacuum. Even if it is not stated explicitly, society influences everything, from the selection of the area on which to focus, the specific aims selected, the methodology employed and the chosen evaluation strategy. Therefore science is not an objective absolute, as it is connected to the researchers themselves and the society, culture and values within which the research takes place. As Kitchen and Tate (2000: 1) explain: 'Research is rarely just a process of generating data, analyzing and interpreting the results. By putting forward answers to questions you are engaging in the debate about what can be known and how things are known. As such, you are engaging with philosophy.' So fundamental questions of what to research and how to do it are not objective, and can frequently be shaped by short-term political priorities or individual values and interests. Even an individual's choice of degree subject to pursue, or thesis topic to select, is taken within the maelstrom of ideas, values and interests whirling round society at large – all of which influence choices, and therefore also objectivity.

Seemingly objective research projects may also use subjective information while pursuing their aims. Not all data is neutral and may be open to competing interpretations depending on individual worldviews. This approach helps to answer what we might call the 'why' questions, which are at their heart subjective themselves. In fact, a large part of the social sciences are focused in this specific area. It is of immense value to society to investigate why particular phenomena may occur, why people may behave in various ways, and how this could be changed. As this may differ depending on whom you ask, where you do it, or even how you phrase it, it is a subjective science and 'facts' are not truth as they rely on context and can be relative. Therefore the links between science and society are more than just individual choices; they are also embedded in the culture within which the research is conducted more generally. For example, aspects such as the openness of science to challenge and debate, or its transparent reasoning and argumentation, are reflected in the wider democratic accountability within societies. As Jasanoff (2009: 1) explains: 'the sound conduct of science and the sound conduct of democracy both depend on the same shared values'.

Given this gradual undermining of the objectivity of science, you may rightly begin to raise questions as to its value and position within environmental planning. There are, however, valuable mechanisms by which the scientific community itself helps to address some of these issues, such as the peer review process and the potential for challenge within academic debate. Polanyi (1962) argued that the community operated akin to a 'Republic of Science', an ideal 'state' where people are free to voice their opinions with impunity, and in doing so help to elevate the contribution and veracity of science as a whole. For example, scientific results are usually published, and during this process they may go through peer review checks by anonymous experts who assess and critique the findings before any publication. If the research reaches the public domain it could be further verified, commented on or challenged by others. As any scientist or academic will recall from personal experience this is frequently a bruising encounter. But it is also a valuable one, with the continual process of debate and analysis, testing and validating providing a seal of quality assurance that helps to mitigate many subjective concerns.

The question of whether science *should* be objective, as perhaps envisaged at the start of this chapter, is also a moot one. Being dispassionate and seemingly value-free led to an accusation of scientists occupying 'ivory towers', a conservative and superior position that resists challenge and erects barriers between the activity and the society within which it is conducted. More significantly from the perspective of this book, a society where the only science that was carried out was as detached or empirical as possible may not be effective at solving many critical environmental planning issues or influencing wider society. Moreover, the environment does not have a voice itself; it relies on people to be concerned enough to mobilize opinion or to pressure governments into action. Therefore, science may not even *address* these issues without subjective advocates, much less being able to resolve them.

Box 6.2 Facts and values

It is worthwhile to pause for a moment to think about what we mean when we use phrases such as 'normative' and 'empirical'. Normative theories are a feature of much contemporary science and generally contain some moral or political prescription; that is, it tells us *how* we should act or what a desired outcome *should* look like. This means that normative statements are: 'suffused with values and embedded within a social and historical context' (Allmendinger, 2002: 89). As described previously, science is believed by some to have little room for normative judgements: it should provide factual descriptions with the aim of uncovering general laws or explanations about the world we live in. This is made possible because the researcher is separate from the object of study: his or her personal values must not affect the research. This is what is inferred by phrases such as 'positivism' or 'empiricism'. However, in reality, differentiating between these two positions is easy to identify but can be difficult to achieve (Gordon, 1991).

The German sociologist, Max Weber (1864–1920), widely regarded as one of the founding fathers of sociology, holds that while the social sciences are infused with values, they can aim at value-freedom. According to Weber, values enter from the very start through topic selection but this does not deem the resulting research to be value-laden. This is done by carefully separating out statements of value (normative) from statements of fact (empirical). The former cannot influence the latter. That is, how the world *ought* to be or how people *ought* to act are normative judgements that cannot influence our consideration of what is happening. Simply put, a fact cannot be derived from value. This means that Weber permits social scientists only to give conditional policy advice. While a social scientist can tell policy-makers how to achieve a desired end state based on their observations, they cannot prescribe what those desired ends should be, as that is a personal judgement.

In a similar vein to Bacon's scientific method, Weber's scheme is an 'ideal type' of achieving a value-free social science to which all research should strive. However, even those theorists who maintain

→

Questions over what governments should do, or how the policy process could be changed to be more effective are important facets of contemporary science. Indeed, if societies denied science the remit to operate subjectively it might spell the demise of the Humanities, and most probably the faculty in which readers are

→

that facts and values cannot be separated think that scientists should aim to make their assumptions and values explicit. As the political theorist, Charles Taylor, observes: 'there is nothing to stop us making the greatest attempts to avoid bias and achieve objectivity. Of course, it is hard, almost impossible, and precisely because our values are also at stake. But it helps, rather than hinders, the cause to be aware of this' (Taylor, 1994: 569).

More recently, planning theorists outline post-positivist approaches. This draws on the work of critical theorists, such as Jürgen Habermas, who argue that the continued maintenance of value-free inquiry and knowledge is mistaken. For Habermas, interests pervade every aspect of the social sciences; the claim to value-freedom is, in essence, delusional, and serves only to maintain potentially unjust and ideologically dominant positions. Indeed, a social scientist's role should recognize this context and be partly emancipatory. These issues are explored in more depth in Chapters 9 and 10.

With regard to environmental planning, the normative/empirical distinction is a useful one to make. Here, the distinction can be regarded less as two polar opposites, but rather as a relationship where we move from factual observations that can be used to help develop theories that are, in turn, used normatively to discuss intervention. How we understand the environment (empirical) is very different from designing interventions into it (normative) – but it is important to engage with both. As the urban designer, Anne Vernez Moudon, explains: '*understanding* a city or part of a city and *designing* it are two different things' (Moudon, 1992: 332; emphasis in original). Formulations of social policy need both to draw on substantive facts about a situation and be ethically informed to mitigate concerns about subjectivity (Howe, 1990). In this view, a planner's role may be to evaluate both the outcomes of a policy as well as the means by which that outcome is reached, which inevitably includes considering empirical and normative approaches. Examples of normative environmental planning are commonplace, and Patsy Healey's (2006) *Collaborative Planning* and Susan Fainstein's (2010) concept of the 'Just City' expand this debate in Chapters 9 and 10, respectively.

studying. Subjective science that engages with values brings additional benefits to society that a focus on science as a purely objective fact-driven pursuit cannot, influencing important aspects such as culture, human experience and philosophy. A critic of this approach may argue that it is not the remit of science to stray from a value-free, neutral position, as by doing so it essentially occupies the realm of politics. However, a narrow focus on objective 'facts' may actually restrain the intellectual power of humanity in a regressive fashion and affect a whole host of areas detrimentally, not least environmental planning. Box 6.2 discusses facts and values in more detail.

In summary, scientific training promotes an *ideal* of how research should be conducted, whereby results can still be deemed objective even if the choice of experiments may be subjective. It essentially acknowledges areas of subjectivity and gives due recognition to the inevitable value judgements or biases that are inherent within scientifically rigorous approaches. Indeed, a strong case can be made that value-free planning is simply unattainable because the subject: 'is itself *essentially* political' (Klosterman, 1978: 39, emphasis in original). It should be noted, therefore, that value oriented research is a feature of environmental planning, where, for example, facts and values questions commonly operate in tandem. Here, the onus is on highlighting areas of subjectivity and perhaps limiting its influence, rather than completely dispelling it. More detail on this issue is provided in the final section of this chapter, which covers the science–policy interface.

Certainty and doubt

In addition to seeing science as a less stable, linear and objective process, there is also a perception, particularly among policy-makers, that science should be about providing certainty: more data equals more evidence, which equals more confidence. This surety is a prerequisite to identifying and justifying intervention strategies, and may be how one envisages the scientific community contributing to effective environmental planning, and society more generally. However, this perception of science as the search for 'truth' or 'proof' may place unreasonable demands on research and researchers, and become a communication barrier inhibiting action. Perhaps more significantly, the political demand for certainty raises fundamental tensions with the foundation of scientific inquiry, which is essentially about doubt.

As the sociologist, Robert K. Merton (1979: 265), underscores, scepticism is key to science in a way that political and social institutions can find hard to grasp: 'most institutions demand unqualified faith; but the institution of science makes skepticism a virtue'.

It can even be accurate to view science as a form of 'organized scepticism', since it is explicitly designed to question anything in the absence of clear evidence. This attitude makes reason and rationality an asset and can be seen to provide an opposition to blind faith or irrationality. As such, it is vital for civic society and democracy more generally. As introduced in Chapter 2, the scientific method is commonly viewed as the best approach for empirical investigation, the starting point of which is observation leading to the formulation of a hypothesis – an assumption to be explored. Within this framework the theory must be testable; that is, it needs to be able to be supported or refuted. However, the philosopher Karl Popper (1968) argued against the classic interpretation of the scientific method in favour of what he called empirical falsification. From this 'Popperian' perspective, science must be falsifiable; that is, there must be an opportunity to test and potentially nullify (rather than prove) the statement, otherwise the argument is unscientific.

For example, while atheists such as Richard Dawkins may argue against the existence of God, it cannot be absolutely proved that this is the case, and in practice the discussion encompasses aspects such as the 'weight of evidence', leading to a probabilistic opinion. As evidence is gathered during research, scientists may gradually develop more confidence in a hypothesis, but critically, there may always be a degree of doubt, however small. Perhaps surprisingly, many theories will never be proved true; instead, they may advance through not being refuted. So while a researcher does not actually prove something, he or she becomes more certain that a theory is unable to be *disproved*; an easy point to misunderstand, and confusing when certainty is seen to be king by decision-makers.

This argument is easily illustrated by examining the theory of gravity. We know a dropped object will fall to the floor because we have observed it happening countless times. But this is not absolute proof; it is a theory supported by a huge weight of evidence of similar occurrences. It is impossible to 'see' gravity, but as the theory has not yet been refuted there comes a point when opposing views lack credibility. The example of climate change also provides insight into the issue of proof, or certainty, in science, and how it can be distorted within politics. Some opponents of measures to address climate change, most notably a number of US politicians, situate their counter-argument around comments such as 'the theory of man-made climate change' – a phrase laden with an inherent scepticism. As it is only a theory we should not necessarily alter economic practices, particularly as scientists cannot predict for certain what the future holds, ergo it is not *proven*. If scientists had to prove beyond any possible doubt, by testing and experimentation, that humans had a clearly understood cause–effect relationship on climatic change, the time spent observing and recording evidence would necessitate a serious gamble with both life support systems and human lives. Or, perhaps more powerfully, from Lunney (2012: 29) 'if the first demonstration is affirmative, there will be no world left'.

Related to certainty, the history of science is replete with examples when the overwhelming weight of evidence in favour of a new theory eventually brings about scientific consensus, which is different from proof. For example, the idea that the continental plates were drifting horizontally over a layer of molten magma, known as plate tectonics, was not accepted by geologists until the 1960s. However, new techniques of mapping the oceans began to provide evidence that existing theories could not explain. Such overwhelming evidence can bring agreement among the scientific community, and unless significant anomalies occur that are inconsistent with the consensus, logic dictates that the emerging theory should be accepted. Therefore, use of the word 'theory' does not indicate automatically that a hypothesis is undecided; it could mean that scientists are actually as certain as they can possibly be, but in practice the phenomenon is as yet impossible to 'prove'.

As environmental planning inevitably navigates the political sphere, questions of certainty or doubt resonate strongly. There are tools to cope with uncertainty, from commissioning research to collating evidence to engaging with specialist stakeholders, but there is a parallel need to adopt a critical edge to this rationality concerning aspects such as how the science was conducted as well as what the data suggests. As Popper (2002: 34) explains: 'The proper answer to my question "How can we hope to detect and eliminate error?" is, I believe, "By criticizing the theories or guesses of others and – if we can train ourselves to do so – by criticizing our own theories or guesses.".' This reflective approach also extends logically to another important environmental planning issue: who should provide the evidence? In practice, there are competing authorities as well as knowledge, all trying to influence decision-making, an issue introduced in Chapters 3 and 4 that will also be picked up in Chapter 9.

The high degree of uncertainty characterizing many environmental planning issues was highlighted by Funtowicz and Ravetz (1991), who advocated that we should move towards 'post-normal' science, as traditional techno-scientific managerial approaches may not be sufficient to address all environmental problems. Post-normal is described as a situation where: 'facts are uncertain, values in dispute, stakes high and decisions urgent' (Ravetz, 2004: 249). This contrasts with the concept of normal science described previously. Simply put, the concept of post-normal science is reflective of a situation where data may be limited or contested, and environmental planning approaches may not be equipped to provide timely interventions. In conventional decision-making there is a need for evidence to justify and determine intervention, but in some cases this may be difficult to achieve. Critically, however, even though we do not yet possess strong data, the potentially high risks in some areas mean that societies should act.

Figure 6.1 describes the relationship between system uncertainty and decision stakes in more detail. Here we see that applied science works well when both aspects are low, but as uncertainty and decision stakes rise this may require more skill, expertise and subjective

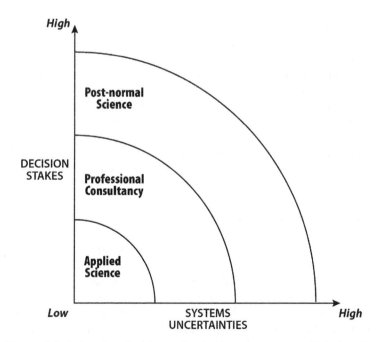

Figure 6.1 *Increasing decision stakes and systems uncertainties require new intervention strategies*
Source: Funtowicz and Ravetz (1993).

judgement, and aspects such as professional consultancy start to come to the fore. Finally, we see post-normal science operating beyond these boundaries, a thorny problem where the significant uncertainty prevents action, but the high stakes demand it. Here politicians may have to accept that science will be more subjective and uncertain within decision-making.

The uncertainties and challenging scale evident in many contemporary environmental problems suggest that the subject is linked closely to post-normal science (Funtowicz and Ravetz, 1985), both having potentially severe consequences and a degree of uncertainty. However, this model conflicts with the conventional science policy paradigm, whereby science would initially quantify problems accurately, thereby providing an evidence base to influence politicians and policy-makers to act. In practice, though, certainty may not be attainable, the facts required to act will not be forthcoming, and in consequence detriment may be perpetuated. The need for informed environmental planning presents a real challenge to achieving a high level of certainty, as in practice not only do we lack the required data, or potentially the time to obtain it, but the sheer complexity of societies ensures that a convenient simplification of causal links is hard to find. The failure to reach a consensus over international approaches to climate change provides perhaps the best example of high system uncertainties conflicting with long-established policy-making processes. Here, it is clear that many are not used to acting in the absence of clear 'proof', are unable to incorporate multiple frames and institutions, or experience resistance from other stakeholders, such as those who rely on fossil fuels to achieve their aims. This brings us to consider the role of experts and expert knowledge, which forms the basis of our next section.

Experts and knowledge

Science and experts play a key role in environmental planning. However, as the previous sections have highlighted, the subjective processes that go on behind the practice of creating this knowledge ensure that science cannot assert privilege over objectivity or truth. In their classic ethnographical analysis of laboratory life at the Salk Institute, Bruno Latour and Steve Woolgar (1986: 31) demonstrated that scientific knowledge is just another: 'social arena in which knowledge is constructed'. They explain the practices of science-related mobilization; how both actors and their opponents create, consolidate and extend their claims by enrolling other actors and institutions into their expert networks before deploying them to assert power. Ultimately, they show that scientific and political positions are co-produced. In demystifying expert knowledge in this manner, the artificiality of divides between the objective world of scientific fact and the subjective world of human experience are highlighted.

The connection between the apparently objective world of science and the normative world of policy-making raises a number of issues with regard to environmental planning. First, scientific claims are inherently contestable, which raises the possibility of questioning expert knowledge, or even of experts arguing with each other. The debate over the science of climate change clearly reflects this. Second, science tends to operate on different timescales from the development of policy. Doubt over scientific evidence may lead to rigorous and lengthy tests. Yet policy-makers routinely demand timeliness and certainty in outcomes. This tension detracts from the space required to account for risk and uncertainty and can serve to promote a degree of judgement that might not be translated adequately beyond the scientific arena.

In addition, scholars working in the developing world question the very foundations of scientific practice and its inherent reliance on expert, privileged knowledge. Specifically, as a product of Western culture it leaves little room for forms of local and indigenous understanding. Work in West Africa has explored conflicts in the perceptions of ecological environments between policy-makers and inhabitants. By ignoring these variable cultural dynamics, policy interventions often fail to produce the desired outcomes (Leach and Fairhead, 2002). A related issue concerns intervention into the environment based on scientific evidence that may not fully engage with public moral concerns. For example, geoengineering is frequently proposed as a solution to artificially managing the Earth's climate, despite the fact that the technology: 'may yet turn out to be imaginative science-fiction' (Corner and Pidgeon, 2010: 26). This case highlights important questions regarding science, the expert, and the potential for 'moral hazard', a process by which people feel insured against threats and so continue risky behaviour. To take a banal example, this equates to a smoker deciding not to quit because he or she reasons that science will develop a cure for lung cancer in the next 30 years. While there is an element of scientific rationality in geoengineering, intentional manipulation of the global climate may be morally unacceptable and ignores historical lessons, where a lack of knowledge about complex interactions may lead to more problems in the future. Changes on this scale mooted by experts may need global assent, not just from politicians, elites or rich countries, but also from the public around the world. Beck (1992: 59) developed this argument further, asserting that:

> the sciences are entirely incapable of reacting adequately to civilization risks, since they are prominently involved in the origin and growth of those very risks ... the sciences have become the legitimating patrons of a global industrial pollution and contamination of air, water, foodstuffs ... as well as the related generalized sickness of plants, animals and people.

At the heart of this critique is a rejection of the notion that experts, modernization, and in particular technology, are inherently good. The conventional view that scientists are objective experts to which politicians or the public then respond does have the appearance of neutrality, but power relations within the science–policy interface are frequently masked. This chapter demonstrates that expert knowledge can be influenced, biased or favour particular intervention strategies. The lionizing of the expert can also create a distance from moral or cultural issues and facilitate arguments that are difficult to translate for the general public. As a consequence, those affected may not be given an opportunity to influence the expert construction of knowledge or subsequent political decisions. These aspects are discussed further in Chapter 9 on engagement, and Chapter 10 on justice.

The science–policy interface

Ascertaining the exact role of science in shaping environmental planning and policy can pose problems. As readers have no doubt begun to notice, this information, along with its uncertainties and caveats, is not always transferred harmoniously to the policy sphere. Data also has to be interpreted and there are visible tensions with the political role of actors and agencies. This point was recognized by Weber (1949: 56; emphasis in original), who drew attention to the inevitability of subjective judgements by emphasizing the cultural divide between the social and natural sciences on the one hand, and social policy on the other, stating:

The distinctive characteristic of a problem of social *policy* is indeed the fact that it cannot be resolved merely on the basis of purely technical considerations which assume already settled ends. Normative standards of value can and must be the objects of *dispute* in a discussion of a problem of social policy because the problem lies in the domain of general *cultural* values.

As explained in Box 6.2, Weber proposed that the sciences could be more objective by strictly separating statements of fact (what is) and statements of value (how things should be).

Since Weber wrote these words, social scientists have devised methodologies that are transparent, robust and can be understood by policy-makers. All of which can pave the way for a closer association between science and policy. Despite these advances, the interface between the two remains beset with complications. Figure 6.2 outlines two images, typically seen in environmental planning and policy literature, or on government websites, which illustrate the perceived relationship between science and policy.

The one on the left is a linear and simplistic process delineating problem-solving over time. Following the identification of a problem, relevant data is gathered and analysed, after which solutions are formulated and implemented. The second is a cyclical series of actions. While this may initially appear to be more sophisticated, it remains equally deterministic. The only difference is that the impact of any implemented measures is monitored and fed back into the process. However, there are implementation gaps that are not considered by these rational, logical models that can inhibit

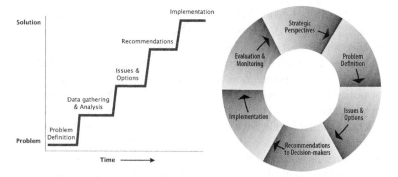

Figure 6.2 *Two examples of how policy-makers may perceive science to contribute to environmental planning*

action, such as hard-to-quantify information, complex problems or the variable distribution of costs and benefits across space and time.

Clearly, neither problems nor science fit seamlessly into any of these neat schematics: what if the problem is difficult to define, or proposed alternatives hard to assess? In these cases the process may not start or could flounder part-way through. Moreover, policy-makers often assume that science is about outputs, but much scientific inquiry is not driven by practical policy problems and is instead related to curiosity or theoretical aspects. Or, as Popper (1972: 191) puts it: 'whatever strikes us as being in need of explanation'. Equally, the problems and solutions may fall into the remit of multiple agencies, an issue discussed in Chapter 3, and may not be able to be addressed within discrete institutions, governments or, as can be seen with many environmental issues, even countries. Models such as these do not necessarily recognize that the science–policy interface is a messy network involving many wider stakeholders who may wish to have a strong say in the matter, whether these are institutions, the private sector or community organizations. Importantly, this is a communicative process rather than a relationship where knowledge produced by science is applied paternalistically down a chain to the next step.

The influential political theorist, Jürgen Habermas (1971), identified three models of transferring scientific expertise to policy. The first is the *decisionist* model. This recognizes that policy choices rely on subjective value judgements. Here, science's role is reduced to being merely an objective knowledge provider that enables decision-making to proceed in the heady political atmosphere of power struggles and debate. While science can appear benign in this model, Habermas draws on the work of Weber (1949) to show that science and experts can wield undue influence and limit the potential scope for policy decisions. The second model is *technocratic* and takes the opposite view. It considers that the very complexity of policy problems means that their solutions lie beyond the ability of politicians. Therefore, the correct role of politicians in the technocratic model is relegated to implementing the optimal choices of scientists. For example, if it were left solely to scientists, fluoride might well be added to the water supply because of its proven ability to reduce tooth decay, yet there is significant public opposition and vibrant ethical debates, such as the balance between a 'common good' and an individual's rights.

Readers might already have detected that both of these interpretations assume science to be value-free, and that there is internal consensus across the scientific community. Yet we know that science can be at odds and socially constructed. Therefore, the final model is *pragmatic*, rejecting both of these standpoints as they bestow too much power on either scientists or policy-makers. Instead, Habermas suggests that knowledge should be produced via a rational discourse among all stakeholders, including the public, to better navigate the juncture between values and facts. In doing so, an interface between science and society is created. It is this final example that most reflects contemporary practice in environmental planning, where collaborative science and co-productive practices are thought to both heighten the possibility of outputs that are likely to be implemented, as well as providing a ready means for knowledge transfer between scientific experts and the wider community (Fischer, 2000). Table 6.1 provides a brief overview of the key points of each of these three models.

In practice, the two communities – science and policy – are working more closely together than ever before, and integrating practices and processes. Yet, with this interface tensions will remain. There are two concerns. The first regards the communication of certainty, where policy-makers tend to talk in a positive, rhetorical manner about solutions and their advantages without

Table 6.1 *Habermas's decisionist, technocratic and pragmatic models*

Model of expertise	View of science	Role of scientific knowledge	Role of policy-makers
Decisionist	Value-free	Provider of objective knowledge	Policy-makers use select scientific results dependent on their own value judgements
Technocratic	Value-free	Governance by scientific experts	Minimal role as a bureaucrat who implements scientific and technical finding
Pragmatic	Value-laden	Scientific knowledge should be collaborative enterprise with policy	Policy-makers work with scientists to find solutions problems in a discursive manner

necessarily reflecting scientific uncertainty because of its ability to undermine political solutions or erode trust and confidence. Second, scientists are more comfortable with carefully caveated observations that may not have strong synergies with the policy requirement for firmly formulated and conclusive solutions. While scientifically accurate, this tentative position can frustrate policy-makers and affect the ability to address environmental problems effectively.

Conclusion

'To my mind the essential thing is that one should base one's arguments upon the kind of grounds that are accepted in science, and one should not regard anything that one accepts as quite certain, but only as probable in a greater or a less degree. Not to be absolutely certain is, I think, one of the essential things in rationality.'

(Russell, 1962: 83)

This chapter has provided insights into the way that science can frame intervention through environmental planning. In doing so, it has shed light on science's strengths and limitations in contributing to effective environmental planning. The discussions clearly outline that there may be tensions between the way that science works and what policy-makers might expect. The demand for certainty, clear evidence and objectivity may place unreasonable expectations on what science can feasibly deliver, and, as the philosopher Bertrand Russell clarified in the quote above, the central rationality of science always leaves the door open to doubt, no matter how small. This does, however, contrast with the similar but competing rationality of decision-making – of which robust evidence and sound science is just a part of the wider political considerations.

Chapter 5 revealed that just as there are nuances regarding how concepts are employed, so science also has its own constraints and idiosyncrasies. But despite these flaws, it remains the most rigorous way to gather evidence of environmental harm and to scope out alternative strategies. Certainty is a human desire that brings comfort and a feeling of control, and is crucial in the world of politics. However, the phrase 'scientifically proven', routinely bandied about in society, may be considered more accurately to be an oxymoron; instead, we should speak in a language that draws on degrees of confidence ranging from infinitesimally low to absurdly high. Consequently, the ability of scientists to be able to quantify and communicate the level of certainty, or perhaps doubt, and the areas of subjectivity, is critical for decision-making and allows science to contribute more fully towards the making of policy. These informed approaches are reflective, involve value judgements and actively engage with the complexities of the human sphere, from politics to ideologies.

Equally, there is a responsibility on those concerned with environment planning policy and practice to understand how science operates, and from there how this might affect their own ability to use science effectively to help manage the environment. As scientific methods need to address the subjective conditions within which they were conducted, and to communicate this to decision-makers, they do not merely provide knowledge, but also meta-knowledge; or, put more simply, knowledge about knowledge (Grunwald, 2007). For example, how is the data collected; which areas fall outside of the scope of the research; and how certain are the findings? The situation of a remote scientist observing society, the policy-maker receiving information and the public accepting decisions is becoming ever rarer: the problem-oriented view of many environmental concerns demands a partnership approach, where scientists, decision-makers and wider stakeholders work together and policy-makers are engaged with questions as to how the data is collected and how robust it may be. As Popper (1972) argued, the objectivity of science rests heavily on the criticizability of its arguments, parts of which are connected to the search for a common language. Therefore, not only do decision-makers require a degree of scientific literacy, as introduced at the start of the chapter, but scientists also need to learn the language of public policy and the nuances of politics to enact change. It is to this we now turn our attention.

Chapter 7

Policy and Regulation

'[T]he very term "planning" implies that society should find a means of handling the uncertainties facing us.'

(Rydin, 2004: 8)

Building on the discussion of concepts and science, we now turn our attention to the way in which science is used in policy, and specifically in environmental planning. In contrast to the discussion in the previous chapter, planning is less constrained by questions of subjectivity or doubt. It is designed explicitly to operate within the political, moral and ethical spheres, and is inherently ridden with competing priorities and contested interpretations. It is also an area that is strategic, future-oriented, and makes plans and policies that have some degree of foresight, whether that is 5, 20 or 50 years in the future. As Rydin states in the opening quotation above, this should serve as a reminder that designing planning policies allow us act despite any uncertainties: there is both a mandate and a requirement to intervene.

The remit of planning to consider multiple policy objectives, such as stimulating economic growth and protecting the environment creates a competition for resources and land use that extends to how evidence is used in decision-making. It also considers the expectation of certainty in the policy sphere, both in terms of informing the design of an appropriate strategy and then in communicating this political decision confidently and unwaveringly to the public. Yet causal links and easy solutions may be rare, particularly concerning the types of issues common to contemporary environmental problems, and there will rarely be agreement on environmental issues, especially where they may challenge economic aims or powerful interest groups. In reality, environmental planning and policy contrasts with the positivism, rationality and objectivism of much scientific endeavour, as it is unavoidably normative and prescriptive in that it often concerns what we *ought* to do, as much as it is about what *is*. To some degree, this is because of the kinds of issues with which environmental planners grapple: to what extent are certain phenomena to be considered as problems; how do we value the environment and how should policies be designed?

Though policy-making strongly connects with science from a complementary perspective to help benefit societies, in modern democracies where people and groups have differing views, it can suffer from a degree of political relativism that presents difficulties. As with planning more generally, it is not only a matter of 'science' or 'policy' because fundamentally it involves people. When we begin to consider this human dimension, we encounter questions such as how importance is determined, or what are people's politics, ethics or values? This places environmental planning at odds with the classic empirical view of science as there may be no single right answer or strategy that is acceptable or appropriate at all times and in all places. Moreover, regardless of the best available evidence, the future is unknowable and may not easily be predicted. Not only is navigating this byzantine intersection of science and politics the *raison d'être* of environmental planning, it is also where the skill and expertise of the discipline offers real value to society.

The previous chapter revealed how science operates and how it influences the framework that permits environmental planners to make interventions. This chapter is a logical extension of those discussions and aims to track how scientific data and evidence is imported into the policy sphere. It first examines the main ways in which environmental planning exerts power through three typical policy instruments: designation, protection and control. We next explore the related debates concerning regulation in more depth before investigating the historical use of evidence in planning to show why it is now considered so indispensable, providing an overview of the issues connected with the underpinning and justification of decisions by recourse to quantitative data. The debate then turns to more qualitative forms of evidence used in policy, in particular, the precautionary principle, before ending with a discussion of the nuances of policy 'transfer' between cities and countries. The main thread running through this chapter is that just as conceptual understanding and scientific endeavours can frame intervention, so too can discussions regarding regulation and the nature of policy development.

Designation, protection and control

While Chapter 2 argued that there has always been some form of 'planning' particularly with regard to land use, resources and the control of polluting activities, the origins of what we now recognize as environmental planning on a larger scale emerged in the late nineteenth century to address public health issues (Wood, 1999). The enormous urban growth during the Industrial Revolution highlighted problems within cities. To some extent, this focused on moral problems, but it began to take an explicitly environmental formulation (Platt, 2005). Aspects such as cholera epidemics, overcrowding and poor sanitation all provided a governance challenge to the unbridled laissez-faire of the Victorian era, particularly as it became increasingly apparent how many problems could be better controlled with some degree of urban planning.

Given the disparities within individual countries, it is difficult to provide a detailed introduction to the nuances of environmental planning everywhere. Yet there are similarities and consistencies regarding the control of land, the treatment of conflict and the regulation of environmental impacts, and so the purpose of this section is to provide a general overview of the field. The UK planning system provides many of the examples, partly because of its longevity: it was one of the first to be institutionalized in professional training and through laws (Cherry, 1996). In addition, because it was an imperial power, for good or for ill it exerted a huge influence on other planning systems (Home, 1997).

During the late nineteenth and early twentieth centuries, there were incremental changes to alleviate overcrowding, poor housing conditions and the management of health in cities. This resulted in new legislation and institutions and, as the urban population expanded, new thinking concerning the requirement to control land use in a more coherent manner. For example, in the USA, the Department of Commerce issued a Standard City Planning Enabling Act in 1928, and in the UK there was a spate of Town Planning Acts in 1909, 1925 and 1932. The origins of town planning are a 'logical extension' of improvements that were happening with regard to housing, public health and environmental conditions (Ashworth, 1954: 181). As a backdrop to this burgeoning legislative and regulatory framework, towns and cities were beginning to be managed on a grander scale. This was also the age of master planning to predefined blueprints, typified by notables such as Patrick Geddes, Raymond Unwin and Patrick Abercrombie in the UK. Similar themes can be found in other cities: Le Corbusier in Paris, Daniel Burnham and Edward Bennett in Chicago, and Henry Vaughan Lanchester in Madras, who also produced ambitious large-scale plans that proposed a desirable future state to transition towards.

Ebenezer Howard is one of the most celebrated forefathers of planning and provides a good example of the strategic, innovative thinking that was apparent at this time. He identified that town and country had their respective pros and cons. Through an analysis of these, he proposed a hybrid of the two, where the high employment and accessibility of towns could be combined with access to nature and a lack of pollution. His seminal book *Garden Cities of To-Morrow* (1902) sets out this argument and is best illustrated by the famed 'three magnets' (see Figure 7.1). The upper two magnets depict the advantages and disadvantages of town or country living, respectively, while the third magnet 'Town–Country' attempts to capture the positives and dispense with the negatives. On close inspection, many of the observations relate to the use and

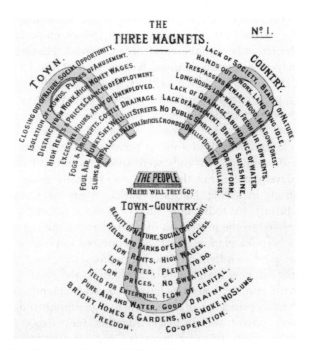

Figure 7.1 *Ebenezer Howard's Three Magnets*
Source: Howard (1902).

control of land: pure air and water, bright homes and gardens, easy access, and no slums.

Legislation was gradually becoming more widely accepted and established as the twentieth century progressed, and a new professional class was emerging. The legacy of the initial social and environmental pioneers was still very much in evidence, however. Using the UK's 1947 Town and Country Planning Act as an example, the more formal development went beyond a desire to control land use and, more broadly, represented: 'a fervent desire to make a better society, one which was fairer, more compassionate and more equal' (Robson, 1999: 168). Acts such as these created new planning authorities, who were given the remit of designating land use strategically through developing comprehensive development plans for their areas. Any private developments would require planning permission for changes to land use, effectively bringing a means of reactive control and enforcement of regulation to the local level.

When the 1947 Act is considered together with the establishment of other developments of the time, such as New Towns designed on Garden City principles, it typifies a shift from managing urban problems at the micro-level of public health and housing to a larger spatial scale, broader in remit, which could capture a city, its hinterlands and the rural areas beyond. Planners began increasingly to influence strategic factors such as the location of industry, the supply of skilled workers, and the economic structure of regions as a means of promoting growth and avoiding some of the disadvantages of development. Regulatory-based environmental planning also exerted a degree of control over air, water and noise pollution. Allied to this, a policy of urban containment gained wide support. Not only were specific areas of land identified for development, but they were also formally designated for conservation, including National Parks, Areas of Outstanding Natural Beauty (AONB), and Sites of Special Scientific Interest (SSSI). Related to the protection of natural areas, the use of 'green belts' as a bespoke planning tool was pioneered in London in 1935 before going on to influence planning regimes across the globe.

Even though new environmental legislation and tweaks to planning systems in many countries have occurred frequently since this time, the main principles of environmental planning to designate, protect and control were in place. Together, these aspects offered planners the ability to exert proactive and reactive influence on differing scales, from the site to the region, and within multiple topics, from controlling pollution to stopping development completely. Other positive changes could take place indirectly, through the relocation of people to areas that could offer a better quality of life and by influencing where industrial activities could be undertaken. Consequently, planners can determine a host of wider environmental factors, from the origin of waste to the location of infrastructure, to the need to travel.

This broader perspective was further advanced by the move from land use planning to spatial planning that occurred in Europe and elsewhere around the start of the twenty-first century (Haughton *et al.*, 2010). Whereas the former had a narrow view of issues relating to land development only, the latter is a more integrative process that links land use with wider policies and programmes affecting the nature of places and their wider social, economic and environmental functions. From this perspective, environmental planning is well placed to engage with the sustainable development movement as well as linking with a variety of environmental concerns, from energy use to climate change to green space provision. Consequently, the contemporary planner has to contend with a wide range of policy remits, some of which are competing with each other, and be able to manage conflict with stakeholders. The transition from a technical and procedural emphasis to a more pluralistic and collaborative model (Healey, 2006) provides both demands and opportunities for environmental planning, not least decisions on to the extent to which activities should be controlled, and the way by which people could influence this. It is to the related issue of regulation that we turn to next.

Regulation

As every developed nation exerts control over the use of land, resources and how people and industries may interact with the environment, the real debate centres on the scope, scale and content of regulation. What is permitted, what needs consent, where are the lines drawn? Where individuals, companies and nations stand on this issue links to the aspects discussed in Chapters 3 and 4 on government and politics, most notably the perception of the desired nature of society as a whole and the role of government within that. Regulation is essentially an attempt by the state to produce outcomes that might not otherwise occur, and is therefore a core rationale for planning as a whole. However, while one may be correct in coming round to the view that planning can be considered to be connected to practically any aspect of the built and natural environment, this is far from true when the extent of regulation is considered, which is often only implemented when there is overwhelming evidence, and is subjected to frequent periodic review. While readers may be familiar with arguments that posit regulation as a constraint on the economy or business, the debates stretch far beyond this simplistic binary and are essentially rooted in political ideologies.

Consideration of the positions of two key thinkers in this area offers us a way to explore more deeply the discourses concerning regulation. The first is the American economist Milton Friedman, and in particular his prominent text, *Capitalism and Freedom* (Friedman, 1962). In a hybrid of economic and political philosophy, he argues that government involvement in society should be kept to an absolute minimum, like a referee who merely enforces law and order or protects property rights, with corporate misconduct deterred via the legal system, as individuals can sue for damages if a detrimental event occurs. From this perspective, not only may government involvement prove to be an unacceptable infringement to individual freedom and liberty, but it can also bring negative unintended consequences and operate in a much less efficient manner than the free market could on its own. For example, Friedman cites the case of the introduction of a minimum wage designed to alleviate poverty among the poorest in society, but as a result of the policy, the unemployment rate in this group actually increased.

The Austrian-born economist and philosopher, Friedrich Hayek (1899–1992) adopted similar political ground in his influential books *The Road to Serfdom* (1944) and *The Constitution of Liberty* (1960), reputed to have influenced a number of world leaders including Margaret Thatcher, Ronald Reagan and a number of modern US Republicans. Hayek also argued against central planning from a core libertarian perspective. He suggested that not only do big governments stifle creativity and entrepreneurship, and create unnecessary taxation through bureaucracy, but they are hallmarks of oppressive societies and therefore to be avoided as a point of principle. From these standpoints, regulation is perceived as being very inflexible compared to market-based mechanisms, such as emissions trading, and in any case it is a feature of competition within capitalist societies that businesses would respond and be 'greener' if consumers demanded that change. In short, in most areas, the market can exert its influence much more effectively and without any loss of freedom.

Occupying right-wing political ground prepared by the pioneering economist Adam Smith, these two authors still have a profound influence on modern discussions connected to government regulation. In this respect, the whole debate may be distilled down to a fundamental tension, but not the familiar one between economic growth and environmental protection as is commonly discussed, rather that between individual freedom and state control. A powerful ideological strand of this position is that economic freedom is a prerequisite of political freedom, therefore if one values the latter so – and people innately do – then one must also have the former.

A connected argument to that of the free market is that, if regulation is simply a means of producing alternative outcomes, could self-regulation operate in the same way? This is an attractive proposition for governments and is related to the issue of governmentality covered in Chapter 3. Regulation brings costs, both economic and political, and the popularity of voluntary approaches has soared in recent decades alongside measures aimed at influencing behaviour more subtly, such as nudge theory (Thaler and Sunstein, 2008). Here, it is argued that decisions can be affected by 'choice architecture', or in simpler terms, the way that options are presented. For example, if a city is easy to walk around, then people may drive less, or if energy bills also compare your use to your neighbours' you may be encouraged to be more energy efficient. Yet, while it may be an effective approach in some regards, it is not able to replace regulation altogether and should instead be considered as part of the wider policy mix.

Thinking back to the discussion on governance, we can see there has been a tendency for smaller, more enabling government over previous decades, with a cutting through of 'red tape' now being a staple feature of elections in many countries. It is exceedingly uncommon, if not impossible, to become elected on a mandate of more 'red tape' or bureaucracy, particularly given the influence of the business sector and lobbying on modern politics. From this perspective, deregulation has become a naturalized process in mainstream politics. Taking a step back and considering the milieu of political debate in many countries, it is clear that regulation is accepted routinely and uncritically as being bad for the economy, bad for jobs, bad for GDP, bad for competitiveness – indeed, bad for everyone. Yet regulation should not be seen so unfairly as a homogenous mass or equated negatively with bureaucracy. There are costs associated with inadequate regulation and it is often borne by those who do not share the benefits. Moreover, many environmental issues fall through the gaps of limited government and may either not be addressed, or only examined after the damage has been done. From this perspective, not only is regulation always playing 'catch up', but its absence can cause major problems, not least demonstrated by the global credit crunch or climate change in recent times. These two high-profile examples emphasize that, in addition to the frequently mentioned costs, regulation can also bring significant economic benefits, from protecting jobs to providing certainty for markets, to providing a more level playing field, and to shielding many against market failure and the inequalities of capitalism.

Now that we understand the broad debates a little better, let us examine some specific examples. One of the core remits of planning is to regulate the use of land, typically by designating or zoning it as having particular uses within a plan. In doing so it can allocate permitted rights (such as the right to develop in a certain way) or responsibilities (for example, the need to protect vulnerable species in valuable natural landscapes). As such, the control of land has huge economic, social and environmental implications and is subject to much lobbying within consultation processes. Rezoning low-grade agricultural land for housing on the periphery of a built-up area can turn landowners into instant millionaires; equally, designating 'countryside' areas, such as new National Parks or Special Areas of Conservation, can greatly limit economic opportunities. The potential value of land and resources also changes in scale and over time, and regulation that is beneficial at one scale may be undesirable at another. For example, fracking is an emerging technique used to extract fossil fuel reserves, but in the UK the land where these reserves are located tends to have been zoned as residential for a long time. Having a new industrial use on the doorstep of residents would undoubtedly have a negative impact, so it is expected that sites would face strong opposition. However, exploiting the resources has been highlighted as a key objective of the government to the extent that it is proposing an Infrastructure Bill to be developed that will give controversial new rights for oil and gas companies to access land (Cabinet Office, 2014).

In addition to having an influence over the decision to make land productive or extract resources, planning also exerts a degree of control over the way that this is conducted. Regardless of whether the discussion is of pollution, waste or any other aspect of environmental planning, a reduction in any side-effects of production can bring costs to the producer, and this can be considered a means of forcing the internalization of external costs, or to use a lay term, used when managing noise: 'quiet costs money'. The issue of water pollution discussed in Box 7.1 provides a good illustration.

The approach of the Water Framework Directive also emphasizes that the effects of pollution may challenge traditional administrative boundaries and demand attention on a larger scale. A further notable example in this areas is the EU Integrated Pollution Prevention and Control Directive, which requires industrial and agricultural activities that have a high pollution potential for air, water or land to apply for a permit. This is only issued if certain environmental conditions are met, such as using the best available techniques for pollution prevention, standards of energy efficiency, and returning the site to its original state when the activity is finished (European Commission, 2008).

When the effects of regulation are considered, one can see how it may be subject to contestation. Regulation allocates responsibilities, creates limits, has compliance costs and can reduce the short-term profits of industries. Yet it does confirm to some of the principles of having a state in the first place, such as acting in the common good and considering longer-term perspectives. Further, air, water and climate do not respect administrative boundaries, challenging traditional ways of governing and, as we shall see in the next chapter, they may be hard to quantify within conventional cost–benefit analyses. Moreover, the sporting analogy of the state limited to the role of a referee as extolled by free market advocates such as Friedman, does not necessarily acknowledge that there are now entire industries set up to lobby for particular players, and, as we shall explore further in Chapter 10 on justice, the notion of a level playing field is far from the truth. Finally, as is apparent with regard to the UK government's push for fracking, it is clear that in some areas the role of the state may appear to be more of a cheer-leader than a neutral arbiter, and new trends in public–private partnerships with the state acting as a developer may blur boundaries even further. Regulation is not only playing catch-up to the sources of pollution, but also to the means by which this may be enacted, placing real demands on the ability to be able to consider a wide variety of information and evidence. It is to this issue that we turn next.

Box 7.1 Water pollution

Poor water quality can bring costs to a host of areas, from tourism to fishing to the expense of providing clean drinking water. Its management has also gained in sophistication as science and policy have developed, and now industries that discharge into watercourses routinely have to adhere to strict levels, with monitoring taking place and fines issued if breaches occur. The effective control of point source pollution in this manner is one of the real success stories of environmental planning, yet watercourses in many areas do not seem 'clean'; why is that? One key downward driver on water quality that is usually entirely unaddressed in regulations is diffuse pollution. The effect occurs in a cumulative manner across an entire catchment as a result of runoff, washing off and carrying contamination from the urban or rural landscape, such as oil from roads or nitrate from fields, and transporting it untreated straight into a watercourse. This source of pollution is rising alongside trends in population, urbanization and agricultural intensification, but it does not mesh well with the typical regulatory measures, as not only is it hard to link to a specific pipe or user, but even if each individual source could be reached it might not be significant enough to trigger pollution control measures.

One attempt to tackle this tricky issue is provided by possibly the most ambitious piece of environmental regulation of recent years: the EU Water Framework Directive (European Commission, 2000). This legislation commits Member States to achieve a 'good' water status in all their water bodies by 2015, and establishes River Basin Districts to manage these on a catchment scale, sometimes across national boundaries. This integrative approach commits all those having an impact on water quality to work together, from planners to industry to farmers. This example is also notable as it has set a target of what good water quality should be, and put the onus on the management of activities in each area to achieve this. While this may seem a reasonable objective, it is rare on an international scale as the emphasis is usually on establishing limits regarding how much a watercourse may be degraded as a whole, or to how much pollution industries may be limited. Or, in simple terms, the Directive aims progressively for the quality that would be desirable, rather than the level we could tolerate.

Evidence-based planning

'So very narrowly, indeed, did he commission them to trace it out, that there was not one single hide, nor a yard of land, nay, moreover (it is shameful to tell, though he thought it no shame to do it), not even an ox, nor a cow, nor a swine was there left, that was not set down in his writ. And all the recorded particulars were afterwards brought to him.'
(*Anglo-Saxon Chronicle*: Ingram, 2009 [1085: 108–9]: 140)

Evidence takes a number of forms, from research, surveys or modelling, to monitoring and expert opinion. Such data can be used to better inform the development of policy, or influence decision-making, and, as demonstrated in the opening quote discussing the *Domesday Book* commissioned by William the Conqueror in 1085, it has a long history. The rise of evidence in decisions is allied to the ascendancy of positivism, which, as we discussed in Chapters 2 and 6, believes firmly in technical and scientific progress and the primacy of the expert (Faludi and Waterhout, 2006). From an environmental planning perspective it is also linked to the instrumental and rational view of land use planning that emerged in the 1960s. Among other factors at that time, innovations in computer technology power led to advances in statistics and mapping that helped to create new ways of envisioning areas and social needs, with the result of fostering a view of the planner as a detached expert, objectively and paternalistically determining the appropriate future of places. Indeed, planning failures from before this time were traced to poor forecasting and evaluation, which gave further support to these methods (Hall, 1980). Since this initial rise to prominence, evidence-based planning has waxed and waned in its policy popularity, but generally speaking, since the mid-1990s it has become a core requirement for decision-making across governments, supranational agencies and the private sector (Wong, 2006).

Because of aspects such as the requirement to identify threats and to justify explicitly any intervention that might inhibit the market, to be effective environmental planning needs to navigate the world of evidence-based planning, which is neither straightforward nor neutral. First, there are issues connected with the robust collection of data and its reasonable interpretation. Those concerned with environmental planning need to have some degree of scientific literacy to understand the evidence, including its methodology, assumptions and caveats and so on. This may be

---

Box 7.2 Wicked problems

The view that some issues are just too complex to be resolved by standard policy approaches is not a new one, and develops previous discussions regarding the boundaries of 'normal' science. Rittel and Webber (1973: 155) compartmentalized problems into two types: *tame* problems and *wicked* problems, where the latter may be multi-causal, dynamic and subject to ambiguity, stating that: 'The search for scientific bases for confronting problems of social policy is bound to fail, because of the nature of these problems. They are "wicked" problems, whereas science has developed to deal with "tame" problems.' Wicked in this sense is not related to notions of evil, rather the ability of certain issues to resist easy resolution, such as terrorism or health care.

Typical policy-making approaches need clear evidence, a responsible agency and an implementable solution that can pass cost–benefit tests and justify action within individual institutions. However, many contemporary environmental planning issues may be subject to uncertain knowledge as well as spanning multiple sectors and scales. In practice, tame problems may be addressed, such as a straightforward cost–benefit decision on building a new road, but wicked ones may not. This is an issue that does not necessarily relate to their urgency, rather to their ungainly fit with existing governance frameworks and decision-making norms. Climate change may be

➔

---

hard to translate or be contested at times, however. For example, John Maynard Keynes famously objected to the use of statistics to analyse the credit cycle, arguing that there was a need to demonstrate that the method was applicable, rather than merely applying it, otherwise it could result in a 'false precision' that neither the method nor the statistics could support (Keynes, 1973: 289).

The view of science and evidence as being objective can also lead a strong and uncritical reliance on it. This may be rooted in both the rational and procedural elements of environmental planning combined with the sometimes rather linear and utilitarian view of policy-oriented research. The information demands on environmental planners are further challenged by the dynamism of evidence, which changes over time as new technologies, governance procedures or legislation all add to the smorgasbord of techniques and information. Just as the rise of technology helped to drive rational planning in the 1960s, so the move towards environmental assessment from

→

described as the archetypal wicked problem: its causes are not identifiable to any one process, there are hard to determine feedback
loops, and dealing with climate change at one level or scale may
only exacerbate its effects elsewhere (Head, 2008). Therefore, it
displays the confusing characteristics of wicked problems, which
can partially explain why it has been so difficult to tackle. For example, it is proving impossible to assign responsibility for climate
change to any single body, to map out all the options for responding to the threat, or even quantifying how much any remedial measures will cost.

The concept of wicked problems was designed to be considered
in the context of a social policy arena within which normal,
evidence-based approaches may not function effectively for decision-makers. For example, there may be an array of areas that challenge the ability to design solutions, from how the problem is
defined to how much it may cost to address. The nature of providing evidence on some issues also challenges the ability to provide
easy answers. For example, what exactly is the social good, or how
may any decision impact on equity? Wicked problems may have no
single correct resolution and be subject to multiple frames.
Therefore they run counter to the typical view of evidence as providing a firm basis for managing environmental concerns – some topics
may confound scientists just as much as they do policy-makers.

the 1970s and collaborative planning moves from the 1990s
onwards similarly changed the nature, volume and composition of
evidence. No longer just statistical balance sheets or lines on a map,
evidence now consists of new methodologies such as scenarios,
stakeholder participation exercises and strategic environmental
assessments, placing new requirements on decision-makers.
Equally, it is clear that evidence-gathering is a continuous process,
with data potentially becoming quickly out of date, therefore
necessitating an ongoing resource commitment (see also Box 7.2).

There are continuing tensions over the relationship between
science and policy. To put the most common debate in a simple
fashion: is it evidence-based policy-making or policy-based
evidence-making? The discussion centres on whether the relationship is a neutral search for problems requiring appropriate policy
solutions, or whether evidence is used retrospectively to justify
politically motivated decisions. For example, tailored calls for

research and tightly constrained data gathering exercises can be used to underpin rather than to shape selected policy agendas. Inevitably the construction and use of knowledge is rooted in social and political processes and is therefore related to power, a point made by Flyvbjerg (1998: 226) who stated that: 'power determines what counts as knowledge, what kind of interpretation attains authority as the dominant interpretation. Power procures the knowledge which supports its purposes, while it ignores or suppresses that knowledge which does not serve it.' This point highlights questions over the impact of engagement exercises, and even the effectiveness of the collaborative or communicative turn more generally (Davoudi, 2006), issues that are discussed in more depth in Chapter 9.

The conundrum regarding evidence-based policy is that the expectation and demand for precision in decision-making may conflict with the variable robustness and mercurial nature of information. Evidence is not neutral, can be selectively commissioned and used, and the nuances poorly communicated to practice. While modellers, statisticians and other researchers may write carefully worded caveats concerning the accuracy of their projections, when this is communicated to environmental planners it may become repackaged as medium or high risk, or a percentage figure in a very short briefing document. Once uncertain data is encoded, translated and interpreted it can appear guileless and effortlessly convincing, and the 'false precision' of which Keynes accused his economic critics is an equal concern for those concerned with the environment. Yet, there is no doubt that a broad variety of evidence can be used effectively for a whole host of environmental planning tasks, from using data to articulate a coherent narrative for place-making, to identifying current threats and future needs, to managing environmental change. The key message is that those concerned with environmental planning need to be critical of data and evidence, which is no easy task, given the prevalence of competing knowledge and agendas, and Box 7.2 explores these issues further.

The precautionary principle

We have already discussed how the world is full of risks, whether small, large, obvious or uncertain. Yet, despite the fears that they might engender, we still need to function as a society. Current ways of dealing with these risks from a policy perspective rely essentially on the ability to produce evidence to justify intervention. However, this approach may not address adequately either future aspects or those where it may be difficult to gather quantifiable data. Once we know that X is a threat, we can act, but what if societies either do not know or do not have the time or ability to discover this before harm is realized?

The complexity of human life combined with its dynamism and rate of change means that new threats will emerge despite the best efforts to prevent them. For example, industrialized societies frequently allow risks to be taken, of which many are unaware, from the degradation of the ozone layer caused by using chlorofluorocarbons (CFCs), to the use of cutting-edge technologies with unrealized side-effects, to the design of the risky short-term financial policies that helped to create the recent global banking crisis. As may easily be observed in many environmental policy debates, from those on climate change to genetically modified crops to geoengineered technologies, that there is also disagreement as to where the burden of proof should lie. Should companies such as Monsanto have to prove that genetically modified crops are safe, or should opponents have to prove that they are unsafe? Where the burden of proof rests with those seeking to establish detriment, the managerial approach may be understood as focusing more on post-damage control, rather than on a strong anticipatory strategy. Consequently, there has been an argument, emerging particularly powerfully from within the environmental sector, that society should take a more cautious view to cope with areas of high uncertainty, a policy stance known as the 'precautionary principle'.

There are a number of definitions of the precautionary principle. One of the earliest derived from the United Nations Conference on Environment and Development in Rio in 1992, which stated: 'Where there are threats of serious or irreversible damage, lack of full scientific certainty shall not be used as a reason for postponing cost-effective measures to prevent environmental degradation' (United Nations, 1992). A higher-profile example was subsequently provided when a group of academics, lawyers, scientists, environmentalists and policy-makers came together in 1998 to try to delineate the principle in more depth. This became known as the Wingspread Conference on the Precautionary Principle, which defined it as: 'When an activity raises threats of harm to the environment or human health, precautionary measures should be taken even if some cause and effect relationships are not fully established scientifically. In this context the proponent of an activity, rather than the public bears the burden of proof.' Together, these statements provide a good overview of both what the precautionary principle stands for and perhaps also an emergent insight into how it may lead to conflict.

Now used in a host of environmental policy areas, from climate change to biodiversity to managing asbestos, and permeating national and international policies across the globe, the principle has become a powerful force to prevent *possible* harm. On one level it can be characterized as a simple common-sense approach along the lines of universal adages such as 'Better safe than sorry'. However, this simplicity belies the significant implications that its implementation has for environmental planning. The first notable change is with regard to the burden of proof, which essentially shifts from the need to collect compelling evidence of detriment to a focus on the potential extent of *harm* and the nature of the *threat*: is it very risky, and could the damage be serious? The issue of scientific certainty and evidence is connected to this. The level of confidence does not have to be clear and incontrovertible, but this does not mean that in the absence of absolute certainty we should maintain the status quo and 'do nothing' as might occur if there was no adherence to the principle. Equally important is the converse of this; that is, a business would not necessarily have to provide absolute proof of safety before beginning any activity – rather that, if there are reasonable grounds for concern then the principle could be deemed relevant.

While it may appear to be a rational logic, the precautionary principle is not immune to criticism. In practice, both of the definitions cited above are intended to be all-encompassing, yet they are also vague. The principle may not provide a clear enough guide to decision-makers and can lead to the creation of a series of legal loopholes over the severity of the threat, who is responsible, or how cost-effective any remedial measures need to be, to take just three examples. The principle can also be used by stakeholders in a relatively arbitrary fashion as a means of justifying any number of contentious views. One way of considering this aspect in more depth is to reflect on which people or institutions might evoke the principle, and for what purposes. It is clear that the change in emphasis would not necessarily be attractive to those concerned with promoting unfettered growth or new technological breakthroughs, indeed opponents would argue that it is mainly attractive to very particular groups or people with certain worldviews. In short, critics argue that it is a tool of those who may consider themselves to be environmentalists, or those who may be against certain scientific advances or business practices.

For example, the principle can be evoked as an argument against a wide range of issues, from the siting of mobile phone masts to the need for new regulations on business – even when the evidence of tangible harm may be lacking. It may even be cited as a rationale for the protection of people, but also have the added benefit of protecting economic interests. In 1999, the French government used the precautionary principle as a justification for maintaining a national ban on British beef imports (put in place in 1996 during the bovine spongiform encephalopathy (BSE) crisis), even after the EU-wide ban had been lifted. The EU declared the beef safe, but the French government defied the ruling because their experts held a different view. This stand-off led to a suspicion in the UK media that the principle was being used as an economic tool to support the French domestic beef industry, and resulted in calls in the UK Parliament to respond, with a spokesman for the prime minister stating: 'We have science and the law on our side and it is regrettable that the French had ignored the science and defied the law' (BBC 1999).

Similarly, the principle may be employed by people who are unduly risk averse; there will always be a level of uncertainty associated with science, technology or new uses of space, but opinion may differ widely as to when risks become unacceptably high. Furthermore, the change of emphasis that the precautionary principle brings means that it may be considered a *moral* doctrine, but whose morals are they? What is the cultural attitude to risk? And how may this posit a challenge to the long-standing, and largely accepted, reliance on evidence-based policy or technological breakthroughs to drive progress? As with many of the concepts discussed so far, it is more controversial and contested than readers might have expected initially. The principle consequently navigates choppy political and social waters, and even this 'common-sense' approach can experience critique and misapplication. Moreover, there is still a requirement for evidence, even though the onus is shifted to the risk rather than the activity itself.

Policy 'transfer'

The encompassing and dynamic nature of environmental policy can be daunting. A host of initiatives, such as sustainability strategies, green infrastructure policies, water efficiency targets and habitat requirements, may all be in force and subject to changes in political emphasis, or wholesale replacement as new trends and ideas emerge. The ongoing demands to design, monitor, integrate and adapt policies, combined with restrictions on staff resources and time, means that the world of policy frequently takes ideas and proposals from elsewhere and seeks to convert these into local solutions. Best practice, exemplar projects and agenda-setting initiatives can provide enormous assistance, but policies that are successful in one place may not be effective in a different social, cultural or political context. The opening of the Guggenheim Museum in Bilbao in northern Spain as a means of driving urban renewal is a case in point. While it is commonly seen internationally as providing the catalyst for significant inward investment and the striking rebranding of the city as a cultural destination, it is a story that is not easy to replicate elsewhere, being a product of a particular place, time and context rather than an off-the-shelf policy product.

Peck (2003) highlights factors such as the internationalization of conferences and consultancy firms, and the formation of new transnational institutions and professional networks as enabling and globalizing the policy transfer process. But the effective proliferation of policy between places is much more complex than a simple focus on appropriation and translation. Policy is territorial and relational; being the product of locally dependent interests, actors and agencies, and its mobility can be dependent on as wide a range of issues as the flow of global capital to the local practice of power (McCann and Ward, 2011). This situation is made even more complex by considering how global capitalism demands competition; cities and nations vie for investment and attention, creating an ever-capricious policy vogue. In addition to the risk of adopting a 'ready made' policy that might not be effective in a new locality, the political emphasis on quick results may also lead to a rapid incorporation that can undermine local democratic processes. Perhaps more fundamentally, it can serve to marginalize planning, and its ability to shape local space and place, in favour of a role centred on enticing flagship projects, enacting international policy ideas or bending to the whims of the global marketplace.

A similar point can be made regarding the ability to implement technological innovations that are frequently mooted as an environmental solution. One of the problems is that experts and policy-makers often assume that their interventions are aimed at calculating, rational individuals where the only imperative is to convince people to use them. Following this assumption, consumers will make the 'correct' choices, and technology will transfer to practice. In reality, this is far from true. Guy and Shove (2000: 10) instead argue that: 'similar technical strategies do and do not make sense for different reasons and at different moments in time, and that their adoption depends on the sometimes competing perspectives and priorities of a whole network of organizational actors. Whatever else, the picture is certainly not one in which proven knowledge is seamlessly transferred from research to practice'.

In a similar vein to policy, the social context of technology is vital to any uptake. Innovation can frequently be resisted by both people and policy-makers, whether because of an uncertainty over costs and performance, a lack of cultural legitimacy, ill-suited legislation, or institutional inertia – all of which can cast doubt on the potential of future technological solutions to solve emerging environmental problems. David (1985) uses the example of the QWERTY keyboard layout to illustrate this argument. This design was originally implemented to slow down manual typewriters, the keys of which had a tendency to stick with high-speed use, but it has continued through to the digital era despite other models being more efficient and easier to master. This societal complexity also provides a challenge to the remorseless rationality of neoclassical economics, where people are frequently assumed to act logically in response to market forces, and where more effective solutions will inevitably prevail.

Even after the process of design and implementation, new policies can be subject to resistance. Actors including policy-makers, the business sector and communities may have long-standing frames, routines and practices through which a prevailing system is reproduced and current trajectories resist change – past decisions, therefore, can lock actors into particular pathways. New practices can also initially be resisted at the level of institutions, technical systems, culture and legislation, which are path-dependent and require reinforcement in social, cultural, economic and technical domains (Geels and Verhees, 2011; Simmie, 2012). Appreciating the issue of resistance to change and territorial inertia can also be used in a positive manner, however, by highlighting the possibility of creating new and more beneficial pathways, and shedding light on the steps needed to secure their eventual 'lock-in'. This is a significant issue for environmental planning, as much of the onus is on engendering changes to the norm.

In sum, policy and technology transfer can play a vital role in effective environmental planning, but both fields need to recognize that the way we know and represent the world is inseparable from the ways in which we choose to live in it (Jasanoff, 2004); knowledge and solutions are embedded in societal contexts, not separate artefacts to be generated and applied. Therefore, aspects such as social learning and effective engagement may need to be considered as part of the strategy of policy or technology innovation.

Conclusion

> 'He did not foresee that within two decades the cow country would become tourist country, and as such have greater need of bears than beefsteaks.'
>
> (Leopold, 1949: 216)

Aldo Leopold used these words to describe what he perceived to be the danger in using economic evidence as the main basis for decision-making, and to highlight how evidence may be ingrained in a time and place and have questionable longevity. In this example, a government trapper had killed the last grizzly bear in eastern Arizona's Blue Mountains, as there was a policy in place to protect the profits of farmers. However, the following decades had witnessed a change in the economic focus of the area, from agriculture to tourism, and so the bear would have eventually become more a resource than a threat; demands for short-term policy or regulatory fixes can therefore have long-term impacts.

The mechanisms selected to obtain data and the way that evidence is weighted means that while there may be a faith in neutral and transparent policy procedures that allow for the consideration of multiple points of view, environmental policy considerations are essentially competing in the rough and tumble of politics and the economically driven market-exchange model. This form of decision-making holds true from the arts to health to the environment, but a narrow focus on profitability or growth can lead to environmental impacts or a degraded global commons. The power of the market to commandeer the use and function of space is such that land designations, regulations and the control of development have been enshrined in policy to facilitate and mitigate these short-term economic priorities for the long-term benefit of societies as a whole. In an era where policy is becoming ever more synonymous with red tape, it is worth noting that, from its earliest incarnation to the present day, environmental planning policy has an element of public good attached to it; those aspects of our natural or built environments enjoyed today may have been fought over decades before we were born.

Though the miserable environmental conditions suffered by people as a byproduct of the Industrial Revolution were a key part of the establishment of environmental planning as a formal process, societies have now established practices and policies to mitigate potential environmental impacts. This may vary from a regulatory and land use perspective to a spatial planning focus that has the potential to engage in environmental issues in a more complex and integrative manner. Using planning and policy-making to control environmental impacts will inevitably involve a mixture of firm legislation and regulation, land designation and protection, and development control and expert negotiation, as well as an engagement with evidence and policy that may vary from the local to the global and incorporate multiple strands of data. Yet the mixture of quantitative and qualitative approaches may not just improve the evidence base and any policy outcomes, but as a corollary can also challenge its integration, weighting and dissemination. Moreover, in a globalized world, successful policies are subject to rapid appropriation but their particular territorial and relational characteristics should not be underestimated; effective policies require bespoke, local expertise.

This chapter has been designed to help readers gain a more sophisticated and nuanced knowledge of the complexities of environmental planning policy, including an overview of some of the more common approaches and the current hegemony of evidence-based planning. While there may be an understandable tendency to focus on practical aspects such as the implementation of policy A, or the monitoring of regulation B, the ways that issues connected with the environment are framed in the policy sphere hold immense power in determining policy design and eventual outcomes. And significantly, the underlying nature of how this influence is gained and exerted often resists attention when attention is drawn to the minutiae of specific policy wording.

Some of the issues raised here are discussed in more depth elsewhere, particularly those connected with politics, engagement and justice; indeed, a key message to be picked up later is that we should not ignore how the policy process needs to involve the views of wider stakeholders to be effective. We now complement the focus of this chapter by turning our attention to the variety of environmental planning 'tools' that routinely enable policy to be developed and support how final decisions are made.

Chapter 8

Decision Support Tools

'I found that nearly all the deaths had taken place within a short distance of the pump ... In five of these cases the families of the deceased persons informed me that they always sent to the pump in Broad-street, as they preferred the water to that of the pumps which were nearer. In three other cases the deceased were children who went to school near the pump in Broad-street. Two of them were known to drink the water, and the parents of the third think it probable that it did so.'

(John Snow, *The Cholera near Golden-square, and at Deptford*, 1854)

While concepts, science and policy all influence the sphere of environmental planning, we now turn our attention to the practical issues that emerge from these more fundamental aspects: the matter of making decisions. We know that there will always be economic pressure to develop land and use resources, and that environmental issues seem to be becoming ever more complex, uncertain and contested. We also know that impacts may be transboundary in nature and can affect people and groups in indirect ways. The challenge is to ensure that under these difficult conditions the decision-making process is as robust and informed as possible and can incorporate a wide range of concerns adequately. In response, a range of decision support tools (DSTs) have been developed that have the potential to provide clarity, integrate data and identify various managerial options.

DSTs refer to a broad array of mechanisms designed to assist the decision-making process. These range from the complicated, such as specialist software or mathematical formulae, to the more familiar written guidance or simple maps, as demonstrated in the words of the physician, John Snow, at the start of the chapter. In this case he mapped the outbreak of cholera cases in 1854 and in doing so provided strong evidence that the disease emerged from a specific water supply pump, and could therefore be managed, rather than

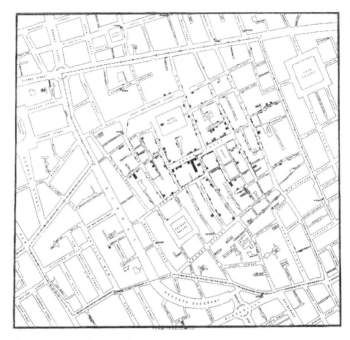

Figure 8.1 *John Snow's map of cholera deaths in London, 1854*
Source: Vinten-Johansen et al. (2003).

being caused by 'bad air'. Figure 8.1 displays the comprehensible map that illustrated this issue. Snow's data not only led directly to the decision to remove the water pump handle by parish leaders, but also helped to provide a breakthrough in epidemiology by linking public health facilities with disease.

Given the variety of DSTs and their varying focus, this chapter is designed both to help in understanding their taxonomy and to give the reader an insight into their use in practice. To provide a broad flavour of their potential they have been split into five different themes of key relevance to environmental planning: economics, measurement, time, space, and scale. First, we explore *economics*, which will include a discussion of cost–benefit analysis and the use of environmental economics in order to attach a price to nature. A separate discussion of the seminal paper 'The tragedy of the commons' in Box 8.1 illustrates the complexities of managing resources through an allegory that is applicable in many societies around the world. The next section emerges naturally from this discussion by unpacking the recent trend for the use of quantitative indicators to *measure*, inform and monitor environmental planning. The following discussion explores *time*, in particular how to consider the future within decision-making norms that are notoriously rooted in the short term. Box 8.2 uses the IPCC greenhouse gas emissions research as an example of how scenarios can be used to inform decisions over the longer term. We next look at *space* and the topic of geographical information systems (GIS), which can be used as a means of spatially representing and analysing data from a variety of sources. The discussion then examines methods to consider issues of *scale*, where impact assessment methods can be used to identify and consider a wide variety of effects of proposals and provide a much bigger picture than would otherwise be the case. Together, these five examples provide a good overview of the scope of DSTs relevant to environmental planning, and some insights into their application.

Cost–benefit analysis and environmental economics

'We destroy the beauty of the countryside because the unappropriated splendours of nature have no economic value. We are capable of shutting off the sun and the stars because they do not pay a dividend ... once we allow ourselves to be disobedient to the test of an accountant's profit, we have begun to change our civilization.'

(Keynes, 1933)

The introductory quote is worthy of a double take and a brief pause to reflect on who uttered these words. Reasonably, one might expect it to be attributed to a Greenpeace activist, or a member of a modern anti-capitalist organization. However, this passionate critic of economics was John Maynard Keynes (1933: 242), arguably the most famous and respected economist of all time. While his views on monetary policy still hold great sway with governments around the world, his opinions on what he called the: 'self-destructive financial calculation [that] governs every walk of life' (ibid.) have a much more muted influence. That said, Keynes was an unusual economist; one who thought that civilization needed to liberate itself from the 'tyranny of financial profitability' (Dostaler, 2007: 242). From this perspective, Keynes essentially drew attention to how the market-exchange model has extraordinary power, yet fails to take into account aspects that are hard to translate into a financial calculus, from the environment, to the arts, to the future; or, more simply, to consider the difference between price and value – a key issue for environmental planning.

People and agencies who commonly make decisions on land, resources or management frequently do so from a financial standpoint; asking questions such as how much will it cost, what advantages will it bring, or how does this compare to other options? This approach has been developed into cost–benefit analysis (CBA), a formal means of determining options that has a long history in decision support. Put simply, CBA involves ascertaining all the relevant benefits and costs of a proposal, assigning a monetary value to these and then analysing the results. This approach is useful as it can include social and environmental aspects and therefore address market failures, which are a key rationale for environmental planning. By distilling complexity down to a single figure or ratio, it also speaks in a language that both those in power and ordinary citizens understand easily and provides a method for justifying decisions, particularly in times when resources are tight and priorities competing with each other. While it does provide a way to analyse trade-offs, economic analyses of this nature can be expensive and time-consuming, and can be skewed by their selected methodology, such as the scope of their calculations or the means by which value is determined. More fundamentally, many environmental pressure groups actively reject the economic pricing of nature, but because many assets are connected to land or controlled within the public or private sectors, this can provide a pragmatic compromise, if unsatisfactory for some.

Before we investigate the ramifications of this approach for the environment, we should first acknowledge that the market-exchange model is firmly established in most societies. As discussed in Chapter 4, the trading of commodities to mutual advantage, usually involving money, has brought stability and enormous advances in standards of living even though these may not be distributed equally. Take a moment to consider the unpalatable alternatives to this bartering system, such as the use of coercion or enforced political ownership as can occur in a dictatorship. The realistic aim here is to find a way for those aspects that resist easy pricing to be included within conventional norms of decision-making; hence the rise of environmental economics.

Environmental economics is based on the view that natural capital can be substituted for human capital. It emerged in the 1960s as a way of incorporating the environment into traditional economic modes of decision-making. We know that economic activity can damage the environment, cause pollution or deplete resources, and create the possibility of present and future loss. Environmental economics is a mechanism to quantify this loss in monetary terms and, in doing so, integrate nature more fully with economic decisions and help to pave the way for new regulation, financial penalties or different land use decisions. The valuation method measures human preferences by assigning *use* and *non-use* values. The former concerns the direct use of a resource, such as fishing or walking in a park. The non-use value is indirect and is trickier to determine. For example, a citizen of the USA might never see a particular endangered species or an environmental resource such as a rain forest, but arguably the protection of these resources does benefit all through the delicate balancing of ecosystems, or just being there as an option to visit. In practice, working out a total valuation that incorporates use and non-use values can be difficult. Often, more causal aspects such as willingness to pay, or damage caused, are easier to agree on than measuring *possible* benefits, which are not normal market transactions.

Environmental economics also concerns the issue of externalities, a cost incurred by an activity, but one not borne by the producer. Again, this is difficult to incorporate within classical market models; for example, air pollution as a result of an industrial process affects many people beyond the source, but it is not necessarily priced within this practice. Externalities are an example of market failure and it is therefore the responsibility of governments to determine if, or how, this cost should be taken into account by an alternative mechanism such as environmental economics. Capitalism automatically pursues the lowest possible production costs and typically views the environment as a resource to be exploited for short-term profit. This factor impinges particularly on 'common' environmental goods: air, water and land. Perhaps the best example of externalities, and the ramifications of a failure to accord value to 'free' environmental goods, is provided by the famous paper 'The tragedy of the commons', discussed in Box 8.1.

While environmental economics does offer a way to consider the environment, offset market failure and help to shape what is 'affordable', this section helps us to appreciate how difficult it may be to achieve. For example, what is in the calculations, how does one attach a value to these, or determine future losses? While the

Box 8.1 The tragedy of the commons

'The Tragedy of the Commons' is the title of a paper by US biologist Garrett Hardin (1915–2003) that appeared in the journal *Science* in 1968. The article has come to represent how a shared resource can swiftly be depleted by individuals acting in their own rational interest. Since its publication it has proved a powerful metaphor for those concerned with protecting the environment. Hardin (1968: 1243) begins by using the future possibility of a nuclear war as an illustration. By observing that the nuclear arms race created the contradictory problem of simultaneously increasing military power and decreasing national security, Hardin writes that 'this dilemma has no technical solution. If the great powers continue to look for solutions in the area of science and technology only, the result will be to worsen the situation'. Drawing on the overriding propensity to consider technical solutions to problems, as opposed to human values or morals, Hardin then illustrates how this may impact on the environment by using the trope of an imaginary tract of common land and how it may be used by the nearby population.

In his example, a pasture is open to everyone and is used to provide grazing for cattle. While the numbers of people and animals are small, the arrangement works perfectly well, but as populations rise the 'commons' logic leads to tragedy. People are rational beings and will seek to maximize their gain. In pursuing their own self-interest they will try to increase their profit by having more cows, as the individual benefits outweigh the collective costs that overgrazing may bring. In economic terms, the profit will be internal and the costs external. This leads inexorably to a situation where the pastureland is used more intensively, becoming increasingly degraded until eventually it is of little use to anyone.

Hardin then drew parallels between this situation and the way that the environment and resources are treated more generally. The natural environment – air, water, land and other resources – is treated as a freely available global 'commons' but, as with the theoretical pasture, there are limits and finite resources that are placed under pressure as the world population grows. The parable could be applied equally to a diverse range of environmental issues, such as carbon emissions, water supply or overfishing, and wider societal issues, from traffic congestion to litter.

Equally, the principle, although in reverse, works with regard to pollution instead of resource use, where discharges rather than

→

→

consumption are subject to the same calculation with regard to individual profit and collective costs. Here, a pipe discharging chemicals into a watercourse creates costs for society rather than the business causing the pollution. The key here is rationality: everyone is behaving in a way that benefits them the most. From Hardin's perspective, a belief in the freedom of the commons therefore brings a remorselessly advancing tragedy and points towards a need for management, regulation and limits, or, as Hardin (1968: 1247) states, 'mutual coercion, mutually agreed upon'.

Despite being a valuable and long-standing illustration of environmental pressure and rational human behaviour, Hardin's article has been criticized. For example, it does not recognize that technology could extend capacity or modify practices, and the argument may amplify unduly the logic of individual freedom at the expense of the potentially significant roles of science, education and notions of community. Equally, Dietz *et al.* (2003) argue that some societies do manage to sustain resources over time, and draw attention to the existence of more than the two institutional arrangements of central government and private property alluded to by Hardin. As a consequence, social organizations and human ingenuity may be able to modify behaviour or design innovative solutions. To describe all people as being driven by self-interest may also be an over-simplification, yet it should be noted that corporations may not be subject to comparable moral codes.

A final interesting point to reflect on is how the article can be used as an argument *against* a freely available commons, rather than the need for better management or regulation. In this case, if unfettered collective access and shared ownership of resources leads to their eventual degradation, then perhaps these areas should be enclosed or privatized for their own protection. While the sale of public goods and an increase in private property is one possible interpretation, one can imagine how this solution of decreasing area of commons can easily lead to inequity or injustice for many, an issue discussed in more depth in Chapter 10. The 'tragedy of the commons' metaphor has become a high-profile framing device within environmental thought, and its principles of management for the collective good are used frequently within multiple debates from sustainability, to the polluter pays principle, to the desired level of government intervention.

worth of nature is determined by humanity – whether by its utility or its beauty – the notion is essentially a process that denaturalizes nature and can create both agreement and division between environmentalists and economists. It also means that those who are concerned with environmental planning need to be aware of how value is attached to nature, and to recognize when this is inadequate or absent. For example, ecosystems provide a service to society, such as providing green spaces that can help to manage water and prevent flooding, but unless their wider value is appreciated and included in decisions they may be treated in the development process simply as uneconomic land ripe for development, rather than part of a natural 'infrastructure' with significant non-monetized functions. Despite areas of potential, environmental economics offers a weak sustainability perspective that supports unashamedly the primacy of the economy: the perspective of the treasury has triumphed, albeit with the environment now entering the debate. We now turn to a related quantitative source of decision support by examining the key issue of indicators.

Indicators

We have already discussed how environmental planning practice and policy-making rely on the use of evidence to inform action. This is a norm of decision-making that commonly is reflected within the approaches and requirements of governments and agencies across the world. This information-centred methodology can take many forms, such as mapping or statistics, but, of these, the use of indicators has been a noticeable trend in environmental planning. Based in the field of statistics, indicators are regarded as a measurement tool to compare phenomena, prioritize decision-making, spend resources wisely and, importantly, to monitor progress. They can be related to numerous fields, from quality of life to sustainable development to biodiversity, and are collected by a large array of agencies, from domestic governments to the United Nations and the World Bank. Mainly quantitative data such as this can provide both huge benefits to guide policy-making and practice, and to track changes over time, but indicators should not be considered as neutral policy instruments. Despite their benign and objective character, the design and interpretation of indicators can greatly influence the distribution of power, and frame intervention (Astleithner *et al.*, 2004).

The use of indicators began in the USA in the 1940s with the release of monthly economic statistics designed to ascertain the health of the economy and spread to the social sphere in the 1960s as their value began to be appreciated more widely. Their first use in this area was a surprising one: a project sponsored by NASA in 1962 to determine how the space programme affected US society. At this time, social indicators were defined by the author of this pioneering research as: 'statistics, statistical series, and all other forms of evidence that enable us to assess where we stand and are going with respect to our values and goals' (Bauer, 1966: 1). After falling out of favour with policy-makers in the 1970s because of concerns regarding aspects such as quantification and value weighting (Carley, 1981), they returned to vogue in the 1990s and have largely retained their position of prominence ever since. In a similar fashion to the evidence-based turn mentioned in the previous section, they were also aided by broader societal aspects, such as the growth in computing power and wider data availability, which led to more bespoke synergies with the requirements of policy-makers.

From an environmental planning perspective, they have found a strong home in the sustainability agenda and with regard to ascertaining the state of the environment more generally. Their ability to monitor change in a wide range of factors, from water quality to ozone depletion to governance, means that they are effective at reviewing progress towards set goals – a key reason why they find favour with the policy-making community. The European Commission (2012) states that useful indicators have three main characteristics: they should be linked to a policy goal, they should be measured regularly and consistently, and they should be reliable and verifiable. At their most effective, indicators can grapple with challenging environmental planning complexities. These include spatial aspects, which can allow for comparison across and between administrative borders, or with regard to rates of environmental or social change over time.

That said, their effectiveness can be limited, particularly if they are not well selected or designed, or if the required data is unreliable, hard to obtain or difficult to interpret. Their complexity also may not translate easily into the policy environment and beyond. For example, in discussing child poverty, Frones (2007: 12) states that the 'mass media seldom informs the recipients that "poor" is a chosen statistical definition and that other indicators might produce different results'. Equally, indicators can suffer from assumptive causal jumps that lead to misleading conclusions. For example, in the aftermath of flood events, the press frequently cite to the number of houses built on floodplains as evidence of previous planning mistakes, commonly asking questions such as: 'If you allow the building of houses on the floodplain, what do you expect?' Yet this ignores a whole host of qualifications, from whether the floodplain is valuable development land that is well protected behind flood defences, whether the land is actually deemed to be at significant risk from flooding, or even whether the flood came from the river and not from another source, such as inadequate drainage.

Connected with this, indicators have also become emblematic of how information is employed to command attention in modern societies. A cursory glance at any newspaper or news website will usually reveal some kind of indicator connected with a story, from economic performance to educational standards, to the volume of CO_2 emissions. It is therefore important to note that indicators have significant power to set agendas and mobilize resources, and that their politically constructed nature may not permeate this narrative. Moreover, though indicators may be seen as a tool to address uncertain situations, quantification and measurement is likely to be at odds with complexity, so it may actually mean that highly uncertain situations do not fit well with this approach. Given this situation, policy-makers may not act if the 'evidence' is not there, but this is an issue more connected with deficiencies in the process rather than the impact of the problem. Also, more information does not necessarily reduce uncertainty; instead, it may simply increase our awareness of a daunting degree of complexity against which traditional disciplinary approaches and policies appear inadequate. Counter-intuitively, therefore, more information may actually mean more uncertainty.

Though indicators can be powerful signs they are also subjective, bounded in cultural contexts and can be variably designed and interpreted by political actors seeking to legitimize their own agendas. For example, the average house price is frequently mentioned in public policy debates, but this data can be used to argue for very different ends. If it is increasing it may be used as a sign of economic buoyancy by some, or an indicator of an overheating housing market by others. Equally, the same sign could be employed as part of the evidence arguing for the additional release of new development land, or even in constructing a case against the restrictive nature of planning laws.

A key issue highlighted here when considering DSTs and environmental planning is that of quantification; not of the 'environment' itself, but rather concerning the ability to balance current effects and possible future changes. Here, hard data, such as that collected by indicators or economics, may need to be considered alongside qualitative information to allow policy measures to be taken. This is particularly the case when considering how some problems are very uncertain or are emerging so rapidly that their impacts occur before societies can experience them, measure them and act. As a consequence, differing ways of gathering evidence and informing decisions may be needed to supplement those discussed so far; it is these precautionary and future-oriented approaches to which we turn next.

Futures and scenarios

In the 1970s, computers were huge mainframes owned by large companies and used to carry out complex tasks, and the extent of home computing – now a societal norm – was not anticipated as much as one might have expected. This was demonstrated by the often-repeated comment by Ken Olsen, Head of Digital Equipment Corp., who in a 1977 speech at a convention of the World Future Society predicted that 'There is no reason anyone would want a computer in their home.' Olsen later complained that his now famously incorrect forecast was referring to the possibility of powerful computers that control aspects in the home, such as regulating temperature and turning on and off lights, rather than those that perform more mundane tasks such as word processing. However, the quote delivered during a speech by the founder of one of the largest US technology companies of the time shows how the future is inherently uncertain and even experts can frequently make predictions that are subsequently proved to be not only just wrong, but appear utterly ridiculous.

Analysing recent trends, integrating varied potential drivers of change and subsequently intervening through policy to shape the future positively lies at the core of environmental planning. There is an implicit need to incorporate a 'futures perspective' in this field, and given this requirement, individuals and organizations should be skilled at responding to the uncertainty and complexity evident when developing long-term strategies and forward plans. However, methods and approaches to analyse and respond to future uncertainties are not, as yet, widely applied (Carter and White, 2012).

Over recent decades, an increased level of awareness of the sheer unpredictability of complex natural and constructed systems has begun to emerge as societies experience the impacts of synergistic crises and powerful individual events. Changing climates, global financial crises and natural disasters affect economies, nations and ecosystems across the globe, highlighting the presence of external forces that lie beyond the control of even the most seemingly sophisticated organizational structures. Anticipating and incorporating these complex future threats within environmental planning can bring significant benefits. However, the development of long-term perspectives is hampered by the often narrow remits, or the limited geographic or temporal foci of the organizations making the decisions.

As understanding of the interconnected and 'glocal' nature of modern society deepens, scientists and policy-makers have a responsibility to recognize and respond to evolving circumstances that influence societies, economies and natural environments. All too often, however, responses materialize after a serious event has been experienced, or a 'weak signal' becomes magnified. The increased risk of New Orleans to catastrophic flooding by a gradual erosion of natural defences and inappropriate development had been highlighted prior to Hurricane Katrina in 2005 (Wisner *et al.*, 2004), yet this insight did not influence policy or practice significantly. While it is reasonable to assume that not all risks can be anticipated, in the case of New Orleans the data was available and the future threat was discussed publicly; however, it was not prioritized or funded. It is clear that evidence of a future problem, even when accompanied by identification of tangible causal chains and the proposal of possible solutions, does not always provide a strong enough argument to motivate changes to policies or decisions until after a detrimental event, which inevitably serves to spur action, generate political will and mobilize capital.

One way to engage in more long-term thinking is via the use of scenarios. A scenario is an imagined sequence of future events. Scenarios are not predictions or forecasts, and levels of probability are not assigned. Instead, they can be viewed most effectively as vehicles through which different possible futures are explored. In some cases their implications are assessed through modelling. The aim of scenario exercises is not to paint an accurate picture of how the future will unfold, however, and so outcomes should be treated with caution to avoid misinterpretation by groups who may not fully understand the nature of the scenario process. Rather, scenarios can help individuals and organizations to develop a longer-term 'futures perspective' that engages with uncertainty and embraces this as a key feature of strategic planning exercises. Scenarios can enable the construction of future visions to be cultivated and in some cases avoided, and used in this way they can provide a powerful nexus for individuals and organizations to collaborate.

In a professional context, scenarios trace their origins back to military planning exercises undertaken around the start of the Cold War. When futures studies became more prevalent during the 1970s, people developing scenarios began to mesh narrative approaches with modelling techniques, often focusing on issues related to environmental sustainability. An early example of this approach can be found in *The Limits to Growth* report (Meadows *et al.*, 1972) that drew attention to the implications of unrestrained economic and population expansion for the Earth's systems. This study used computer simulation to model a dynamic system that could help to develop scenarios to consider the implications of global driving forces on prospects for human development. The research was met with criticism connected to the methodology and conclusions, particularly regarding the tenor of its catastrophic warnings, but it still holds value as a means of understanding how growth interacts with finite resources (Turner, 2008). Very influential current scenarios within environmental policy are the IPCC greenhouse gas emissions (GHG) scenarios (IPCC, 2000), which are discussed in Box 8.2.

The IPCC example demonstrates how the scenario method now finds itself at the heart of global environmental planning and policy, and is used across the public, private and voluntary sectors to push decision-making towards a longer time horizon. This is a valuable asset for policy-makers, since it helps to shift the argument away from short-term gains towards a balance between generations. Scenarios can thus better reflect some of the aims of environmental planning, notably those related to sustainability, climate or future risks. We have examined DSTs that connect to time, so now let us turn our attention to those concerned with space.

188

Box 8.2 The IPCC greenhouse gas emissions scenarios

Climate change is widely held to be one of the most pressing threats of the twenty-first century. Scientists can study tree rings or ice cores to help understand past climates, and may measure the atmosphere to gain an insight into the present situation, but the future is more difficult to predict, as it depends greatly on how societies respond. Will nations progressively cut GHG emissions, or will there be a growth along 'business-as-usual' projections? To what extent will emerging industrial powers such as Brazil, Russia, India and China – the so-called BRIC economies – adapt their energy use, behaviour or political stances? The truth is that no one knows for sure, and so it is difficult to predict the potential trajectory of impacts.

In response, the IPCC first released emission scenarios in 1992, which provided a scientific attempt to inform future global circulation models and help to evaluate the potential consequences of environmental change for policy-makers. This research was updated in 2000 with the release of the *Special Report on Emissions Scenarios* (IPCC, 2000), which was used by the IPCC assessment reports of 2001 and 2007. These scenarios identify the key demographic, technological, social and economic driving forces with the potential to influence levels of future GHG emissions. Even slight variations in the direction of these driving forces and the relationships between them may lead to significantly diverging atmospheric GHG levels over the twenty-first century. Consequently, projections display a wide range of possible outcomes depending on the chosen emissions scenario.

The scenarios show how surface temperature may change in the future depending on how societies respond. For example, the 'A1' storyline describes very rapid economic growth, a global population peaking in the mid-century and the rapid development of more efficient technologies that balances fossil energy resources with other sources. Conversely, the 'B2' scenario has population rising at a lower rate, slower economic development and an emphasis on local solutions. The surface temperature is projected to rise higher and faster in the former scenario than the latter.

A final interesting aspect of these scenarios is how they have designed a formula to translate qualitative and quantitative science into a scalar language that can be understood by decision-makers. For example, 'very high confidence' reflects expert qualitative judgement that predicts the outcome to be correct 9 out of 10 times, while 'low confidence' equates to 2 out of 10.

Geographical Information Systems (GIS)

Mapping has been a key element of planning since its emergence as a discipline. From Ebenezer Howard to the trend for blueprint planning in the 1950s, they have been a core DST. Beyond mere representations of space, mapping approaches can also inform decisions greatly by capturing and displaying data across a variety of fields. For example, the social researcher, Charles Booth, surveyed deprivation levels in late-nineteenth-century London, using colour coding to demonstrate the spatial distribution of economic classes. His approach was a forerunner of the spatial analysis common today and it concluded that around 31 per cent of the city was in extreme poverty, a figure that influenced both the burgeoning socialist movement at the time and government policy (Hall, 2002).

From around the 1990s, information and communication technologies (ICT) have played an ever more central role in informing environmental planning. Developments in computer technology, the emergence of the internet and the World Wide Web, and the spatialization of environmental data have transformed the extent to which we can visualize and analyse decisions over space and resources. The most notable DST in this area has been the widespread adoption of GIS. This approach uses specialist software to link a variety of data to a specific space, to enable its more sophisticated analysis. In environmental planning it is used most commonly with large quantitative datasets such as those connected with managing resources, natural hazards, ecosystems or climate change. A key feature is its spatial versatility and interactivity to aid decision-making; users can flick between layers of data, pan across areas and zoom in to consider different levels of scale.

For example, not only can GIS be used to appreciate which areas are at risk from flooding, but this can be overlaid with socio-economic data concerning deprivation, the location of schools or utility services, or the number of basement flats in an area, say, to gain a much more nuanced understanding of the relative vulnerability of a particular place and help to shape more targeted and efficient intervention strategies (Cavan and Kingston, 2012). It could also be used to aid an appreciation of the various regulatory boundaries or managerial regimes associated with a particular space. In this case, a planning decision could be subject to a host of policy considerations, from habitats to archaeological sites, to soil composition. It can also be used to better understand service provision or those areas of population that have particular socioeconomic profiles. In this case, by using data on existing green spaces and the distance that communities have to travel to access these, we can work out areas of low green space provision that could benefit from investment in new nature parks. Equally, you can use GIS to inform decisions on transport options, new infrastructure or to identify areas with a poor history of engagement in planning that may be in need of outreach investment. The possibilities are limited only by the data and how it is used.

While representing data spatially is not a new approach, the possibilities afforded by GIS go far beyond a traditional understanding of mapping. It allows differing sources of data to be considered alongside each other, thus allowing for deeper analysis and interpretation of relationships and trends, as well as creating innovative visualizations. Its ability to communicate information to citizens also means that it has synergy with trends in engagement and e-government, where technology is seen to play a key role in service delivery. To this end, GIS can also be used as a means to engage directly with citizens and ascertain their views on particular places or environmental planning options (Kingston, 2000). While this development provides the basis for an effective mechanism to allow people to participate, it should be noted that some in society may have neither access to the internet nor the skills to take advantage of its use, and that these groups tend to be among the poorest in society. It also serves to highlight that it is a little too crude to simply caricature GIS as epitomizing a technical–positivist approach that conforms well to empiricist norms; participatory perspectives of this nature can have a strong sociopolitical standpoint.

A key issue with GIS is a function of its close association with data. For example, is it accurate? Is it up to date? How far can we zoom in before scalar differences from the source material may be exposed? Further, data may not be freely available or it may not be in an interoperable format that can be transferred easily between systems or institutions, or it may be costly to acquire and update. More fundamentally, some datasets may also resist their transformation into points, polygons or pixels: geographical functions are bounded, but spatial ones are not – the boundaries of an area of a Site of Special Scientific Interest are much more straightforward to depict than the location of people who may value its existence as a resource. GIS also requires a degree of expenditure and expertise to compile, and has a limited ability to compare and assess differing alternatives, which is the job of the user. At the end of the process there is still the age-old problem of its influence: it is a DST, but perhaps one more comfortable as part of the evidence-gathering phase than in the making of firm choices, as the many factors at play resist quantification in this manner. This should be the case; however, the skill set and remit of the planner goes far beyond the passive interpretation of technical data.

A further concern is methodological. While GIS may appear to be a neutral tool free from bias, its reliance on data collected by people and its subsequent transformation into a spatial format means that it has an element of social construction. Techniques such as these can easily take on an air of technological determinism and inherent authority. Encoding and mapping data can suffer from a degree of 'false precision' inherent in the simplistic spatial interpretations of what may in fact be complex phenomena (White, 2013: 107). The distilling of data down to a line on a map is rooted essentially in positivist approaches and may not reflect, or be able to communicate easily, the uncertainty of the information, the fuzziness of its spatial representation or the degree to which it is subject to dynamic forces.

More critically, notions of space are distinct from notions of place, so to what extent can GIS portray reality? People perceive their environment differently and this social and political dimension can be lost depending on how the data is treated. Poore and Chrisman (2006) highlight the way that discussion of GIS tends to vary between two conflicting metaphors of information. On the one hand there is information visualized as a 'thing' transmitted between actors during the process of communication, while the other views it in a more utopian manner as forming part of a path towards further knowledge, and perhaps even wisdom. These contrasting articulations also serve to demonstrate the wider political, social and ethical concerns inherent in the technical representation of space. That is not to say that these concerns cannot be mitigated, however, either within the platform itself or when considering its use in decision-making. A key message is plurality: other DSTs are available, such as those discussed elsewhere in this chapter, which can offset some of these issues and provide much needed balance – just as environmental planners need to consider a range of views, so too must they be comfortable with dealing with a variety of techniques.

Impact assessment

One of the most significant DSTs introduced in recent decades concerns the development of more sophisticated methods and approaches to better assess the *impact* of changes to land, or the introduction of new policies, projects or programmes. This section will discuss the emergence of this agenda and the role it can play in environmental planning. While there are different types of mechanism under this heading, such as strategic environmental assessment (SEA) or social impact assessment (SIA), we shall discuss in the main the environmental impact assessment (EIA), which is focused on the project level.

In the USA, the 1969 National Environmental Policy Act introduced EIA into the public policy arena. In part, the initiative was a reaction against the changing scale and complexity of development: new technologies and ever-larger schemes were becoming the norm, with impacts clearly stretching beyond local boundaries. It was also a result of increased public interest in the quality of the environment, and a concern that the process of decision-making was weighted too heavily towards economic aspects, with social and environmental factors struggling to exert their influence. Since this time, EIA has been adopted in many countries, such as via the 1985 European EIA Directive, and more generally recommended on an international scale. For example, it was formally recognized in principle 17 of the 1991 Rio Declaration.

While there are many differing definitions of EIA, simply put, it is a systematic process that is designed to identify, predict and evaluate the environmental impacts of major decisions. An EIA is required for proposals that are likely to bring significant environmental effects, and as such is oriented towards larger developments such as a new port or industrial complex. Beyond these clear examples, a screening process can determine if something is required or not. By conducting an EIA in advance there should be more information on the consequences of actions and increased insights into how these may be mitigated. The assessment should also enable more long-term objectives to be achieved, such as to protect valuable natural resources or to avoid irreversible environmental change. The overall aim is to ensure that part of the portfolio of evidence under consideration includes a more nuanced and integrated view of environmental impacts.

At this point, some readers may be thinking that planners should be assessing the environmental impacts of development in any case – and if that is so, then what is new? The main difference is concerning the systematic, holistic and multidisciplinary approach of EIA (Glasson *et al.*, 2012). Not only does it have the ability to identify and address specific impacts, but its encompassing scope also means that it has a good potential to integrate decisions across areas of public policy and provide the basis of a more informed negotiation of trade-offs. It can also help to bring more balanced and sustainable outcomes, provide a forum to engage with the community, and potentially speed up some decisions by allowing areas of conflict to be addressed early in the process.

EIA has not been without criticism, however. Developers may instinctively rail against the monetary and time costs of preparing the document, or point towards its complex nature. Perhaps more fundamentally, it cannot ensure that environmental impacts do not occur and its project emphasis is not designed to address the uncertain, cumulative and fuzzy nature of many contemporary environmental concerns. Moreover, there is still the perennial problem concerning its actual influence, which can be limited and opaque, and at times the degree of interpretation and flexible weighting in the practice of EIA has been accused of supporting preconceived judgements (Owens *et al.*, 2004).

At its heart, any form of impact assessment is a process – from determining whether it is needed to establishing the scope and evaluating possible impacts. Figure 8.2 provides an insight into the various steps to be followed in this regard. It should be noted that while this describes a generic linear procedure, there should be feedback at each stage and EIA practices may vary slightly across national boundaries. Here, for example, preparatory activities such as screening and scoping pave the way for the prediction and evaluation of impacts before they can influence decisions.

Reflecting on this process, readers should be starting to make connections with discussions in previous sections, in particular those in Chapter 6 concerning science, objectivity and expert knowledge. EIA has a clear positivist genealogy rooted in neutral scientific authority, but we now know that these aims are not uncontested and it is no surprise that in some cases the overtly technical and rational approach has been accused of painting an ethical and political judgement as a technical one (Owens *et al.*, 2004). However, trying to shift the emphasis from procedural rationality to pursuing more deliberative outcomes could mean that EIA loses legitimacy and is more subject to the use of power.

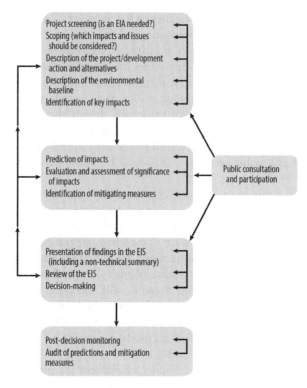

Figure 8.2 *Important steps in the EIA process*
Source: Glasson et al. (2012: 4).

Conclusion

Making decisions is at the centre of environmental planning, and mechanisms to improve this are welcomed by practitioners. At its heart, decision-making is essentially a choice between alternatives: Do we develop or not? Is there evidence of impact, and how could it be mitigated? Which policies support this, and which may be against it? Who receives the benefits and who bears the costs? The process of decision-making is designed to consider all these issues, and in this respect choices may be understood as a series of trade-offs. And while individual problems may be unique, there are standard tools available that are transferable and can help greatly to inform the activity. In the main, this chapter has been designed to provide a brief overview of some of the more common DSTs and their relationship to environmental planning. While this has an undeniably practical dimension it is also designed to provide a rounded critical perspective where underlying methodologies and caveats are also considered. As the British economist, Joan Robinson (1980: 17), argued: 'The purpose of studying economics is not to acquire a set of ready-made answers to economic questions, but to avoid being deceived by economists.'

To this end, when considering tools such as these there can be an emphasis on results – the comforting reliability of technical information at one's fingertips. However, this often belies what is going on underneath and it is easy to forget to question how data is compiled and maintained. Fundamentally, tools represent a way of assembling, presenting and analysing data that has inherent power. In all this discussion it should not be forgotten that information is both a thing and a relation; it is both tangible and helps us to understand the complex world of environmental planning. Of course, DSTs have technical and practical applications, but when we analyse the air of rationality we can also see its political power to frame and transform. This holds true from the hand-drawn maps of new towns in the distant past of planning to the modern scope of CBA or EIA. Some readers may even be slightly uncomfortable with some of the tools mentioned here. For example, movements to attach a value to nature may initially seem counter-intuitive and indicative of all that is wrong with the world, but the pragmatic counter-argument is that it is a realistic alternative to complaints concerning the marginalization of the environment in policy decisions. While tools do conform to the demands of normal practice, they also allow a more integrated debate to take place and may level the playing field with regard to the effect of environmental representation in decision-making. To this end, we should also acknowledge that the perception of a single decision-maker using tools to inform a 'choice' may not represent how the process operates in modern democracies.

Finally, while DSTs have the potential to alter our perceptions of economics, measurement, space, time and scale, there will also be an enormous amount of information available that fails to influence policy or practice (Owens *et al.*, 2004), or does so in a manner that brings further impacts connected to a whole host of areas, from justice to accessibility to privacy. The deeper foundation of understanding provided by examining governance, politics, concepts, science, policy and tools means that we are now well placed to investigate Chapters 9 and 10, which turn the debate towards people and decisions.

Chapter 9

Engaging with Stakeholders

'The majority is never right. Never, I tell you! That's one of these
lies in society that no free and intelligent man can help rebelling
against. Who are the people that make up the biggest proportion
of the population – the intelligent ones or the fools? I think we
can agree it's the fools, no matter where you go in this world, it's
the fools that form the overwhelming majority.'

(Ibsen, 1882 [1999: 76])

The opening quote is from *An Enemy of the People*, a play by the
influential Norwegian playwright, Henrik Johan Ibsen
(1828–1906). It can be read as containing fears about democracy, or
more specifically where decisions may suffer from 'the tyranny of
the majority' (Tocqueville, 2003 [1835]). The main protagonist in
the play, Dr Stockmann, has discovered that a nearby tannery is
polluting the town's public baths, making them unsafe to use. Yet
because of the financial benefit of the facility to the community
there is resistance and even disbelief in his findings. Despite his
strong moral conviction that he is in the right it makes him deeply
unpopular and leads him to be labelled: 'an enemy of the people'.

Dr Stockmann's passionate tirade highlights that popular public
opinion can often be biased, unethical and unduly influenced by
short-term financial concerns. The 'truth' argued for by a minority
may be outweighed by the concerns of others: policy directions in
harmony with the wishes of most people may seem sensible, but
can cause the oppression of marginal views in a similar way that a
tyrant might. Stephen Spielberg's film, *Jaws* was also reputed to be
inspired by Ibsen's play, with Chief Brody reprising the role of the
ostracized lone voice, whose concerns about safety were not heeded
by the wider townsfolk for economic reasons. Environmental
protection agendas frequently suffer from similar accusations. For
example, opponents of action to mitigate climate change cite the
economic costs of measures on the business sector, or question the
veracity of scientific studies as a means to maintain the status quo.

In addition to managing the varied weight of opinion, engagement practices are further complicated as citizens and groups hold some-times equally persuasive but opposing views. The public interest used to be relatively clear: early environmental planning had an accepted public health component, while there was a noticeable post-war consensus based on collectivism and welfare objectives, but now there appears to be little widespread agreement among the public. To bedevil the issue further, engagement occurs with multiple 'publics'. For example, environmental planning plays a part in enabling both public- and private-sector interests to be achieved. New development and infrastructure are vital for economic growth and will serve the interest of capital and certain stakeholders, but they also have impacts. Navigating these tensions productively is an inherent feature of engagement, which, in turn, leads to related debates regarding ethics, advocacy and whose interests are being served.

Discussions concerning the outcomes of planning inevitably lead to questions of process. As environmental concerns have moved up the political agenda, they have posed particularly searching ques-tions regarding the extent to which 'the people' should have a say in decisions. Is it just a matter of providing information? Experts are experts, after all. Or is it something more collaborative and inclusionary? If policy-makers recognize that moving towards sustainable development or managing environmental risks requires behavioural change or more responsibility to be taken at all levels of society, then shouldn't people have a say? Yet, while this may seem to be a democratic good, some people and groups are much more able to exert influence than others. Moreover, engagement can slow down decisions or even undermine the value of planning as a discipline – just as the rational planner of the 1960s was criti-cized for not incorporating public views, we could now be swing-ing too far in the opposite direction, where strategic oversight or hard-earned skills are marginalized. So dependent on the issue at hand, and the interests affected, there may need to be a degree of flexibility with regard to the level of engagement and how this might be pursued – all of which serves to challenge both environ-mental planning procedures and the professionals themselves.

In this chapter we shall first investigate how engagement became part of environmental planning and explore the advantages it can bring to decision-making. We shall then examine the theoretical foundation before introducing the challenges in translating this promise into reality. Finally, we shall discuss engagement in practice and the professional demands it may place on those concerned with environmental planning.

The rise of engagement

As we know from the previous two chapters, engagement in environmental issues can take place among a variety of groups and occur throughout the political process. More specifically with regard to the use of land or resources, the planning system provides the key forum to soften market forces, temper techno-rational tendencies and consider a wide range of social, environmental and community views. Indeed, this is a central purpose of environmental planning: changes in the use of resources or land tend to be driven by those with power in society, and outcomes may not be beneficial beyond these groups.

Until around the late 1960s, planning was implemented at a nation-state level as a top-down form of rational decision-making based on professional knowledge and techniques wielded by elite experts. Stemming from essentially good intentions to improve public health, environmental conditions or the nature of cities, planning was seen as the rational mastery of the irrational (Mannheim, 1940). While the planner was firmly in charge, participation did still take place at this time, though it was limited to the provision of information. This quote from Keeble (1961: 161) colourfully sums up the stance:

> Resort has often been had to the pernicious practice of canvassing nearby residents for their views on the application before determining it. To those unfamiliar with the real circumstances this might appear an example of what the Americans call grass roots democracy, but it is quite indefensible. It is the Local Authority's duty to determine applications in the light of the facts surrounding them and on the advice tendered to them by their officers.

The tone both neatly defines this paternalistic view and points towards the rationale for its eventual change: regardless of the quantitative techniques or expertise available, planning was about people and for people, therefore they should be allowed a voice in decisions – something that overly rational and state-centred approaches often failed to appreciate.

An important intellectual counter-argument was provided by Jane Jacobs in her influential 1961 book, *The Life and Death of American Cities*. Now regarded as a modern classic, it served to highlight many of the flaws in the rationalist approach to planning, and in particular how its preoccupation with order and detached expertise struggles to recognize the organic complexity and vibrancy of cities that can make them such enjoyable places for people. Healey (1992: 145) summarizes the dominating authority of this position, stating: 'Reason, understood as logic coupled with scientifically-constructed empirical knowledge, was unveiled as having achieved hegemonic power over other ways of being and knowing, crowding out moral and aesthetic discourses.'

The accepted wisdom of zoning land uses provides a good example. While it can appear to be logical on a master plan, the strict demarcation of space into separate functions can create an unnatural city monoculture that separates and isolates in much the same way as a field growing a single crop will contrast unfavourably with one teeming with biodiversity. Jacob's work served to ignite debates concerning what kinds of places planning should be trying to foster, and more pointedly to this chapter, provided a devastating critique of the relationship between the existing processes and ideologies and the people they were designed to serve. Engagement beyond the realm of the experts in planning was gradually coming to be seen not just as a way to improve results, or as a means to gain agreement, but as a democratic necessity.

The context of the changing political discourse in the 1960s discussed in the previous chapter now becomes more relevant. While we are now familiar with the view that planning is political, at that time this debate was still playing out and was becoming manifest in local opposition to unpopular top-down decisions. Planners were urged increasingly to make more effort to consult with the public and other governmental actors and agencies, with legislation gradually changing to formalize this role. However, while engagement was becoming accepted as a part of both strategic and local planning, there was still uncertainty over what exactly it would mean in practice. For example, in the UK, the influential Skeffington Report (1969) marked a change in approach by recommending that participation should go beyond talking or consultation, with citizens playing an 'active' role, while at the same time arguing that decision-making power was to be retained in the hands of the existing parties. More people were being invited to the table, but it would take time for their voices to exert substantial influence.

From the 1970s onwards, decision-making structures have changed greatly, with a move away from universalistic authoritarian rationality to more post-positivist approaches. Alongside these pluralistic and inclusive intentions, governance changes meant that

Box 9.1 Arnstein's ladder

Arnstein depicted engagement techniques as occupying a scale of eight potential steps, each with its own characteristics, ranging from non-participation at the bottom to complete citizen control at the top. On the lower rungs of the ladder the emphasis is on 'education'. Essentially, this can be seen as non-participation in a similar vein to 1950s approaches. Not only is control retained, but power can also be used to sway opinion. As we progress upwards, Arnstein draws attention to 'tokenistic' approaches where voices may be heard but not necessarily heeded. Strategies that are usually termed 'informative' or 'consultative' are included here: they often create the veneer of engagement, and may arguably conform to regulatory requirements, but still retain significant authority in the hands of established decision-makers. An example may be a simple survey that canvasses opinion, but it is unclear as to what effect it might have in practice. Finally, approaches near the top can bring genuine citizen control, such as by formal power sharing or taking complete ownership of local services or issues.

The ladder is essentially an illustrative tool. It links engagement to the redistribution of power and emphasizes that the relationship is relative. It further connects processes with outcomes: is it an empty ritual or is there significant ability for citizens to influence proceedings? The discussion has strong ties to previous sections on power, the capacity to act, governance and politics.

Despite its longevity in appreciating the shades of participation, the approach has not been without criticism. For example, in practice, the simple continuum may not reflect the complexity and subtleties of engagement: there are many different types of 'partnership' that could be used and it may be unhelpful to characterize these as being similar. The ladder analogy also assumes implicitly that the higher rungs are incrementally better: essentially that citizen control is an ideal goal to be achieved. However, sacrificing direction and control can inhibit strategic outcomes or

→

regulation was becoming increasingly decentralized and involved numerous actors. Understanding this changing role brought new critical insights into the nuances of planning practice. Involving stakeholders either in a minor way or at the end of the process merely to rubber-stamp decisions, can be democratic to some extent, but is far removed from what we may term 'true' engagement. The process of engagement comprises multiple methodologies; some are more

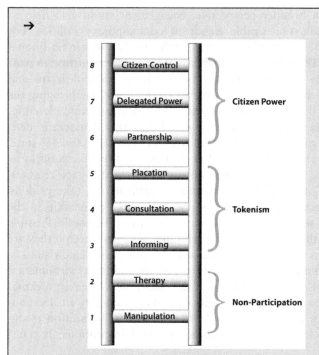

Figure 9.1 *The ladder of participation*
Source: Arnstein (1969).

unacceptably slow down decisions. Further, some participants may not wish to engage in these time-consuming practices and actually prefer experts to act on behalf of society. Yet its value as a simple metaphor of an intricate issue has helped it to retain classic status since its publication. It emphasizes that 'engagement' does not equate automatically to a redistribution of power; the associated epistemologies and practices also need to be put under the spotlight.

consultative while others are deeply embedded within communities from the outset. Comprehending the differences between these and their respective impact on power and outcomes is a key recurring theme for environmental planning. One of the first academic attempts to explain the differing approaches and their consequences still provides a very effective way to introduce these issues. Box 9.1 discusses a seminal 1969 paper by Sherry Arnstein.

Taking a broader perspective, engagement could also help to address some undesirable trends of contemporary politics. For example, the noticeable decline of public involvement in traditional decision-making processes, such as voting, or the reduction in trust between the general public on the one hand and politicians and experts on the other (Rueschemeyer *et al.*, 1998). By bringing the views of stakeholders more centrally into environmental planning, engagement practices can serve to address this democratic deficiency in a small way. As Wondolleck and Yaffee (2000: 248) state, even if people aren't interested in politics: 'most people want to be neighbourly, solve common problems, have face-to-face relationships with others that are pleasant and affirmative, take pride in their organizations and communities, and take ownership in the directions set by public decision making processes'. Possible changes within local areas hold relevance for many, even if they are not engaged in national politics or interested in strategic visions.

International action regarding an impending environmental crisis, the rise of uncertainty and the recognition of environmental injustices have all further challenged state authority in decision-making. For example, principle 10 of the Rio Declaration recognizes local knowledge and empowers local institutions. It states that:

> Environmental issues are best handled with participation of all concerned citizens, at the relevant level. At the national level, each individual shall have appropriate access to information concerning the environment that is held by public authorities, including information on hazardous materials and activities in their communities, and the opportunity to participate in decision making processes. (United Nations, 1992)

Bringing the story up to the present, it is now commonplace for engagement practices to be enshrined in local, national and international policy. For example, in 1998, most European countries signed up to the Aarhus Convention (UNECE, 1998). The Convention ensures that the public has access to information and justice in environmental matters and recommends that they be given opportunities to participate in decision-making. Subsequent initiatives, such as the Water Framework Directive and the Strategic Environmental Assessment in the EU, have been designed specifically both to promote and to require greater public participation. Together, these socio-political and legislative trends have led to engagement becoming a key requirement for environmental planning.

To summarize, a focus on effective engagement promises a number of substantive benefits. In addition to forming a better fit with the nature of the contemporary world, it serves to mitigate accusations of instrumental rationality by engaging explicitly with values and recognizing how knowledge is socially constructed. It can also provide a valuable mechanism to explore uncertainties regarding space and resources, facilitate public debate and create the potential for better outcomes. Further, collaborating in this manner can make decision-making speedier and more effective by identifying common ideas, beliefs and aspirations, and deal with potential problems at an early stage. Finally, there is a significant capacity building and social learning element; not only are traditional boundaries eroded, but stakeholders involved in collaborations may develop new skills to help them deal with future environmental challenges.

The theoretical foundation

The ongoing movement of the planner from being detached expert to grounded communicator has brought different intellectual demands and as a consequence new theoretical understandings connected with power, dialogue and consensus have gradually entered into academic discourse. These debates started to coalesce around a possible new 'communicative' paradigm for planning (Sagar, 1994), a more inclusive grand narrative more appropriate to the changing societal and democratic trends. Drawing on the social theories of Anthony Giddens (1984) and Jürgen Habermas (1984), it deliberately places planning as operating in a very different milieu from that earlier in the century. An emphasis on managing urban expansion in a top-down manner could be deemed appropriate where there was a broad consensus on objectives and where the nation state held huge authority. But what about a situation where the boundaries between local and international concerns are blurred, where globalization and the market wield a huge influence, or where agreement is in short supply?

Given these institutional, economic and societal realities, it was argued that the role of the planner should be much more action-oriented and cognizant of the environment within which decisions are made in order to achieve the best outcomes for shared spaces and environments (Forester, 1989; Healey, 2006). A more communicative and collaborative approach can better manage the spatiality of economic activity, reflect a broader array of stakeholder views and acknowledge wider post-modern concerns regarding the role and process of planning (Healey, 1992). This perspective recognizes how societal norms, values and cultures provide an influential framework that shapes the ability to act, but planners can also be equally active in pursuing change and empowering actors within these overarching structures. Not only is the previous claim of value-free freedom seen as unachievable, but planners should purposely intervene and help to mitigate unjust or dominant positions. This is a relational stance where individuals, agencies and issues are interconnected, with the spotlight focused on how planners navigate these critical junctures.

It is an interesting angle for environmental planning, as people and groups do have universal interests concerning spaces or resources – from a local urban renewal project to the global commons. Also, environmental planning is strongly normative; that is, it is grounded in competing assumptions concerning what we ought to do. It will therefore be influenced by various organizing ideas that frame intervention and the sometimes passionate opinions of stakeholders within these. A challenge for engagement within environmental planning is connected with making sense of various claims and appreciating the sometimes contradictory objectives within the decision-making process. This stance encourages a degree of reflexivity and balance that could lead to more informed local planning and help to resist the power of the state, institutions and economy, or long-held habits of thinking or acting.

Here, decision-making unfolds by a process of dialogue between stakeholders. Theoretically, this open conversation should foster a consideration of what is of value in the natural world or a locality before attention turns to appraising the tools necessary to achieve a particular outcome. Significantly, these views may not be fixed, but may be formed by the communicative process itself as stakeholders interact. This means that the discourses surrounding our relations with the environment become important. For example, decision-makers need to ask which metaphors and storylines are invoked, or which power structures could skew outcomes unfairly or disadvantage vulnerable groups (Rydin, 2003). The role for planners is to act as facilitators by enabling engagement, to make links between competing economic, environmental and social aspects, and attempt to negotiate towards a consensus.

Connected to this point, it is emphasized that engagement should be a vehicle to better understand the positions of others, and in doing so revise existing stances (Forester, 1989). This ability to foster learning within engagement is central to the approach, as communicating and arguing are seen as aiding the ability to achieve mutual understanding, consensus and co-operation. Habermas (1984) referred to an 'ideal speech' situation; a principle of what he called 'communicative action'. Here, the planner needs to move beyond technocratic leadership and understand the *process* of learning and attaining agreement. This view has a very progressive element; indeed, argument is widely renowned as the classic intellectual tool to address elite power. However, the 'better' argument does not always win, even leaving aside notions of 'better for whom?': democratic pluralism operates in a climate of harsh political economy.

Regardless of the logic associated with parts of this agenda, the next section will show that, while it aimed to carve an intellectual niche to challenge the hegemony of scientific and technical rationality, engagement is markedly easier to write about than to achieve in practice.

The promise and the reality

While there is widespread agreement regarding the need to pursue a discursive and reflexive approach to environmental planning, in reality it is valid to remain sceptical of realizing its theoretical promise. For example, there may still be resistance within institutions to cede power to wider stakeholders or to do more than fulfil minimum requirements. There is a persistent risk with regard to this entire topic that engagement occurs too often in name only just to tick a regulatory or legislative box, rather than becoming embedded in institutional change. Moreover, related to the topics of governmentality and power discussed in Chapter 3, some actors, such as environmental NGOs, may choose deliberately to remain apart from formal processes of government for fear of being co-opted into agreeing with organizing frames and wider agendas, thereby losing their ability to be critical about fundamental aspects of capitalism or globalization.

However, reticence to buy into the agenda is not just limited to institutions; citizens may also not wish to devote the necessary time or resources that engagement requires. In practice there is often a reliance on certain types of actors, or more colloquially what may be called 'the usual suspects' – people who frequently attend meetings and may be very vocal about certain issues but may not be representative of the wider community. There are also collective action and 'free-riding' problems. Put simply, individuals may refuse to co-operate in initiatives of this nature as the costs of engaging far outweigh any perceived benefits. Further, even where common goods or issues are identified, individuals may benefit more by sitting back while other members of the group or society take action. As a result, no one may act.

When the public are motivated to engage it is often because they are protesting against a potential development or activity change. While they may have valid concerns about an economic or quality of life impact, in opposing the proposal they tend to run the risk of being termed a NIMBY ('not in my backyard'). It should be noted that NIMBY is a pejorative and antagonistic term. It is used in a dismissive fashion to characterize actors crudely as selfish or relying on simplistic emotive arguments connected with location. Here, the development is painted as being subject to conflict over a particular space, but moving the proposal elsewhere may well elicit a similar response – no local residents want to have their quality of life affected by the negative externalities that some undesirable new development may bring. Therefore, while the process of engagement provides a forum to pursue consensual policy or practice outcomes, this desirable result is far from certain. In practice, some values and beliefs will always be in opposition, and discord will be absolutely inevitable. For example, bringing stakeholders together to debate a proposal to build a wind farm or a fracking site may not result in anything even approaching agreement; here there is no middle ground, whether the proposal is given permission or not, some will be bitterly disappointed. It also emphasizes the need to maintain an ongoing relationship with stakeholders. If there is a history of inadequate democratic systems or disillusionment with previous attempts to engage, then the public response may either be muted or people will feel they have little option but to resort to direct action.

Consequently, scepticism regarding whether increased collaboration leads to better outcomes is a valid stance. Logically, it may be assumed that the participation of NGOs, industry, academics and the public will result in a higher-quality plan or proposal. However, competing interests and multiple conflicting voices could prove the opposite. Wide stakeholder engagement can mean that the final plan only implements the lowest common denominator – a decision that is not desired by anyone, but is the least unacceptable for all. The inherent nature of a democratic forum may also inhibit debate; radical but politically unacceptable solutions may not emerge in this public arena. Yet setting agendas in advance or holding deliberations behind closed doors with a more manageable array of stakeholders can lessen legitimacy and fail to offset power inequalities, such as the construction of certain 'storylines' that may be preferred by dominant economic and political interests.

Thinking back to Arnstein's ladder in Figure 9.1, there are also limits in the ability to share power. Residents frequently may not want to be involved in service delivery, as that is perceived to be the job of those in public administration. Equally, they do not want to be consulted on everything, as that can cause consultation fatigue. A balance may involve initiating an open dialogue to establish the desired boundaries of the relationship. That said, it should be noted that community groups are not representative, they are indicative: in the absence of a ballot box they do not hold the clear legitimacy or democratic mandate that elected members may possess. Some power and decisions can be devolved, but in many cases it may require decisions in the broader public interest.

Regardless of the theoretical promise of engagement, in practice it may neither be feasible nor effective to base all environmental policy purely on collaborative principles. For example, given the contentious nature of many issues, the engagement process may yield no consensus outcome, or perhaps a policy recommendation that is incompatible with a wider commitment to sustainability or other policy objectives. Equally, some issues require a degree of technical knowledge that may make any engagement difficult. Consequently, there will be a role for an educator and adjudicator, not just a facilitator. And when this occurs, some of the promise of collaboration is softened, with experts playing a more muscular role. Ultimately, therefore, centralized planning still has a place in environmental policy-making, such as by merging short- and long-term perspectives and balancing strategic policy goals and stakeholder views. In the light of critiques of this nature, some commentators question the view of a paradigm shift, instead suggesting that communicative theories are just one of a number of ways to think about planning (Huxley and Yiftachel, 2000). This is not to undermine the discussion so far, however. Part of the value in understanding engagement within environmental planning is to better understand the relationship between the state, the various actors and agencies, and how decisions over space and resources are made.

Now that we appreciate some of the positives and negatives, let us now turn to the issue of practice.

Engagement in practice

Given that greater public participation is enshrined in local, national and supra-national conventions, questions such as who participates, and when and how, are germane. If environmental planning aims to engage the 'community', the first question is what is meant by this term, and who might it encompass? In this respect it generally refers to the population of a discrete area, which could pertain to the local residents or people who use the space, or it could bypass geographical boundaries and refer to a community of interest, such as those who identify with a specific topic. In reality, we all belong to multiple communities connected to various facets of our life – from our local area or hobbies to our views on national parks. This fluidity and sprawling scale may not be overly helpful for those in public administration, however.

Given the theoretical foundation of engagement and the variety of stakeholders affected, there should also be some insights into the types or make-up of communities that may benefit from more targeted action. For example, where are the pockets of disadvantage, or whom might be affected the most? Do some ethnic or social groups have a history of non-engagement, which means they do not have a voice in decisions? This reflective aspect is vital for achieving some of the stated aims of the engagement turn: acknowledging and respecting diversity and difference, appreciating power differentials, and emerging with consensus decisions. Accordingly, analyses of effective engagement tend to stress that it is not only about initiating a process; rather, it relates to whether approaches are able to achieve a more effective management strategy or better outcomes (Rydin, 2003). The dual consideration of process and outcomes is an important distinction; while some issues can be standardized, such as at what stage should communities be meaningfully involved, there is clearly a need for expert interpersonal skills and insights into which measures may elicit the best response for particular groups.

The value in designing engagement strategies to engage explicitly with specific groups can be extended to also include key professional groups. Yet, while these stakeholders have expertise and are used to negotiation, this does lead us on to more subjective territory. For example, who are these parties, and does this represent collaboration, or is it a form of selection that is based around privileged knowledge? Haas (1992) used the term 'epistemic communities' to describe groups of experts who hold knowledge within a discrete domain. While they can provide very useful information to decision-makers, significantly they may also share beliefs, values and practices that can underpin existing policies or methodological approaches. Perhaps more fundamentally, this also highlights how some aspects of the collaboration agenda may not be as open, accountable and transparent as they promised initially. In a globalized world, hugely influential and mobile actors, such as multinational corporations, can be informal, relatively invisible and far removed from the ecosystems from which they draw resources. These stakeholders can also be funded and motivated by power structures that are not always immediately apparent, such as the work of NGOs who lobby political members in private. As Hillier (2000: 34) observes: 'the energies and power of these networks may influence planning decision making in ways which may never formally enter the public domain, may never be publicly expressed, visible, or recorded. They are unlikely to be normalized into a rational, communicative, consensus-seeking debate'.

The next issue to grapple with is when it is required to happen, or when it may be desirable to facilitate. The distinction here is deliberate as there are statutory and non-statutory opportunities. While individual countries or cities may each have their own regulations, generally speaking a degree of engagement is mandatory during the long-term process of developing a strategic or local plan, or when deciding individual development proposals. But engagement can go beyond the regulatory minimum and be much more proactive and creative to engender wider participation. From this perspective, interaction in itself is seen as beneficial, almost regardless of the outcomes; engagement is not merely a series of procedures, nor about delivery, but a chance to further the learning and development of those involved. It is also part of the mandate of planners to support the creation and maintenance of vibrant local areas; to move towards that valuable intangible commodity: a sense of community. Notions such as these are persuasive and desirable as they tend to have strongly positive connotations: from a bygone age when people could leave their doors unlocked, to a ready supply of people willing to contribute to strategic discussions or service delivery.

As a consequence, it is important to distinguish between formal and informal aspects of environmental planning and the variable ability of stakeholders to participate. Formal planning refers to institutionalized activity that is normally carried out under the auspices of the state, whether at the national or local level. Formal actors include national governments, regulatory agencies and international actors, such as the United Nations or the EU, and their involvement is often a result of statutory demands. However, as we know from previous chapters, policy development and decisions concerning space and resources can hold huge interest for non-profit and private-sector interests such as NGOs, the business community, and citizens more generally, all of whom can be motivated by the issue at hand. While formal actors are used to the processes and skills that engagement requires, informal ones may not be. Where knowledge is lacking, there may be a need to support more informal processes and explicitly to build capacity. However, this can mean that engagement is often seen as a drain on scarce resources and a candidate for budgetary cuts in resource competitive institutions.

Yet, as many planners would readily acknowledge, in some circumstances people are only too willing to become involved in environmental planning, in particular if the subject affects them directly over the short term. While this is a form of engagement, it also highlights how notoriously difficult it is to involve people in designing plans, projects or programmes, such as those connected with sustainability or climate change, which may not appear to have a huge impact on one place or stretch far into the future. Part of the challenge for environmental planning is to try to address this long-standing impediment, and aspects such as transparency, clear levels of influence and engaging early become important in building ongoing relationships with stakeholders. Here, centralized top-down planning may need to play a strong part initially in supporting engagement, such as by creating best practice within local institutions or capacity-building processes, which will enable both the space for debate and the emergence of wider views.

Connected to this, there are also opportunities to design processes that reduce the financial or social costs of participation in order to facilitate action. Technological developments have opened up room for new approaches that can incorporate local knowledge in a remote fashion. The use of GIS provides one example. Here, interactive, web-based mapping tools can be used to provide stakeholders with access to information and an ability to target comments spatially from the comfort of their own homes (Kingston, 2000). This can cut costs and make it easier for people to become involved, but it should be noted that not all groups have access to the internet, some are uncomfortable engaging in this manner, and there are still the familiar problems connected to its opaque influence on decisions.

As an interesting aside, it should be noted that engagement in practice is not just a matter for policy or development proposals. There have been recent initiatives to expand this approach further into the conduct of science, particularly where it involves communities or will lead eventually to policy outcomes. Citizen science movements can provide informal observations of local environments that objective, expert, quantitative approaches may miss. Used in combination with traditional academic methods, such contextual knowledge can broaden environmental understanding, help research to have a greater grounding in society, and generate the potential for real-world impact. Box 9.2 discusses issues surrounding the co-production of research with members of the public.

Reflecting on the chapter so far, it is now apparent that interpersonal and negotiation skills are becoming as central to the planners' armoury as the technical knowledge of policy and regulation. For example, to include the views of various interest groups effectively there is a need to recognize that those having opinions would range from the well-funded elite organizations to those with neither the finances nor the expertise to contribute. In short, people are entitled to their opinions as per recognized societal norms, but inequality is rife with regard to both the opinions themselves and the abilities of those expressing them. Considering the effect of expertise, power and negotiation, some people and groups will be much more adept at this than others. Or, put more simply: 'the power of words depends on the power of the speakers' (Fainstein 2000: 458).

Consequently, it has long been argued that planners may need to adopt an advocacy role, in much the same way that lawyers represent people in legal matters. A seminal paper by Davidoff (1965: 423) first argued that, given the evident disparity in the ability and capacity to influence, the role of the planner should go beyond explaining possible courses of action and rather become: 'an advocate for what he deems proper'. This extends the discussion of the potential roles of planners from facilitators, educators

---

Box 9.2 Co-production in science

As was discussed in Chapter 6, the science–policy interface can be seen as a social process, but engagement can equally occur with regard to the production of knowledge and data, or in conducting science more generally. On the one hand, scientists could work in isolation, tackling difficult issues and then aiming to make their work influence public policy – this is effectively the traditional approach. At the other end of the spectrum, citizens can be included from the outset and essentially work to 'co-produce' knowledge. This latter strategy is rooted in a recognition of the value in involving what may be considered service users with service delivery; stakeholders outside the scientific community may themselves possess valuable knowledge and increase the efficiency of any transfer to practice. This innovative approach can also empower communities, take advantage of existing networks, provide deep levels of learning, and conform to democratic principles.

More fundamentally it goes back to relationships within society. Co-production recognizes the pervasive nature of the 'social'; knowledge is embedded within society, not merely a separate artefact to be generated and then applied. Fischer (2000: 44–5) highlights how science is essentially an interpretive enterprise and, given this, 'science loses its privileged claim as superior knowledge. Empirical science need not fold up shop, but in a practical field like

→

---

and adjudicators, to include the possibility of being political actors in their own right, with a core remit to offset power inequalities. However, this raises valid questions concerning how planners adapt to this changing responsibility, and emphasizes that topics such as ethics and values are not just for theoretical debate but have real-world practical implications.

It also brings life to discussions concerning the public interest. There is a general consensus that representing the public interest is desirable, and that it should influence environmental planning. Indeed, one could create a strong argument that upholding the public interest is the entire rationale for planning. But what is this, and how is it represented? It claims to refer to 'general wellbeing' or something that is of 'interest' to the public; but there is no single public interest, and decisions over space can affect almost everyone. This situation also highlights a common environmental planning tension: that between local and national interests. Take the

→

public policy, it has to establish a new relationship to the other relevant discourses that bear on policy judgements'. This view also undermines the habitually lazy uses of homogeneous categories such as 'scientific experts' or 'lay citizens' in a way that puts them at odds with one another. Scientists are themselves citizens, albeit with specialized knowledge in a particular area. Here, shared citizenship, social learning and clear processes can provide a basis for overcoming divides between cultural and technical values. Moreover, the contextual knowledge of local people can substantially enrich traditional scientific knowledge as well as enabling engagement aims to be achieved.

With regard to engagement, the co-production of knowledge involves the joint framing of problems, processes and outputs. More than merely involving participants in projects, it also has the potential to question underlying facts and social norms that may otherwise appear fixed and can therefore be a mechanism to engage and share power in a meaningful way. It does present problems, however. Participants can frequently have different values, expectations and aims, or there may be a lack of clarity over roles or responsibilities. Further, in merging rights and responsibilities, as can occur in co-production approaches, it should be noted that not all citizens are 'responsible', nor even helpful. Science or policy aims can easily be subverted from their original intention.

example of airport expansion; it may generate economic growth for the country but have a negative impact on local residents. Therefore, as public interests change over space and time, part of the training of those concerned with environmental planning is to navigate these occasionally byzantine philosophical, moral and ethical matters. All of which reinforces the importance of professional conduct. As Howe (1992: 245) states: 'planners should be as clear as possible about the kinds of justifications we give for the public interest. It is the clarity and openness of these justifications that protect us'.

To sum up this section, trends in engagement have led to a less visible role for the state, with interests seemingly entering into a much higher degree of competition with each other. As the planner plays a key role in this new arena, the professional consequences are significant; once just a detached neutral expert – a professional with a 'special claim on disinterested morality' (Fainstein, 2000:

456) – the planner is now an organizer, mediator, advocate and a political actor. This means that, in addition to debates about deliberative processes or tangible outcomes, there is a need to consider the impact of engagement on the practitioners themselves. Influential work by Schön (1983) and Forester (1999) both challenged practitioners to be reflective and to revise theories of action before and during engagement in order to be more effective. The instrumentalist view of environmental planning as being about a resource, a decision or a space is thus challenged by new understandings concerning the potential effect on participants – both citizens and professionals.

Conclusion

This chapter has outlined how and why engagement has become an integral part of environmental planning, and introduced some of the issues associated with putting the approach into practice. Despite appearing to be a radical shift, we can see that it does still share similarities with previous agendas. For example: 'there is the same sense of searching for the right decision-rules – be they rational-comprehensive or rational-communicative, universal or local' (Huxley and Yiftachel, 2000: 102). Moreover, elements of the technical and analytical skill set of planners are eminently transferable to these new demands, such as when identifying common interests and points of convergence, outlining issues and options, and determining set criteria (Innes, 1995). However, while communicative approaches provide a clear focus on the 'arena of struggle' (Healey, 1993), power inequalities within this forum are very much in evidence.

Theoretically, collaborations and stakeholder engagement hold a great deal interest for environmental planning. The issue links closely to debates over the use of land, the impacts of pollution, behavioural change, shared responsibilities and increased citizen responsibility, all of which are fundamental to managing contemporary issues. They can have a positive value by increasing the capacity of hitherto ignored actors to contribute to decision-making, lending a greater degree of legitimacy to intervention than top-down decisions alone can achieve. It can also lessen or remove opposition to proposals and speed up the development process. Yet while there is value in understanding how engagement can assist in managing the environment, the subject is accompanied by several notes of caution. Effective collaboration depends on the issue, and when it is applied uncritically it can deliver poor results. Moreover, the optimistic potential of engagement to deliver consensus or better outcomes may not reflect the reality that it depends on the issue, or how the questions are phrased. Finally, issues that attract community opposition are often those that are the most controversial. Outside of these high-profile proposals it can be challenging to involve the public in strategic-plan-making and to foster social capital more generally.

When reflecting on the topic it is also apparent that there is a degree of natural acceptance – where engagement is widely seen as being a 'good thing' almost regardless of how it is manifest or what the alternative outcomes may be. Arnstein (1969: 216) compared engagement to eating spinach: no one is against it in principle because it is good for you, but in the same way as spinach doesn't seem to find its way into everyone's weekly shopping basket, so too engagement struggles to achieve its theoretical promise in reality. Regardless of all the advances in process and practice, processes to involve the community are still occasionally accused of adopting a 'decide–announce–defend' (DAD) approach, where decisions are announced and, in the absence of a substantial role in forming plans or proposals, communities have no reasonable option other than opposition and the risk of being depicted as NIMBYs. A key message is that engagement can often suffer from a reductionist tendency to be thought of as an activity in itself, a separate procedure that is minimized to adhere to basic ethical expectations or bureaucratic regulation. This does, however, lessen the potential benefits associated with pursuing advocacy or power inequalities proactively, and serve to mask the central aim of this entire debate: 'whether an emphasis on improving the procedures of planning results in a better place to live in' (Rydin 2011: 128).

Finally, while engagement practices can be seen as a foundation of fairness, they do not provide an unequivocally 'just' outcome. Unthinkingly employed, they can have the opposite effect of facilitating unjust and illegitimate exercises of power. This is well highlighted in the eye-catching title of Cooke and Khotari's (2001) book *Participation: The New Tyranny*. Here they argue that without reflexive practitioners and critical application, systemic tendencies can lead to the dominance of certain agencies and funders, a failure to address local power inequalities and the unthinking selection of participatory methods instead of other approaches that could provide better outcomes. Overall, it should not be forgotten that in many cases paternalistic modes of decision-making could produce more desirable results and be effective at offsetting inequalities (Fainstein, 2000). Discussions with regard to engagement and outcomes have prepared the ground for our next chapter, on justice.

Chapter 10

The Question of Justice

'The growth in public concern over environmental problems was thus widely interpreted as being primarily concerned with distributional issues, that is, issues concerning "who decides" and "who gets what, when and how".'

(Eckersley, 1992: 9)

Previous chapters have paved the way for our discussion of justice. Environmental planning is concerned centrally with balancing demands, and turning our attention towards justice will help to widen our appreciation of the consequences of the eventual decisions. As the opening quote by Eckersley highlights, this is connected to resource distribution and so raises questions about who wins and who loses, or who is involved (or not) in making such decisions. It therefore brings *injustice* into view. Campbell and Marshall (2006: 240) explain further: 'We regard planning as an activity which is concerned with making choices about good and bad, right and wrong, with and for others, in relation to particular places. It is about making ethical choices over issues which are often highly contested. Planning is therefore profoundly concerned with justice.'

A veritable who's who in the history of ideas has grappled with what it means to be 'just', from Plato to Nietzsche. Culturally, the notion is equally pervasive; the Ancient Romans had a goddess named 'Justitia', while the Ancient Greek deity was 'Diké', both were deemed to rule over human justice and fair judgement. Yet despite this substantial legacy, what it means to be 'just' is still debated. Rather than attempting to give a 'correct' answer, this chapter is designed rather to provoke readers towards a deeper consideration of the relationship between environmental planning processes and decisions and the concept of justice.

Justice has always been closely linked to the practice of law. Consider the modern terminology of the 'judicial process' to see how this relationship retains a strong legacy. Further, Lady Justice,

217

modelled on 'Justitia', is a statue that is commonly found erected near courthouses around the world. She provides an iconographic personification of how the term is now understood: the scales of truth and fairness in one hand to represent balance; a blindfold to symbolize impartial objectivity; and a sword depicting the power to carry out reasoned decisions.

The design of the statue is a useful route into understanding an inherent tension when we speak of justice. On the one hand, it relates to the sense that everyone should be treated equally; but on the other, that someone may receive punishment for a misdemeanour. In a similar fashion to our discussion on engagement in the previous chapter, this is essentially a distinction between a just *process* and a just *outcome*. These two interpretations can be in conflict, however. If everyone is treated alike there is less scope to give someone what they may 'deserve'. A person convicted of a crime may get fair treatment according to historical precedent, but this can frequently dissatisfy those who hold a different opinion regarding what their punishment should be. Discussions of justice are therefore open to everyone in society, not just from a legal perspective but also to the humdrum everyday; from being dissatisfied with the weak sentencing of a criminal to the turned-down penalty appeal in sport.

Frequently, this is not a clear-cut issue of right clashing with wrong; it is more a problem of right clashing with right. Consider most of the conflicts going on in the world at the present time: a common characteristic is multiple parties strongly believing that they have a 'just' cause. The Middle East conflicts provide an ample demonstration of this impasse in practice. Therefore, the challenge with justice, and allied concepts such as morality and fairness, is not only to decipher its meaning, but also to determine application: notions of just and unjust can be appropriated by particular moral or political frameworks; different cultural or social contexts may have alternative views on what is just.

Moreover, there is the question of justice for whom or what. While it is accepted in most societies that humans have a right to equity, do concepts such as justice and fairness apply to other species, people not yet born, or even to the planet more generally? If responsibility can be assigned then justice may often follow; that is, if notions of environmental stewardship are accepted it could be argued that there are duties to manage related aspects such as pollution, biodiversity loss or common goods.

This chapter outlines the main issues that the question of justice poses for environmental planners, particularly with regard to normative claims: statements of what should happen rather than what is a matter of fact. This perspective helps to reinforce the view that environmental planning is not a detached rationality, as has been the case in the past, but one related to society and its cornucopia of worldviews. But here, again, there are nuanced interpretations. For example, environmental justice debates can be centred on responsibility and the public good or, alternatively on equity and need, both of which are valid. A change to any aspect of the environment has effects, and discussions of justice will also help readers to appreciate more advanced environmental planning issues, such as power, engagement and difference, in more depth.

The first section begins by considering the notion of justice generally and its application to the environment. We shall then look at the development of the environmental justice movement, its roots in environmental racism, and its key concerns, drawing a distinction between the USA and the UK in particular. We shall also cover notions of 'equity' and 'fairness', by looking at the implications of environmental justice for planners. The final part links with the related topic of sustainability before a conclusion highlights the key messages.

Conceptions of justice

In considering to what extent a society is just we need to reflect on how it allocates aspects we value, not just tangible things such as money or resources, but also more abstract notions such as rights, duties and power. Sandel (2009) identified three ways of thinking about justice that can help in understanding these issues: *welfare*, *freedom* and *virtue*. Taking welfare first, an idea of justice may revolve around utilitarianism. This was a doctrine founded by the philosopher Jeremy Bentham (1748–1832) that rested on right and wrong being guided by the simple premise of the greatest happiness for the greatest number. While the focus on welfare may appear to be a rational logic, it has been criticized as potentially overriding individual rights and distilling justice to a simplistic, anthropocentric cost–benefit calculation that may bring injustice for many. For example, from this perspective, utilizing fossil fuels may benefit more people, while only a minority experience the bad effects; but can this be considered to be just?

We could turn to the second of these aspects – freedom – as an answer. One of Bentham's students, John Stuart Mill (1806–73) responded to some of the problems associated with the utilitarian thinking on individual freedom by modifying the thesis slightly. He summed up this stance in his influential book of 1859, *On Liberty*, with the simple position that people should be free to act as they wish as long as they do not harm others. This has the advantage of protecting the minority against the injury that might occur in the previous example, and it is centred on potent issues such as free speech, religious freedom and individual human rights. Yet proponents of this libertarian approach typically emphasize a small state, low regulation and unfettered markets – all of which are deemed to be a restraint on 'freedom'. This stance can provide a problematical issue for environmental planning as it may be in direct opposition to enforcement or regulatory mechanisms, or common discourses, such as those that apply to limits or the distribution of resources.

Finally, justice could be centred on notions of virtue. This may be most simply understood as legislating around morality, as a just society will uphold and value what is good and right; that is, what is considered to be virtuous. It therefore contrasts with the idea of liberty by prizing certain behaviour or practices, with a particular conception of what is 'good' and 'right'. Yet this approach can be prejudiced, as it could be dominated by particular sections of society, such as fundamental religious groups, so that laws are constructed around a conception of morality that may not be shared by all members of that society. As can easily be seen, these three perspectives of justice are embedded in culture and politics, making the question of what is the 'right' thing to do a highly subjective one.

Justice within society can also take on different forms. For example, should murderers face capital punishment from a retributive justice standpoint, or should there be a focus on restorative justice, which may advocate rehabilitation of criminals and consider the needs of the victim? Furthermore, environmental issues often touch on justice from a more abstract, and less legal, perspective. If we recall our previous discussions on resources and impacts, they may concern the subject of a 'fair' allocation or the concept of inter- and intragenerational 'equity' that is so central to sustainability. This may be understood as relating to distributive justice: the just distribution of goods. Justice has a tendency to become much more salient when it moves beyond theory and is considered alongside the perennial environmental frames of scarcity and limits. But once we scratch the surface of this it raises very difficult questions, such as which goods are relevant, and what is a socially just allowance.

So how could resources, opportunities, costs and risks be distributed fairly among the members of a given society? John Rawls offered a highly influential account of just decision-making in his *Theory of Justice*. Modern democratic societies are characterized by disagreement and conflict, so Rawls asks us to perform a thought experiment. All persons are placed in the 'original position' under a 'veil of ignorance', within which they are deprived of knowledge regarding the social class, ethnicity, gender and talents of people, and of their personal costs or benefits of any decisions on distribution (1971: 118–43). As a consequence, they are compelled to make impartial choices regarding who gets what on the basis of a moral *principle* of fairness rather than any other influence. Given this, rational individuals tend to consider all perspectives and agree a social contract that distributes societal goods in a way that is fairest to those who will potentially be the most disadvantaged. Or put most simply, there is little difference between the allocations. The focus here is not on determining the outcomes of society – variances in talent and opportunity are a given and will inhibit any attempts to control outcomes. Rather, the veil of ignorance is a device to highlight how the *process* of decision-making needs to be fair and removed from bias. This is known as 'justice as fairness' and brings the spotlight on to the *procedures* active in environmental planning.

While this remarkably simple analysis has been highly influential, it has not escaped criticism. From a practical basis, a selected process may never be accepted as 'fair' by all involved, thus leading to impasse. The powerful underlying currents of capitalism and globalization can also underpin existing inequalities regardless of the processes followed. Perhaps more significantly, by playing down the differences between individuals, it could be argued that 'justice as fairness' will only reinforce existing power imbalances that may be the result of a person's characteristics, such as those relating to race, class or gender; in practice, these may need to be known about and addressed to pursue equity effectively.

These arguments lead us to our final contrasting conception of justice, which is provided by the notion of capabilities. This view is centred on two connected premises: first, that enabling human, and even non-human, life to achieve well-being (however defined) is the key aim; and second, that this should be considered in the context of people's capabilities – that is, their opportunities to pursue this goal. It emphasizes a flexible and holistic approach to understanding human life, drawing attention to pluralism and needs beyond a narrow focus on the distribution of goods and resources. The key distinction between this and other discussions of justice is the recognition that there is a huge range of human diversity, and people may have different requirements and opportunities. For example, many may value a just society over a just distribution of resources, while marginalized people or groups may be ill-served by impersonal notions of faceless rational actors, each able to access justice equally.

Justice and the environment

The linkages between the environment, justice and social difference are visible in many ways, from the exposure to risk, to the access to benefits, to the consumption of resources, and to the power to influence change. As a consequence, there is considerable potential for the environment to be discussed in relation to justice. Agyeman (2005: 26) drew on existing notions of justice and applied them within an environmental perspective. He identified three key aspects, which help to develop the discussion we have had so far. First, 'procedural justice', which refers to the ability of people to be meaningfully involved; second, 'substantive' justice, relating to the right to live in a healthy environment; and third, 'distributive' justice, relating to the equitable distribution of environmental benefits. Walker (2012: 10) provided a similar interpretation, similarly identifying procedural and distributive justice, but adding the specific issue of justice as recognition, which links to decisions and corresponds to who is given respect and who is valued.

As a result, justice in environmental planning can be viewed as stretching beyond specific legal decisions on the use of land – the just process – to include also more intangible notions such as equity, fairness and representation, and their spatio-temporal considerations. For example, environmental justice may be intra- and intergenerational and may even include consideration of those who are excluded from the decision-making process.

While it can be a useful learning exercise to initially view these aspects of justice in a separate manner, in reality not only can it be difficult to highlight clear boundaries between the elements, but they may also be mutually reinforcing. Recognizing that injustice has an *interplay* helps us to understand the issue in more depth, and links this chapter with previous discussions regarding power and engagement. It can be helpful to outline with an example how the same groups may experience multiple injustices. Groups who are campaigning against the environmental impacts of a new development in their area, or an uneven allocation of environmental goods, also commonly argue that their voices are not heard in the decision-making process. Put simply, if their views were given due weight, this situation would not occur. However, this is a function of inequality more generally; those who have few resources or little recognition are likely to find it more difficult to participate in, never mind influence, the relevant discussions. Therefore, environmental injustice can be related to uneven power relations in society more generally; a vicious and self-sustaining circle of inequality where the poor have little influence and as such are less able to control the distribution of resources to become wealthier.

As raised in the previous chapter, engagement is not just a matter of advising people of decisions, or giving them information via a 'deficit' model, but considering the nature of the communities it may involve working with them to alleviate disadvantage. For example, online information may not be able to be accessed equitably by poorer groups, and their voices may subsequently be excluded. However, the influence of structural factors such as globalization and capitalism means that justice is not just a matter of adopting a different process, its dominance influences decision-making and creates an inherent unevenness for those involved – procedural idealism cannot operate outside material reality. Fainstein (2000: 469) argues that participation in public decision-making is part of the ideal of a 'just city', not just as a worthy goal, but rather as: 'benevolent authoritarianism is unlikely'. While this is no guarantee of acceptable outcomes – or procedural justice is not necessarily substantive – an awareness of principles such as democracy, diversity and equity should be part of the remit of environmental planners.

The complexity is heightened when discussions turns to context. For example, when considering the subject of justice, you may initially feel that everyone deserves a completely equal share of resources, as may occur when Rawl's veil of ignorance is applied. This is normative and simplistic, however. Inequality is a descriptive term that depicts an aspect of *difference* between groups, and while in society it is usually seen as negative or unfair, this may not necessarily be the case. Inequality in *itself* is not necessarily unjust, patterns of variability are visible everywhere and are absolutely impossible to prevent, rather it is more concerned with our cultural notions of fairness. Inevitably this is connected to value and has a relative quality. Harvey (1996) expands on this theme, arguing that it is important to understand how disparities in social conditions are produced, and from there to evaluate the justice implications rather than simply focusing on an uncritical assessment of difference.

The possible tensions between environmental and social justice complicate the topic further. The commonly advocated measure of taxation on domestic fuel to encourage changes in fossil fuel consumption is an easy illustration. It is commonly assumed that the rich consume the most fuel – they have bigger cars and use less public transport, therefore taxation in this area will hit them the hardest. However, relatively speaking, the proportion of their outlay on domestic fuel as a percentage of their earnings is significantly smaller than those who have less income. As a result, taxation to benefit the environment in this manner will affect those on the smallest incomes the most. This does not mean that financial mechanisms will always be unfair on the deprived; rather, it highlights a need for sophisticated interventions that take into account social and environmental factors.

Now that we have explored the environment and justice a little, let us start to consider the subject of environmental justice in more depth. The concept is similarly connected to equality of treatment, both with regard to accessing a clean environment and protection from harm. Much research on this topic seeks to establish whether these aspects are unfairly distributed on the basis of aspects such as class, ethnicity or income and, connected with this, whether environmental planning processes and practices are just. There are multiple definitions of environmental justice, all centred on the themes introduced at the start of this section. One clear example is: 'Environmental justice's two basic premises are first, that everyone should have the right and be able to live in a healthy environment, and second, that it is predominantly the poorest and least powerful people who are missing these conditions' (ESRC Global Environmental Change Programme, 2001: 3).

Considering this definition for a moment, we can see that it appears to have strong links to the emergence of sustainability and of the transboundary nature of many issues in environmental planning. There is also a social element that means it is associated to the politicization of the environment and related elements such as democracy and the ability to engage as discussed in the previous two chapters. Further, there is a strong anthropocentric focus, which creates a noticeable difference between ecological justice – that between species – and environmental justice more specifically. Finally, the scope of those affected and the reasons for the injustice is also broad. Justice here is not just a matter for an individual, as can frequently be seen from a legal perspective, but has a wide social range, be it a group, community, race, income class or gender. Similarly, the environmental factors in question could encompass a broad array of aspects, from contaminated land to flooding to noise.

Environmental justice is therefore a valuable addition to our understanding of the consequences of human interaction with the environment. Here, the discourse has moved on from that of conservation or stewardship as described in Chapter 2 of the book, to a more reflective and inclusive one related to people and the outcomes of their interactions with society, decisions and the environment. The concept also links to notions of sustainability; justice and equity have long been identified as being at the very heart of the sustainability discourse. It is an idea that also breaks down the persistent perceptual, if not spatial, boundaries between the wilderness and the city, or 'urban' areas and 'natural environments', to include all the areas where people live, work or spend time. Finally, it helps to highlight difference, not just between resources or places, but also between people. Indeed, as we shall see in the next section, this is where the topic originates.

Environmental racism

While there had been earlier developments in understanding the related area of social justice as a theory (for example, Harvey, 1973) and numerous examples of disaffection from this perspective coalescing into social action, environmental justice has a slightly different history. As a movement, commentators identified a number of notable examples in the 1970s and early 1980s in the USA that helped in its eventual emergence. Bullard (1999) highlights a specific incident, in 1982 in Warren County, North Carolina, which he argues proved the catalyst. More than 500 people were arrested trying to stop the state dumping contaminated soil into a landfill site located in a deprived area. As a result of this protest, a study was conducted regarding the siting of hazardous waste more generally, which identified how the sites were located disproportionately in predominantly African-American areas (US General Accounting Office, 1983). A powerful term was coined to describe this uneven situation: environmental racism.

Bullard's *Dumping in Dixie: Race, Class and Environmental Quality* (1990, xv) is one of the key accounts that links environmental justice explicitly to ethnicity, highlighting the insidious and often unfair consequences of environmental pollution. In his examination of four US states, Bullard found that, because of their economic and political vulnerability, African-American communities in the South have been targeted routinely for the siting of noxious facilities, locally unwanted land uses and environmental hazards. As a consequence, they are likely to suffer greater environmental and health risks than the general population. Bullard argued there were four causes of this unequal distribution. First, potential polluters chose to site facilities where they were least likely to face resistance from inhabitants. Second, this was more likely to be in poorer communities that were underrepresented in political processes that tended to be dominated by white, wealthy and educated citizens. Third, there was an illusion of choice; even if they wished to move from the site, poverty renders inhabitants immobile. Finally, crime, housing and the short-term economic gains of having employing industries nearby may be higher on the list of priorities than environmental matters.

Though situated within the realm of social justice, the early emergence of environmental justice was connected to race and fuelled by a grassroots activist base. It grew in response to information becoming known regarding the nature of toxic and hazardous waste material on the health of certain communities, but as the subject matured it was found that other disadvantaged groups, irrespective of their race or ethnicity, might be deprived of justice in this area. Box 10.1 describes a high-profile example that highlights how injustice can occur, and how residents may mobilize in response: the tragedy of Love Canal in New York in 1978.

Along with examples such as the Love Canal tragedy, researchers began to examine the theoretical and practical basis of environmental injustices. However, unpicking the nuances of data to prove the reasons for injustice can be problematic. For example, is the main cause of a problem systemic racism, or is it a one-off case? Malicious intent by decision-makers on this specific basis can be difficult to prove. Pulido (2000) invoked the term 'white

Box 10.1 The Love Canal tragedy

In the late nineteenth century, an entrepreneur, William T. Love, wanted to build a new US city and planned to build a kilometre-long canal from Niagara Falls to provide hydroelectric energy. The canal was completed but remained dry when his plans failed to come to fruition. The pit was subsequently purchased as a convenient site for the dumping of municipal refuse by the City of Niagara Falls, and later the disposal of toxic waste by the Hooker Electrochemical Company, until it was eventually sealed in clay, covered in soil and declared safe. The land was sold in 1953 to the Niagara Falls School Board for only US$1, with a somewhat suspiciously detailed caveat that limited the liability of the selling company with regard to hazardous waste. The land was subsequently used to build an elementary school and houses.

In 1976, heavy rains caused some seepage of toxic waste to come to the surface. The building work had damaged the integrity of the clay seal and because of a lack of monitoring or any general warnings to residents concerning the hazardous history of the site no one acted on the potential danger. Soon afterwards, the effects of this were felt: sickness, miscarriages and birth defects were at abnormally high levels, and reporters and residents began to campaign for an investigation. Eventually, the toxic causes were discovered and the residents evacuated after the area was formally declared unsafe (see Blum 2008 for an in-depth study).

In the absence of official action, grassroots groups mobilized to, first, demand that attention was paid to the problem, and then that there was redress for the harm provided. This was a notable example of an environmental movement that was not based on politics or worldviews as in the past, but rather on directly experienced injustice. Moreover, a link was made between environmental harm and poverty: the inhabitants were predominantly working-class and engaged in a battle with powerful institutions. The incident led to new legislation and, perhaps more importantly, changes in perception among Americans concerning risk, responsibility and social justice. The case linked the environment beyond issues of process or regulation to social issues connected with the distribution of power, such as class, income or race. The year 2000 film *Erin Brockovich* is based on a similar environmental justice battle, with citizens investigating and then campaigning against the presence of hazardous industrial pollution that has contaminated groundwater.

privilege' to highlight how it is not always empirically easy to identify the person or agency that is definitively responsible: even a society that purports to be 'colour-blind' may unwittingly be reinforcing structural inequalities. An example here would be the suburbanization of Los Angeles, where the increased mobility of people with money, the so-called 'white flight', left inner-city ghettoes that were predominately black. Therefore, the typical social and spatial processes of urban development, which are absent from any specific malicious intent, can also create disadvantaged spaces within which environmental injustice can occur.

This argument brings us to our final issue: determining the relationship between race and low income. Or, put simply, is the injustice caused by racism or poverty? A pioneering paper by Freeman (1972) correlated US census data on income, housing and race with information on exposure to pollution, and demonstrated that there was a relationship between wealth distribution and environmental quality – something one may instinctively suspect but it can be difficult to prove. More recently, in a study of disaster recovery in New Orleans after Hurricane Katrina, it was discovered that lower-class and even middle-class African Americans, Latinos and Asians were disproportionately exposed to environmental risks (Pastor *et al.*, 2006). So, injustices may be compounded, because wealth disadvantage exacerbates other disparities, including race. The converse is also true, of course: those in a higher income bracket, regardless of race, wield a disproportionate amount of power. The ability to move away to a better neighbourhood or to 'buy' their way out of a risk depends greatly on income. The affordability of insurance is a good example here. In addition to the complicating factor of wealth, asserting race as the primary injustice may also serve to marginalize other significant cleavages, such as class and gender, which may also be at play. Here we can also see how the development of the subject of environmental racism, with its heightened appreciation of difference, disadvantage and the environment, led us to the broader concept of environmental justice.

Environmental justice

As a social movement, environmental justice was slow to spread beyond the USA with its particular demographic composition, well-established civil rights movements and heightened awareness of difference. For example, Agyeman (2000: 7) claimed that for many people in the UK:

> 'environmental' and 'justice' do not sit easily together. At best, their combination evokes a memory of some distant news report or documentary of how communities of colour and poor communities in the US face a disproportionate toxic risk when compared with white middle class communities, and at worst the combination fails to register a signal.

Since this time, however, researchers across the globe are finding similarly strong correlations between environmental harm and the most deprived sectors of society. There is, however, a noticeable divergence in how difference may become manifest as environmental injustice across cultural contexts.

Initially, the focus of environmental justice research was on specific environmental exposures contained within a discrete locality or country. Research typically focused on issues relating to land use or waste facilities, often reflecting the concerns of ordinary citizens. For example, in the UK it was discovered that the distribution of Industrial Pollution Control sites were disproportionately clustered in deprived areas (Walker *et al.*, 2005). These visible, and local, spatial impacts are not the only concern, however. In a national study of air quality it was discovered that it was the poorest communities that both receive the most pollution and emit the least (Mitchell and Dorling, 2003). The early focus of environmental justice here had a substantive element. It was essentially reacting to what Beck (1992) referred to as manufactured environmental risks – for example, toxic sites or air pollution. Significantly, a factor that exacerbated inequality and highlighted the importance of wider procedural justice is that the burden of proof tended to be on the victims.

This does, however, lead to a debate on the ability to prove injustice. There are some important qualifications over the interpretation of statistical data that can occur when plotting environmental exposures. In particular, we should be cautious about making wider generalizations and drawing hasty conclusions, since there may be high levels of empirical uncertainty (Bowen, 2002). As in the previous section, claiming that there is an identifiable pattern of inequality is not the same as discovering what caused that inequality. Moreover, it is difficult to maintain that inequality is necessarily unjust. Issues of justice may be a matter of opinion – that is, they are felt subjectively. This can be hard to assess quantitatively and implies a certain amount of ethical judgement in considering what a disproportionate impact might be, and how environmental planning should respond. A further qualification is the spatial scale on which such research is conducted, which can influence the strength of the correlation between factors such as race or poverty and environmental pollution. It follows from this that it is difficult to apportion responsibility and blame for environmental injustice, and that we must be careful in formulating policies and regulation. Equally, in practice there may also be differences in the ways that researchers interpret notions of justice and how the courts do so, with difficulties experienced with regard to proving intent, or the links between environmental impacts, particular social groups and demonstrable harm (Mitchell and Dorling, 2003).

From this overview we can see that environmental justice has a number of conceptual and empirical considerations, and that the focus can differ between cultural and legal contexts. Moreover, applying notions of justice to the environment does raise a number of questions, most notably what should (or shouldn't) be distributed, among whom and when? Or what should the process be? We can also begin to appreciate how the topic may link with environmental planning more fundamentally because of its focus on land, resources and pollution, its capability to address social concerns, and with key issues such as sustainability, all of which can further complicate matters. For example, is justice to be applied simply to those humans currently alive in particular countries, or is there a deeper understanding that expands the concept beyond these narrow spatio-temporal boundaries?

Justice and sustainability

As a concept, justice clearly has a number of similarities to sustainability. Indeed, it fits remarkably well with what we already know of key themes associated with the concept; in particular, that of a better quality of life, principles of fair engagement in decision-making, or equity within and between generations and species. Distributive justice can also link to core sustainability debates, such as resource allocation, access to environmental goods and protection from harm. Yet there are also noticeable differences related to approach, scale and those interested in the subject. Sustainable development can be viewed as being oriented towards policy and has a strong top-down element, while environmental justice has its roots in a bottom-up movement. Environmental justice can also tend to have a reactive, short-term focus on a site scale, while sustainability can be viewed as more proactive and related to integrated, strategic issues. Finally, advocates of sustainable development are also more likely to be more professional, better educated and live in differing areas in comparison to the more activist-orientated nature of environmental justice (Agyeman, 2005).

The *principles* underlying social and ecological justice apparent in the sustainable development discourse do, however, have a resonance to that of environmental justice. One of the values of combining an understanding of environmental justice with that of the more common social justice is with regard to synthesis. Environmental problems, resource use or land use change all have social implications and: 'by seeing social justice issues through an environmental lens, and vice versa by analyzing environmental issues more clearly in terms of social justice, new and more effective ways for dealing with each can be developed than if, as is usually the case at present, each is dealt with separately' (ESRC Global Environmental Change Programme, 2001: 3). Expanding on this integrative view, Dobson (1998) argued that the conceptualization of justice could have a triangular design, where the present and future generations of humans occupy two points, and with non-human species represented in the third. Interestingly, arguments linking justice with sustainability emphasize that consideration should be given to the effects that intervention strategies may have on future generations and non-human species, which, considering that neither has a voice, can be both a speculative endeavour and be difficult to prove from a legal perspective.

While some interpretations of justice do resonate with sustainability, it should not be assumed that pursuing a policy focused on one will automatically achieve the other. For example, Dobson (1998: 24) noted that the environmental justice movement in the USA: 'seems, stubbornly, to be much more about human justice than about the natural environment – or, rather, it is only about the natural environment inasmuch as it ... can be seen in terms of human justice'. This may provide a narrow, anthropocentric lens that can restrict non-human issues. Furthermore, from what we know so far, both justice and sustainable development have a multiplicity of meanings, which will challenge the synergistic application of these topics in practice. For example, social justice goals will depend on the concept of sustainability that is used; do we preserve what we already have, or do we search for alternative ways of renewing existing sources? Perhaps more critically, since justice concerns the distribution of goods with no real specification that these goods may actually be finite or in need of conservation, it may conflict with notions of limits and needs that are critical to sustainability.

Agyeman and Evans (2004) are less convinced that sustainability and justice are conceptually incompatible. They propose the notion of 'just sustainability' in recognition that there are enough overlaps to suggest that environmental justice and sustainability can come together. They reject the idea that environmental justice is only ever about sharing risk equally rather than getting rid of risk altogether. Further, in recognition that outside the USA there may be a lack of a grassroots movement, they suggest that the principles may be equally valid when applied by centralized policy actors and professionals, such as those concerned with environmental planning. This in turn highlights the importance of social justice to this field, since: 'the unjust society is unlikely to be sustainable in environmental or economic terms; the social tensions that are created undermine the recognition of reciprocal rights and obligations, leading to environmental degradation and ultimately to political breakdown' (Haughton, 1999: 234). Justice can therefore be thought of as operating both as a critical part of sustainability and as a stand-alone principle for consideration.

Conclusion

> 'In arguing about environmental justice, we are not addressing nature, but humanity. Nature does not know justice, and if we try to derive values from any other source other than humanity we get into trouble.'
>
> (Low and Gleeson, 1998: 33)

While the idea of environmental justice is relatively new, *injustice* relating to the environmental can frequently be found in the pages of history: it is a perennial issue related to differences and inequalities in societies more generally. Though the most striking practical examples may be at the local level, the concept can provide more than an insight into the distribution of what may be called environmental 'bads', such as pollution or the location of certain undesirable sites, or even unequal access to environmental 'goods'. It is, as the opening quote from Low and Gleeson suggests, connected with humanity and its values.

The focus in environmental planning on aspects such as distribution, recognition, participation and capabilities means that it has strong synergies with many conceptions of justice. Environmental planning also concerns space, materials, costs and benefits, but frequently the approach can be a simplistic one centred on location, design or construction – or, in short, the 'where'. An appreciation of environmental justice deliberately tests this bounded rationality and links well with 'moral' traditions connected with the environment, such as ethics and stewardship. Yet, while it can supplement discussions concerning 'where' its application can experience difficulties regarding 'what' it stands for and 'how' this should be realized.

Beyond this there may well be tensions between aspects of justice, such as can be observed between globally distributed justice and justice to future generations, or social and environmental goals. Arguments that wish to restrict fossil fuel use in developing nations may bring a global benefit but it will slow development and affect the wealth of both current and future generations in the countries concerned. Justice is also not just a matter of *opposition* to possible environmental harm, because sites such as nuclear power stations and waste facilities can provide employment opportunities as well as making environmental impacts in an area, and as a result they can be seen as attractive or unattractive propositions dependent upon people's views. If the development goes ahead, this can provide an example of a just process, an uneven distribution, but a just outcome. Equally, restricting the development of housing in desirable rural areas to preserve environmental goods may not only bring justice for local people; it might also bring injustice by restricting economic opportunities and affordability for younger generations. In this way, 'the project of maintaining capital, far from being a means to securing intergenerational justice, is simply a way of translating present injustices into the future' (Holland, 1999: 68).

Academic literature on environmental justice has usually explored either the philosophical and political conditions, or specific cases of inequality, and as such this chapter has tried to bridge the gap between the two. As occurs with the case of engagement, just *processes* may not in themselves create just *outcomes*. What becomes immensely important when considering issues of justice and equity is being very careful about the design of the process, the information used to make decisions, and how people are involved. For example, as explored in Chapter 6, if science, rationality or expert knowledge is privileged in the construction and framing of problems or risks, then arguably it is part of the system that can perpetuate injustice. A narrow focus on limited public engagement processes may mean neither procedural nor substantive justice may be achieved. Equally, just providing more opportunities to participate can favour those with resources, expertise and time available; and more governance or expanded processes may mean that those who are already well represented in the processes of public decision-making have even greater access. Effective environmental justice may demand something more interventionist than a level playing field or a broad-brush approach, which places real demands on those concerned with environmental planning.

Chapter 11

Conclusion

'The environment, which seems to be no more than an independent parameter of human existence, actually is its opposite: nature as thoroughly transfigured by human intervention.'

(Giddens, 1994: 77)

Initially, the area of environmental planning seems to be a very practical subject: one concerned with designation, regulation or consents, and where there is a series of resources or processes that needs to be *managed*. This is an instrumental view, which fits well if, for example, we understand the purpose of politics and policy to be organizing activities similarly concerned with the control and distribution of resources. But when one delves deeper into the broad area of environmental planning it quickly becomes apparent that this perception is not just inaccurate, but may actually serve to underpin many of the 'environmental problems' present in contemporary societies. As the opening quote from Giddens illustrates, not only are issues rooted in culture and society, but their categorization as a concern is itself a construct. Inevitably, some will capture the public imagination while others appear more marginal or do not link well to self-interest arguments where environmental planning can be framed as a means of improving our own lives or those of future generations. Critically, this is not always connected to the magnitude of an issue; rather, to a host of wider aspects such as their ease of identification, public profile, possible impact on powerful lobby groups or the costs of management. Reflecting on these factors also highlights why certain concerns remain stubbornly unaddressed. From this perspective, environmental planning, politics and policy are much more than a mere contest over space or resources; they are opportunities to reconsider the connectivity between human and natural systems.

If one thing is clear from this book, it is that 'nature is nothing if it is not social' (Smith, 1990: 30). As outlined in the opening quote to this chapter, this goes beyond a mere changing of the landscape to be so comprehensive a socialization that it leads some to suggest that we have witnessed the 'end of nature', a situation where the natural world is now affected by humanity to such an extent that it can arguably be deemed artificial (McKibben, 1989). For example, even the climate, the air or the seas – those most fundamental of environmental processes – are not immune to change. As such, it is important to note that we do not simply do 'things' to the environment, in doing so we alter something we ourselves are part of and sometimes in a wholly unforeseen manner. In 1876 Frederick Engels outlined this dialectical relationship with the following observation:

> Let us not, however, flatter ourselves overmuch on account of our human victories over nature. For each such victory nature takes its revenge on us. Each victory, it is true, in the first place brings about the results we expected, but in the second and third places it has quite different, unforeseen effects which only too often cancel the first. (1978: 13)

The local impacts of transformed landscapes or the global effects of any altered atmospheric composition provide evidence of this interconnectivity.

Understanding this complexity is part of designing effective intervention strategies, but it may also stray too far from the comfort of rational processes and norms to the extent that some may be left with the opinion that, if environment planning is everything, then maybe it is nothing – a loose term that could be used to encompass anything you would like to see changed. This is a tricky question that has been raised in a comparable manner with regard to similarly inclusive topics, such as planning (Wildavsky, 1973), sustainability (Næss, 2001) or nature (Castree, 2005). But while the subject is inclusive there are still defined parameters and rationalities in existence, which, combined with long-standing processes and practices, can help us to bridge the divide between the theory and practice of environmental planning.

In Chapter 1 it was argued that, while humans and the environment are inextricably linked, in practice this symbiotic relationship may not be reflected in how the environment is perceived, managed or interacted with. This is neatly outlined by Leopold's (1949: 6) famous allegory: 'There are two spiritual dangers in not owning a farm. One is the danger of supposing that breakfast comes from the grocery, and the other that heat comes from the furnace'. Chapter

2 in particular discussed the forces that drive and perpetuate this dualism, and introduced how these intellectual legacies found their way into environmental planning. Rooted in the advances of the Enlightenment, the Industrial Revolution and 'Western' thought more generally, this view tends to divide the world into two: whether built and natural, town and country, or urban and rural, erecting barriers between the environment and society more generally.

This perspective has resulted in what Castree (2005: 224) refers to as an 'ontological schism', one that inevitably sets these sequestered elements on collision courses, with the environment, or nature, being considered to be what society is not, and vice versa. This separation may also lead to a distorted perception of the environment and society relationship and lead to more hierarchal thinking, where humanity is usually considered as being superior. Harvey (1996) highlights how the dominant Western worldview actively perceives the world as a series of things that can be isolated, deconstructed and analysed; where nature is thought to be subject to immutable laws that operate outside and beyond our narrow and transient social perspectives. This is an essentialist view, one that reduces the environment to an unchanging essence that masks its mutability and contrasts sharply with society's dynamism. Freudenburg *et al.* (1995: 388) argue that the uncritical acceptance of this dualism can inhibit the ability to manage the environment, suggesting that: 'we run the risk of having our vision distorted by the very taken-for-grantedness of our socially agreed upon definitions – the risk of being prisoners of our own perspectives'.

This, in turn, links the field to socio-cultural perspectives concerning the persuasiveness of intervention arguments, which were subsequently explored in Chapter 3 on 'Governance and Power' and Chapter 4 on 'Politics and the Media'. Knowledge and thoughts about the environment are socially constructed: that is, their meaning is determined through culturally variable lenses. In this sense, it is the social context of the inquiry, not the independent variable, that constructs the reality. In practice, views of the environment are subject to the competing worldviews of a multiplicity of actors and agencies. The environment is tangible, and performs practical roles, but it is also helpful to understand that the sense of what is 'real' is also imagined, it is subject to our individual perception. In much the same way that a landscape painting may depict a vision of the environment that may differ from person to person, culture, experiences and sources of information, from the media to our hobbies, all contribute to how people individually 'see' the world. This is important to bear in mind in later parts of the book, when consideration of engagement and justice help to shed light on why there may be disagreement on environmental planning interventions, and why this changes spatially and temporally. This relative and dynamic viewpoint may be feel odd initially, especially if one is used to seeing nature as 'real', something static or fixed 'that stubs your toe when you trip over it' (Whatmore, 1999: 7).

Significantly, this stance also has a legacy for how the central topics in this book are considered within scientific and policy decision-making spheres, as explored in Chapters 5 to 7. The environment, planning, politics and policy are often researched and studied independently of one another, in accordance with long-standing empiricist scientific approaches and disciplinary norms. This includes, but is by no means confined to, the artificial divisions placed between the natural and social sciences, human and physical geography, or urban and environmental planning. Such an approach may constrain the importance of these relationships, but while notions of systems, networks, hybrids or 'post-natural' thinking actively reject this standpoint, they may not mesh well with norms of science, policy-making or decision support tools.

In this context it is not surprising that consensus on environmental concerns can be difficult to achieve. For example, the IPCC represents an attempt to provide a strong, clear view from the scientific community that dangerous climate change is occurring due to human activity. Yet significant action still does not occur and it is commonplace for the public across the world to express doubt regarding both the causes of climate change and the level of scientific agreement (Anderreg *et al.*, 2010). It is not only aspects of politics, media balance or general risk communication that obscure messages such as these, there may also be vested interests who benefit from the status quo deliberately aiming to manufacture doubt (Oreskes and Conway, 2010). This is a critical issue, since perceived scientific consensus is pivotal to a public acceptance of science and the associated requirement for action. While multiple truth claims are an essential function of democracy, it does make effective environmental planning a problematic subject – and one with which scientists, policy-makers and institutions of governance occasionally struggle to negotiate.

The issues discussed in this regard will also continue to evolve, and perhaps ever more rapidly. New media configurations and academic forays into the social media and blogging may improve communication skills, public engagement and impact, all of which can enhance the understanding of environmental planning and loosen the shackles of traditional media imperatives. Yet, while these media have the potential to better communicate issues, these are not neutral and objective, and in some cases can even provide a legitimate platform for more extreme views. What we know from the material covered so far is that the way environmental issues are conceptualized, framed or understood will influence the extent to which they can be politicized and acted upon.

The focus of the discussion in this book has been relatively anthropocentric, in that environmental concerns are commonly analysed and considered in respect of how they interact with the institutions and processes that shape intervention, including reference to particular sections of society, whether it is an individual, a private sector company or a government agency. Such a cacophony can blur the relationship between environmental and social concerns. While nature may not have a 'voice', it does have many who opt to speak on its behalf, or, perhaps more accurately, multiple representatives, each arguing its own interpretation (Latour, 2004). These crowded political arenas within which environmental discourses of cause, effect and intervention take place demand the attention of a wide array of stakeholders. They not only represent the natural world and compensate for its muteness, but also champion the causes of specific sections of society as the socio-economic ramifications of changes to the status quo draw in actors and agencies beyond the traditional academic and policy spheres. These groups can operate across national boundaries and are engaged in a discursive competition to frame environmental concerns and mobilize action to correspond with their own worldviews or interests. Beck (2009: 86) argues that this encompassing reach is not necessarily a function of the globality of problems as diagnosed by science, rather of the 'transnational discourse coalitions' that place environmental threats on public agendas on a global scale. Environmental planning is truly both a global and local activity, and, as explored in Chapters 9 and 10, issues connected to engagement and justice challenge the bounded nature of many traditional processes and practices.

In conclusion, projections regarding nature are inescapably tied up with the broader socio-cultural forces that shape how it may be valued. From the locally focused farmer to the internationally oriented government minister, the interplay between environment, people and society will differ. Notions of the environment therefore do not start beyond the city limits, nor might they be thought of as being a discrete physical space. The natural world and our interactions with it are dynamic and may be better understood by reflecting *inwards*, engaging with the kinds of societies we wish to inhabit, as well as *outwards* to particular places or spaces.

So, while it seems clear that the environment may be everything around us, there is a more philosophical question with which to grapple: to what extent do we consider ourselves to be a part of it? When we discuss the environment, we do not simply pass comment on something 'out there'; the ways in which we give it meaning provide an accurate reflection of how we see society. It reveals itself to be a strong cultural signifier that can shed light on a host of issues, from one's upbringing to one's political views. In this sense, the environment can be thought of as a proxy battleground, not with regard to notions of economic growth versus conservation, or simply trying to stop unwanted development, but as a deeper narrative concerned with the kinds of societies we would like to inhabit in the future.

References

ABC News (2005) *Poll: Most Say God Not a Factor in Hurricanes*, 2 October. Available at: http://abcnews.go.com/Politics/PollVault/story?id=1174220&page=1; accessed 22 August 2014.

Adams, J. (1995) *Risk*, London: University College London Press.

Adger, N. (2000) 'Social and ecological resilience: are they related?', *Progress in Human Geography*, Vol. 24, pp. 347–64.

Agyeman, J. (2000) *Environmental Justice: From the Margins to the Mainstream?*, London: Town and Country Planning Association.

Agyeman, J. (2005) *Sustainable Communities and the Challenge of Environmental Justice*, London: New York University Press.

Agyeman, J. and Evans, B. (2004) '"Just sustainability": the emerging discourse of environmental justice in Britain?', *Geographical Journal*, Vol. 170, No. 2, pp.155–64.

Allmendinger, P. (2002) 'Towards a post-positivist typology of planning theory', *Planning Theory*, Vol. 1, pp. 77–99.

Anderreg, W. R. L., Prall, J. W., Harold, J. and Schneider, S. H. (2010) 'Expert credibility in climate change', *Proceedings of the National Academy of Sciences*, Vol. 107, No.27, pp. 12107–09.

Aristotle (1965 [350 BC]) *Historia Animalium*, trans. A. L. Peck, Cambridge: Harvard University Press.

Aristotle (1977 [350 BC]) *Politics*, trans. B. Jowett, Pennsylvania: The Franklin Library.

Arnstein, S. R. (1969) 'A ladder of citizen participation', *American Institute of Planning Journal*, Vol. 35, No. 4, pp. July, pp. 216–24.

Arrhenius, S. (1908) *Worlds in the Making: The Evolution of the Universe*, trans. Dr H. Borns, London/New York: Harper & Brothers.

Ashworth, W. (1954) *The Genesis of Modern British Town Planning*, London: Routledge & Kegan Paul.

Astleithner, F., Hamedinger, A., Holman, N. and Rydin, Y. (2004) 'Institutions and indicators – the discourse about indicators in the context of sustainability', *Journal of Housing and the Built Environment*, Vol. 19, pp. 7–24.

Bacon, F. (2001 [1627]) *The New Atlantis*, Raleigh, NC: Alex Catalogue.

Barry, J. (1999) *Rethinking Green Politics: Nature, Virtue and Progress*, London: Sage.

Bauer, R. A. (ed.) (1966) *Social Indicators*, Cambridge, MA/ London: MIT Press.

BBC (1999) *France Keeps British Beef Ban*, 8 December. Available at: http://news.bbc.co.uk/1/hi/world/europe/556089.stm; accessed 5 April 2014.

Beck, U. (1992) *Risk Society – Towards a New Modernity*, London: Sage.

Beck, U. (2009) *World at Risk*, Cambridge: Polity Press.

Bennett, W. L. (1996) 'An introduction to journalism norms and representations of politics', *Political Communication*, Vol. 13, No. 4, pp. 373–84.

Berdyaev, N. (1962) *The Meaning of History*, Cleveland, OH: The World Publishing Company).

Berkes, F. (2002) 'Cross–scale institutional linkages: perspectives from the bottom up', in E. Ostrom, T. Dietz, D. Nives, P. C. Stern, S. Stonich and E. U. Weber (eds, pp. *The Drama of the Commons*, Washington: National Academies Press, pp. 293–321.

Bernoulli, J. (1713) *Ars conjectandi, opus posthumum. Accedit Tractatus de seriebus infinitis, et epistola gallicé scripta de ludo pilae reticularis*, Basel: Thurneysen Brothers.

Bevir, M. and Rhodes, R. (2003) *Interpreting British Governance*, London/ New York: Routledge).

Black, J. T. (1996) 'The economics of sprawl', *Urban Land*, Vol. 55, No.3, pp. 52–3.

Blum, E. D. (2008) *Love Canal Revisited: Race, Class, and Gender in Environmental Activism*, Lawrence, KS: University Press of Kansas.

Blumer, H. (1955) 'Collective behaviour', in A. McClung-Lee (ed.), pp. *Principles of Sociology*, New York: Barnes & Noble, pp. 165–98.

Bosher, L. S. (ed.) (2008) *Hazards and the Built Environment: Attaining Built-in Resilience*, London: Taylor & Francis.

Botero, G. (1956 [1589]) *Reason of State*, trans. P. J. Waley and D. P. Waley, London: Routledge & Kegan Paul.

Bowen, W. (2002) 'An analytical review of environmental justice research: what do we really know?', *Environmental Management*, Vol. 29, No. 1, pp. 3–15.

Boykov, M. T. and Boykov, J. M. (2004) 'Balance as bias: global warming and the U.S. prestige press', *Global Environmental Change*, Vol. 15, No. 2, pp. 125–36.

Boykov, M. T. and Boykov, J. M. (2007) 'Climate change and journalistic norms: a case-study of US mass-media coverage', *Geoforum*, Vol. 38, pp. 1190–204.

Bradley, R. L. (2009) *Capitalism at Work: Business, Government, and Energy*, Salem, MA: M & M Scrivener Press.

Brand, F. S. and Jax, K. (2007) 'Focusing the meaning(s) of resilience: resilience as a descriptive concept and a boundary object', *Ecology and Society*, Vol. 12, No. 1, pp. 1–16.

Brulle, R. J., Carmichael, J. and Jenkins, J. C. (2012) 'Shifting public opinion on climate change: an empirical assessment of factors influencing concern over climate change in the U.S.', *Climatic Change*, Vol. 114, No. 2, 169–88.

Bucchi, M. (1998) *Science and the Media: Alternative Routes in Scientific Communication*, London: Routledge.

Bullard, R. (1990) *Dumping in Dixie: Race, Class and Environmental Quality*, Boulder, CO: Westview Press.

Bullard, R. (1999) 'Dismantling environmental racism in the USA', *Local Environment: The International Journal of Justice and Sustainability*, Vol. 4, No. 1, pp. 5–19.

Burby, R. J. (2006) 'Hurricane Katrina and the paradoxes of government disaster policy: bringing about wise governmental decisions for hazardous areas', *The Annals of the American Academy of Political and Social Science*, Vol. 604, No. 1, pp. 171–91.

Cabinet Office (2014) *Her Majesty's Most Gracious Speech to Both Houses of Parliament at the State Opening of Parliament 2014*, London: Cabinet Office.

Callendar, G. S. (1938) 'The artificial production of carbon dioxide and its influence on temperature', *Quarterly Journal of the Royal Meteorological Society*, Vol. 64, No. 275, pp. 223–40.

Campbell, H. and Marshall, B. (2006) 'Towards justice in planning: a re-appraisal', *European Planning Studies*, Vol. 14, No. 2, pp. 239–52.

Carey, J. (ed.) (2000) *The Faber Book of Utopias*, London: Faber & Faber.

Carley, M. (1981) *Social Measurement and Social Indicators: Issues of Policy and Theory*, London: George Allen & Unwin.

Carson, R. (1962) *Silent Spring*, Boston, MA: Houghton Mifflin.

Carter, J. and White, I. (2012) 'Environmental planning in an age of uncertainty: the case of the Water Framework Directive', *Journal of Environmental Planning and Management*, Vol. 113, pp. 228–36.

Carvalho, A. (2007) 'Ideological cultures and media discourses on scientific knowledge: re-reading news on climate change', *Public Understanding of Science*, Vol. 16, pp. 223–43.

Carvalho, A. and Burgess, J. (2005) 'Cultural circuits of climate change in U.K. broadsheet newspapers 1985–2003', *Society for Risk Analysis*, Vol. 25, No.6, pp. 1457–69.

Castells, M. (1978) *City, Class and Power*, London: Macmillan.

Castells, M. (1996) *The Rise of the Network Society*, Oxford: Blackwell.

Castree, N. (2005) *Nature*, London: Routledge.

Catton, W. R. Jr and Dunlap, R. E. (1978) 'Environmental sociology: a new paradigm', *The American Sociologist*, Vol. 13, pp. 41–9.

Cavan, G. and Kingston, R. (2012) 'Development of a climate change risk and vulnerability assessment tool for urban areas', *International Journal of Disaster Resilience in the Built Environment*, Vol. 3, No.3, pp. 253–69.

Cherry, G. E. (1996) *Town Planning in Britain since 1900: The Rise and Fall of the Planning Ideal*, Oxford: Blackwell.

Chhotray, V. and Stoker, G. (2008) *Governance Theory and Practice: A Cross-Disciplinary Approach*, New York: Palgrave Macmillan.

Clegg, S. R. (1989) *Frameworks of Power*, London: Sage.

Clegg, S. R. and Haugaard, M. (eds) (2009) *The Sage Handbook of Power*, London: Sage.

Commoner, B. (1966) *Science and Survival*, New York: Viking Press.

Connelly, J. and Smith, G. (2003) *Politics and the Environment: From Theory to Practice*, London and New York: Routledge.

Cooke, B. and Khotari, U. (eds.) *Participation: The New Tyranny*, London: Zed Books.

Copernicus, N. (1995 1543*) On the Revolutions of Heavenly Spheres*, New York: Prometheus Books.

Corner, A. and Pidgeon, N. (2010) 'Geoengineering the climate: the social and ethical implications', *Environment: Science and Policy for Sustainable Development*, Vol. 52, pp. 24–37.

Correia, D. (2013) 'F**k Jared Diamond', *Capitalism Nature Socialism*, Vol. 24, No. 4, pp. 1–6.

Cosgrove, D. (1984) *Social Formation and Symbolic Landscapes*, Madison, WI: University of Wisconsin Press.

Cronon, W. (1993) 'The uses of environmental history', *Environmental History Review*, Vol. 17, No. 3, pp. 1–22.

Cronon, W. (1995) 'The trouble with wilderness; or, getting back to the wrong nature', in W. Cronon (ed.), *Uncommon Ground*, New York: W. W. Norton, pp. 69–90.

Crosby, A. W. (1995) 'The past and present of environmental history', *American Historical Review*, Vol. 100, No. 4, pp. 1177–89.

Dahl, R. A. (1957) 'The concept of power', *Behavioural Science*, Vol. 2, No. 3, pp. 201–15.

Darwin, C. (1859) *On the Origin of the Species*, London: John Murray.

David, P. A. (1985) 'Clio and the economics of QWERTY', *American Economic Review*, Vol. 75, No. 2, pp. 332–7.

Davidoff, P. (1965) 'Advocacy and pluralism in planning', *Journal of the American Institute of Planners*, Vol. 31, No. 6, pp. 331–8.

Davoudi, S. (2006) 'Evidence-based planning: rhetoric or reality', *DISP*, Vol. 165, No. 2, pp. 14–24.

Defra (Department for Environment, Food & Rural Affairs) (2011) *The Natural Choice: Securing the Value of Nature*, London: The Stationery Office.

Diamond, J. (1997) *Guns, Germs and Steel: The Fates of Human Societies*, New York: W. W. Norton.

Dietz, T., Ostrom, E. and Stern, P. C. (2003) 'The struggle to govern the commons', *Science*, Vol. 302, pp. 1907–12.

Dimitrov, R. S. (2010) 'Inside Copenhagen: the state of climate governance', *Global Environmental Politics*, Vol. 10, No. 2, pp. 18–24.

Dobson, A. (1998) *Justice and the Environment: Conceptions of Environmental Sustainability and Theories of Distributive Justice*, Oxford: Oxford University Press.

Dobson, A. (2003) *Citizenship and the Environment*, Oxford: Oxford University Press.

Dobson, A. (2012) *Green Political Thought*, London: Routledge.

Dobson, A. and Eckersley, R. (2006) *Political Theory and the Ecological Challenge*, (Cambridge: Cambridge University Press).

Doherty, B. (1992) 'The fundi–realo controversy: an analysis of four European green parties', *Environmental Politics*, Vol. 1, No. 1, pp. 95–120.

Donner, S. and McDaniels, J. (2013) 'The influence of national temperature fluctuations on opinions about climate change in the U.S. since 1990', *Climatic Change*, Vol. 118, No. 3, pp. 537–50.

Dostaler, G. (2007) *Keynes and his Battles*, Cheltenham: Edward Elgar.

Douglas, M. (1992) *Risk and Blame: Essays in Cultural Theory*, London: Routledge.

Douglas, M. and Wildavsky, A. (1983) *Risk and Culture: An Essay on the Selection of Technical and Environmental Dangers*, Berkeley, CA: University of California Press.

Dryzek, J. (1997) *The Politics of the Earth: Environmental Discourses*, Oxford: Oxford University Press.

Eckersley, R. (1992) *Environmentalism and Political Theory*, London: UCL Press.

Eckersley, R. (2004) *The Green State: Rethinking Democracy and Sovereignty*, Cambridge, MA: MIT Press.

Ehrlich, P. (1968) *The Population Bomb*, New York: Buccaneer Books.

Ehrlich, P. and Ehrlich, A. (1990) *The Population Explosion*, London: Hutchinson.

Ellis, E. C. and Ramankutty, N. (2008) 'Putting people in the map: anthropogenic biomes of the world', *Frontiers in Ecology and the Environment*, Vol. 6, No. 8, pp. 439–47.

Emerson, R. W. (2009) *Essays and Lectures*, Lawrence, KS: Digireads.com Publishing).

Engels, F. (1978) *The Part Played by Labour in the Transition from Ape to Man*, Moscow: Progress Publishers.

Entman, R. M. (2004) *Projections of Power: Framing News, Public Opinion, and U.S. Foreign Policy*, Chicago: University of Chicago Press.

Environment Agency (2000) *An Environmental Vision*, Bristol: Environment Agency.

Environment Agency (2006) *Using Science to Create a Better Place: Environment Agency Scenarios 2030*, Bristol: Environment Agency.

Environment Agency (2009) *Flooding in England: A National Assessment of Flood Risk*, Bristol: Environment Agency.

Environment Agency (2011) *Understanding the Risks, Empowering Communities, Building Resilience: The National Flood and Coastal Erosion Risk Management Strategy for England*. Available at: http://www.official-documents.gov.uk/document/other/9780108510366/9780108510366.pdf; accessed 27 June 2014.

ESRC Global Environmental Change Programme (2001) 'Environmental justice: rights and means to a healthy environment for all', Special Briefing Note No. 7, Brighton: University of Sussex.

European Commission (2000) 'Directive 2000/60/EC of the European Parliament and of the Council establishing a framework for the Community action in the field of water policy'. Available at: http://ec.europa.eu/environment/water/water-framework/index_en.html; accessed 18 June 2014.

European Commission (2007) 'Directive 2007/60/EC on the assessment and management of flood risks'. Available at: http://eur-lex.europa.eu/LexUriServ/LexUriServ.do?uri=CELEX:32007L0060:EN:NOT; accessed 24 March 2014.

European Commission (2008) 'Directive 2008/1/EC of the European Parliament and of the Council of 15 January 2008 concerning integrated pollution prevention and control'. Available at: http://europa.eu/legislation_summaries/environment/waste_management/l28045_en.htm; accessed 18 June 2014.

European Commission (2012) *Evalsed: The Resource for the Evaluation of Economic Development*, Brussels: European Commission.

Evans, E., Ashley, R., Hall, J., Penning-Rowsell, E., Saul, A., Sayers, P. and Watkinson, A. (2004) *Foresight: Future Flooding Scientific Summary: Volume 1, Future Risks and their Drivers*, London: Office of Science and Technology.

Evans, J. P. (2011) 'Resilience, ecology and adaptation in the experimental city', *Transactions of the Institute of British Geographers*, Vol. 36, No. 2, pp. 223–37.

Evans, J. P. (2012) *Environmental Governance*, London: Routledge.

Fainstein, S. S. (2000) 'New directions in planning theory', in S. Campbell and S. S. Fainstein (eds), *Readings in Planning Theory*, Oxford: Blackwell, pp. 173–95.

Fainstein, S. S. (2010) *The Just City*, New York: Cornell University Press.

Faludi, A. and Waterhout, B. (2006) 'Introducing evidence based planning', *DISP*, Vol. 165, No. 2, pp. 4–14.

Febvre, L. (1925) *A Geographical Introduction to History*, New York: Alfred A. Knopf.

Fischer, F. (2000) *Citizens, Experts, and the Environment: The Politics of Local Knowledge*, Durham, NC/London: Duke University Press.

Flyvbjerg, B. (1998) *Rationality and Power*, Chicago: University of Chicago Press.

Foreman, D. (1991) *Confessions of an Eco-Warrior*, New York: Crown.

Forester, J. (1989) *Planning in the Face of Power*, Berkeley, CA: University of California Press).

Forester, J. (1999) *The Deliberative Practitioner: Encouraging Participatory Planning Processes*, Cambridge, MA: MIT Press.

Foucault, M. (1979) *Discipline and Punish: The Birth of the Prison*, trans. A. Sheridan, New York: Random House.

Freeman, A. M. III (1972) 'Distribution of environmental quality', in A. V. Kneese and B. T. Bower (eds), *Environmental Quality Analysis: Theory and Method in the Social Sciences*, Baltimore, MD: Johns Hopkins University Press, pp. 243–78.

Freudenburg, W. R., Frickel, S. and Gramling R. (1995) 'Beyond the society/nature divide: learning to think about a mountain', *Sociological Forum*, Vol. 10, No. 3, pp. 361–92.

Friedman, M. (1962) *Capitalism and Freedom*, Chicago: Chicago University Press.

Frones, I. (2007) 'Theorizing indicators: on indicators, signs and trends', *Social Indicators Research*, Vol. 83, pp. 5–23.

Funtowicz, S. O. and Ravetz, J. R. (1985) 'Three types of risk assessment: a methodological analysis', in C. Whipple and V. T. Covello (eds), *Risk Analysis in the Private Sector*, New York: Plenum, pp. 217–31.

Funtowicz, S. O. and Ravetz, J. R. (1991) 'A new scientific methodology for global environmental issues', in R. Costanza (ed.), *Ecological Economics: The Science and Management of Sustainability*, New York: Columbia University Press, pp. 137–52.

Funtowicz, S. and Ravetz, J. R. (1993) 'Science for the post-normal age', *Futures*, Vol. 25, pp. 735–55.

Garner, R. (2000) *Environmental Politics*, London Macmillan.

Geels, F. W. and Verhees, B. (2011) 'Cultural legitimacy and framing struggles in innovation journeys: a cultural–performative perspective and a case study of Dutch nuclear energy (1945–1986)', *Technological Forecasting and Social Change*, Vol. 78, pp. 910–30.

Gerth, H. H. and Wright Mills, C. (1948) *From Max Weber: Essays in Sociology*, London: Routledge.

Giddens, A. (1984) *The Constitution of Society*, Cambridge: Policy Press.

Giddens, A. (1991) *Modernity and Self-Identity*, Cambridge: Polity Press.

Giddens, A. (1994) 'Living in a post-traditional society' in U. Beck, A. Giddens and S. Lash (eds), *Reflexive Modernization: Politics, Tradition and Aesthetics in the Modern Social Order*, Cambridge: Polity Press, pp. 56–109.

Glacken, C. J. (1967) *Traces on the Rhodian Shore: Nature and Culture in Western Thought from Ancient Times to the End of the Eighteenth Century*, Berkeley, CA: University of California Press.

Glasgow City Council (2010) *Climate Change Strategy and Action Plan*, Glasgow: Glasgow City Council.

Glasson, J., Therivel, R. and Chadwick, A. (2012) *Introduction to Environmental Impact Assessment*, London: Routledge.

Godschalk, D. (2003) 'Urban hazard mitigation: creating resilient cities', *Natural Hazards Review*, Vol. 4, No. 3, pp. 136–43.

Goffman, E. (1974) *Frame Analysis: An Essay on the Organization of Experience*, New York Harper & Row.

Gordon, S. (1991) *The History and Philosophy of Social Science*, London: Routledge.

Gore, A. (2005) 'On Katrina, global warming'. Speech given to the National Sierra Club Convention, 9 September, San Francisco. Available at: http://www.commondreams.org/views05/0912-32.htm: accessed 6 April 2014.

Gramsci, A. (1995) *Further Selections from the Prison Notebooks*, London: Lawrence & Wishart.

Gray, J. (2009) *Straw Dogs: Thoughts on Humans and Other Animals*, London: Granta Books.

Grove, R. H. (1992) 'Origins of Western environmentalism', *Scientific American*, Vol. 267, No. 1, pp. 42–7.

Grove, R. H. (1995) *Green Imperialism: Colonial Expansion, Tropic Island Edens and the Origins of Environmentalism*, Cambridge: Cambridge University Press.

Grunwald, A. (2007) 'Governance for sustainable development: coping with ambivalence, uncertainty and distributed power', *Journal of Environmental Policy and Planning*, Vol. 9, No. 3–4, pp. 245–62.

Guardian, The (2010) *Women to Blame for Earthquakes, Says Iran Cleric*, 19 April. Available at: http://www.theguardian.com/world/2010/apr/19/women-blame-earthquakes-iran-cleric; accessed 22 August 2014.

Guy, S. and Marvin, S. (1999) 'Understanding sustainable cities: competing urban futures', *European Urban and Regional Studies*, Vol. 6, No. 3, pp. 268–75.

Guy, S., Marvin, S., Medd, W. and Moss, T. (2011) *Shaping Urban Infrastructures: Intermediaries and the Governance of Socio-Technical Networks*, London: Earthscan.

Guy, S. and Shove, E. (2000) *The Sociology of Energy, Buildings and the Environment: Constructing Knowledge, Designing Practice*, London: Routledge.

Haas, P. M. (1992) 'Introduction: epistemic communities and international policy coordination', *International Organization*, Vol. 46, No. 1, pp. 1–35.

Habermas, J. (1971) *Towards a Rational Society. Student Process, Science and Politics*, Boston, MA: Beacon.

Habermas, J. (1984) *The Theory of Communicative Action: Volume 1 – Reason and the Rationalization of Society*, Oxford: Polity Press.

Hall, P. (1980) *Great Planning Disasters*, Berkeley, CA: University of California Press.

Hall, P. (2002) *Cities of Tomorrow*, Oxford: Blackwell.

Hardin, G. (1968) 'The tragedy of the commons', *Science*, Vol. 162, No. 3859, pp. 1243–8.

Harvey, D. (1973) *Social Justice and the City*, Baltimore. MD: Johns Hopkins University Press).

Harvey, D. (1974) 'Population, resources and the ideology of science', *Economic Geography*, Vol. 50, No. 3, pp. 256–77.

Harvey, D. (1996) *Justice, Nature and the Geography of Difference*, Oxford: Blackwell.

Haughton, G. (1999) 'Environmental justice and the sustainable city', *Journal of Planning Education and Research*, Vol. 18, No. 3, pp. 233–43.

Haughton, G., Allmendinger, P., Counsell, D. and Vigar, G. (2010) *The New Spatial Planning, Territorial Management with Soft Spaces and Fuzzy Boundaries*, Abingdon: Routledge.

Hayek, F. A. (1960) *The Constitution on Liberty*, Chicago: Chicago University Press.

Hayek, F. A. (1944) *The Road to Serfdom*, London: Routledge.

Hays, S. P. (1982) 'From conservation to environment: environmental politics in the United States since World War Two', *Environmental Review*, Vol. 6, No. 2, pp. 14–41.

Head, B. W. (2008) 'Wicked problems in public policy', *Public Policy*, Vol. 3, No. 2, pp. 101–18.

Healey, P. (1992) 'Planning through debate: the communicative turn in planning theory', *Town Planning Review*, Vol. 63, No. 2, pp. 143–62.

Healey, P. (1993) 'The communicative work of development plans', *Environment and Planning B*, Vol. 20, pp. 83–104.

Healey, P. (2006) *Collaborative Planning: Shaping Places in Fragmented Societies*, Basingstoke: Palgrave Macmillan.

Heywood, A. (2003) *Political Ideologies: An Introduction*, Basingstoke: Palgrave Macmillan.

Hillier, J. (2000) 'Going round the back? Complex networks and informal action in local planning processes', *Environment and Planning A*, Vol. 32, No. 1, pp. 33–54.

Hippocrates (1881) *On Airs, Waters and Places*, trans. F. Adams, J. A. van der Linden, J. Cornarius and E. Littré, London: Wyman & Sons.

HM Government (2005) *Securing the Future*, Norwich: HMSO.

Hobbes, T. (1962 [1651]) *Leviathan*, London: Cox & Wyman.

Holland, A. (1999) 'Sustainability: should we start from here?', in A. Dobson (ed.), *Fairness and Futurity*, Oxford: Oxford University Press, pp. 46–69.

Holling, C. S. (1973) 'Resilience and stability of ecological systems', *Annual Review of Ecology and Systematics*, Vol. 4, pp. 1–23.

Holling, C. S. (1996) 'Engineering resilience versus ecological resilience', in P. C. Schulze (ed.), *Engineering Within Ecological Constraints*, Washington, DC: National Academy Press, pp. 31–44.

Home, R. (1997) *Of Planting and Planning: The Making of British Colonial Cities*, London: E. & F. N. Spon).

Hood, C. (1991) 'A public management for all seasons', *Public Administration*, Vol. 69, Spring, pp. 3–19.

Howard, E. (1902) *Garden Cities of To-Morrow*, London: Swan Sonnenschein.

Howe, E. (1990) 'Normative ethics in planning', *Journal of Planning Literature*, Vol. 5, No. 2, pp. 123–50.

Howe, E. (1992) 'Professional roles and the public interest in planning', *Journal of Planning Literature*, Vol. 6, No. 3, pp. 230–48.

Howlett, M. (2000) 'Managing the "hollow state": procedural policy instruments and modern governance', *Canadian Public Administration*, Vol. 43, No. 4, pp. 412–31.

Hughes, J. D. (2006) *What Is Environmental History?*, Cambridge: Polity Press.

Hughes, J. D. (2009) *An Environmental History of the World: Humankind's Changing Role in the Community of Life*, Abingdon: Routledge.

Hulme, M. (2009) *Why We Disagree About Climate Change: Understanding Controversy, Inaction and Opportunity*, Cambridge: Cambridge University Press.

Hume, D. (1987 [1742]) *Of National Characters*, Indianapolis; Liberty Fund.

Huxley, A. (1932) *Brave New World*, London: Chatto & Windus.

Huxley, M. and Yiftachel, O. (2000) 'New paradigm or old myopia? Unsettling the communicative turn in planning theory', *Journal of Planning Education and Research*, Vol. 19, No. 4, pp. 333–42.

Ibn Khaldun (1969 [1377]) *Muqaddimah: An Introduction to History*, trans. F. Rosenthal, Princeton, NJ: Princeton University Press.

Ibsen, H. (1882 [1999]) *An Enemy of the People, The Wild Duck, Rosmersholm*, Oxford: Oxford University Press.

Inhofe, J. (2003) 'Science of climate change', *Congressional Record*, 28 July, S10012–S10023.

Ingram, R. J. (trans.) (2009) *The Anglo-Saxon Chronicle*, London: Echo Library.

Innes, J. E. (1995) 'Planning theory's emerging paradigm: communicative action and interactive practice', *Journal of Planning Education and Research*, Vol. 14, April, pp. 183–89.

International Air Transport Association (IATA) (2010) 'Volcano crisis costs airlines $1.7bn in revenue – IATA urges measures to mitigate impact', Press release 21 April. Available at: http://www.iata.org/pressroom/pr/Pages/2010-04-21-01.aspx; accessed 6 April 2014.

IPCC (Intergovernmental Panel on Climate Change) (2000) *IPCC Special Report: Emissions Scenarios Summary for Policy Makers*, New York: IPCC.

IPCC (Intergovernmental Panel on Climate Change) (2007) *Climate Change 2007: The Physical Science Basis: Contribution of Working Group I to the Fourth Assessment Report of the IPCC*, Cambridge: Cambridge University Press.

Ipsos MORI (2011) 'Key environmental concerns by nation', April. Available at: http://www.ipsos-mori.com/Assets/Docs/Polls/

sri-environment-global-advisor-april-2011-presentation-slidepack.pdf; accessed 6 April 2014.

Jacob, M. C. (2009) *The Scientific Revolution: A Brief History with Documents*, Boston, MA: Bedford/St Martin's.

Jacobs, J. (1961) *The Death and Life of Great American Cities*, New York: Random House.

Jacobs Engineering UK (2004) *Strategy for Flood and Coastal Erosion Risk Management: Groundwater Flooding Scoping Study (LDS 23) Final Report, Volume 1 of 2*, London: Defra.

Jacobson, M. Z. (2002) *Atmospheric Pollution: History, Science, and Regulation*, New York: Cambridge University Press.

Jamieson, A. (2001) *The Making of Green Knowledge: Environmental Politics and Cultural Transformation*, Cambridge: Cambridge University Press.

Jasanoff, S. (ed.) (2004) *States of Knowledge: The Co-Production of Science and Social Order*, London: Routledge.

Jasanoff, S. (2009) 'The essential parallel between science and democracy', *SEED Magazine*, 17 February.

Jessop, B. (2008) *State Power*, Cambridge: Polity Press.

Jevons, W. S. (1866) *The Coal Question: An Enquiry Concerning the Progress of the Nation, and the Probable Exhaustion of our Coal-mines*, London: Macmillan and Co..

Jowett, B. (1977) *Aristotle: Politics – A Translation by Benjamin Jowett*, Wawa, PA: The Franklin Library.

Kaplan, H. B. (1999) 'Toward an understanding of resilience: a critical review of definitions and models', in M. D. Glantz and J. L. Johnson (eds), *Resilience and Development*, New York: Kluwer Academic.

Kaufman, L. and Zernike, K. (2012) 'Activists fight green projects, seeing U.N. plot', *New York Times*, 3 February. Available at: http://www.nytimes.com/2012/02/04/us/activists-fight-green-projects-seeing-un-plot.html?pagewanted=all&_r=0; accessed 20 August 2014.

Keeble, L. (1961) *Town Planning at the Crossroads*, London: Estates Gazette.

Keynes, J. M. (1933) 'National self-sufficiency', *The Yale Review*, Vol. 22, No. 4, June, pp. 755–69.

Keynes, J. M. (1973) *The Collected Writings of J. M. Keynes, Volume XIV, The General Theory and After: Part II, Defence and Development*, London: Macmillan for the Royal Economic Society.

Kingdon, J. W. (1995) *Agendas, Alternatives, and Public Policies*, New York: HarperCollins.

Kingston, R. (2000) 'Web-based public participation geographical information systems: an aid to local environmental decision-making', *Computers, Environment and Urban Systems*, Vol. 24, pp. 109–25.

Kitchen, R. and Tate, R. (2000) *Conducting Research into Human Geography*, Harlow: Prentice Hall.

Klein, R. J. T., Nicholls, R. J. and Thomalla, F. (2004) 'Resilience to natural hazards: how useful is this concept?', *Environmental Hazards*, Vol. 5, pp. 35–45.

Klosterman, R. E. (1978) 'Foundations for normative planning', *Journal of the American Institute of Planners*, Vol. 44, pp. 37–46.

Knight, F. H. (1921) *Risk, Uncertainty and Profit*, Chicago: University of Chicago Press.

Kuhn, T. S. (1957) *The Copernican Revolution: Planetary Astronomy in the Development of Western Thought*, Cambridge, MA: Harvard University Press.

Kuhn, T. S. (1962) *The Structure of Scientific Revolutions*, Chicago: University of Chicago Press.

Labour Archive (2014) 'Smoke from chimneys not from guns!', Poster, 1935. Available at: http://www.labourarchive.com/843/; accessed 8 April 2014.

Laffety, W. M. and Eckerberg, K. (2009) *From Earth Summit to Agenda 21*, London: Earthscan.

Latour, B. (2004) *The Politics of Nature*, Cambridge, MA: Harvard University Press.

Latour, B. and Woolgar, S. (1986) *Laboratory Life: The Construction of Scientific Facts*, Princeton, NJ: Princeton University Press.

Leach, M. and Fairhead, J. (2002) 'Manners of contestation: "citizen science" and "indigenous knowledge" in West Africa and the Caribbean', *International Social Science Journal*, Vol. 173, pp. 299–312.

Leal, D. R. and Meiners, R. E. (2002) *Government vs. Environment*, Lanham, MD: Rowman & Littlefield.

Leftwich, A. (1983) *Redefining Politics: People, Resources, Power*, London: Methuen.

Leiserowitz, A., Maibach, E., Roser-Renouf, C. and Hmielowski, J. D. (2011) *Politics and Global Warming: Democrats, Republicans, Independents, and the Tea Party*, New Haven, CT: Yale University and George Mason University, Fairfax, VA, Yale Project on Climate Change Communication. Available at: http://environment.yale.edu/climate/files/PoliticsGlobalWarming2011.pdf; accessed 6 April 2014].

Lemke, T. (2002) 'Foucault, governmentality, and critique', *Rethinking Marxism*, Vol. 14, No. 3, pp. 49–64.

Leopold, A. (1949) *A Sand Country Almanac: And Sketches Here and There*, New York: Oxford University Press.

Lester, L. and Cottle, S. (2009) 'Visualising climate change: television news and ecological citizenship', *International Journal of Communication*, Vol. 3, pp. 920–36.

Lindblom, C. E. (1979) 'Still muddling, not yet through', *Public Administration Review*, Vol. 39, pp. 517–26.

Lovelock, J. (2000) *Gaia: A New Look at Life on Earth*, Oxford: Oxford University Press.

Low, N. and Gleeson, B. (1998) *Justice, Society and Nature: An Exploration of Political Ecology*, London: Routledge.

Lowe, P. and Goyder, J. (1983) *Environmental Groups in Politics*, London: George Allen & Unwin.

Lukes, S. (2005) *Power: A Radical View*, Basingstoke: Palgrave Macmillan.

Lunney, D. (2012) 'What's the difference between climate science and climate journalism?', in P. Banks, D. Lunney and C. Dickman (eds), *Science Under Siege: Zoology Under Threat*, Sydney: Royal Society of New South Wales.

Lupton, D. (1999) *Risk*, London: Routledge.

Macnaghten, P. and Urry, J. (1998) *Contested Natures*, London: Sage.

Malthus, T. (1993, original edn 1798) *An Essay on the Principle of Population*, London: Dent.

Mannheim, K. (1940) *Man and Society in an Age of Reconstruction*, New York: Harcourt Brace.

Marx, K. (1975) *Early Writings*, Harmondsworth: Penguin.

Marx, K., Proudhon, P.-J. and Engels, F. (1910) *The Poverty of Philosophy (Being A Translation of the Misère de la philosophie) (a reply to 'La philosophie de la misère' of M. Proudhon)*, Chicago: C. H. Kerr & Company.

Maslow, A. H. (1943) 'A theory of human motivation', *Psychological Review*, Vol. 50, No. 4, pp. 370–96.

McCann, E. and Ward, K. (eds) (2011) *Mobile Urbanism: Cities and Policymaking in the Global Age*, Minneapolis, MN: University of Minnesota Press.

McCright, A. M. and Dunlap, R. E. (2011) 'The politicization of climate change and polarization in the American public's views of global warming, 2001–2010', *Sociological Quarterly*, 52, 155–94.

McHarg, I. L. (1969) *Design With Nature*, New York: Natural History Press.

McKibben, W. (1989) *The End of Nature*, New York: Anchor Books.

McManus, P. (2000) 'Beyond Kyoto? Media representation of an environmental issue', *Australian Geographical Studies*, Vol. 38, No. 3, pp. 306–19.

Meadows, D. H., Meadows, D. L., Randers, J. and Behrens, W. W. III (1972) *The Limits to Growth: A Report for the Club of Rome's Project on the Predicament of Mankind*, New York: Universe Books.

Merchant, C. (1982) *The Death of Nature: Women, Ecology and the Scientific Revolution*, London: Wildwood House.

Merton, R. K. (1979) *The Sociology of Science: Theoretical and Empirical Investigations*, Chicago: University of Chicago Press.

Mignon, E. (1962) *Les Mots du Général*, Paris: Librairie Arthème Fayard.

Mill, J. S. (1859) *On Liberty*, London: The Walter Scott Publishing Co.

Miller, A. A. (1947) *Climatology*, London: Methuen.

Miller, D. (2005) *Market, State, and Community: Theoretical Foundations of Market Socialism*, Oxford: Oxford University Press.

Ministry of Environmental Protection of the People's Republic of China (2011) *Report on the State of the Environment in China*. Available at http://english.mep.gov.cn/standards_reports/; accessed 6 April 2014.

Mitchell, D. (1995) 'There's no such thing as culture: towards a reconceptualisation of the idea of culture in geography', *Transactions of the Institute of British Geographers*, Vol. 20, No. 1, pp. 102–16.

Mitchell, G. and Dorling, D. (2003) 'An environmental justice analysis of British air quality', *Environment and Planning A*, Vol. 35, No. 5, pp. 909–29.

Moivre, A. de (1718) *The Doctrine of Chances: Or, a Method for Calculating the Probabilities of Events in Play*, London: W. Pearson.

Moore, G. E. (1903 [2004]) *Principia Ethica*, London: Cambridge University Press.

More, T. (1982 [1516]) *Utopia*, London: J. M. Dent & Sons.

Moudon, A. V. (1992) 'A catholic approach to organizing what urban designers should know', *Journal of Planning Literature*, Vol. 6, pp. 331–49.

Mumford, L. (1961) *The City in History: Its Origins, Its Transformations, and its Prospects*, London: Secker & Warburg.

Mythen, G. (2004) *Ulrich Beck: A Critical Introduction to the Risk Society*, London: Pluto Press.

Næss, P. (2001) 'Urban planning and sustainable development', *European Planning Studies*, Vol. 9, No. 4, pp. 503–24.

National Audit Office (2001) *Inland Flood Defence*, London: The Stationery Office.

National Commission on the BP Deepwater Horizon Oil Spill and Offshore Drilling (2011) *Deepwater: The Gulf Oil Disaster and the Future of Offshore Drilling*, January. Available at: http://www.gpo.gov/fdsys/pkg/GPO-OILCOMMISSION/content-detail.html; accessed 6 April 2014.

Nelkin, D. (1987) *Selling Science: How the Press Covers Science and Technology*, New York: W. H. Freeman.

Newman, P. W. G. and Kenworthy, J. R. (1989) 'Gasoline consumption and cities: a comparison of US cities with a global survey', *Journal of the American Planning Association*, Vol. 55, No. 1, pp. 24–37.

New Statesman (2010) 'The NS interview: Noam Chomsky', 13 September. Available at: http://www.newstatesman.com/internationalpolitics/2010/09/war-crimes-interview-obama; accessed 6 April 2014.

O'Connor, M. (ed.) (1974) *Is Capitalism Sustainable? Political Economy and the Politics of Ecology*, New York: Guilford Press.

O'Hare, P. and White, I. (2013) 'Deconstructing resilience: lessons from planning practice', *Planning, Practice & Research*, Vol. 28, No. 3, pp. 275–9.

Olson, M. (1965) *The Logic of Collective Action: Public Goods and the Theory of Groups*, Cambridge, MA: Harvard University Press.

Oreskes, N. and Conway, E. M. (2010) *Merchants of Doubt*, New York: Bloomsbury Press.

O'Riordan, T. (1976) *Environmentalism*, London: Pion.

O'Riordan, T. (1995) 'Frame works for CHOICE: core beliefs and the environment', *Environment: Science and Policy for Sustainable Development*, Vol. 37, No. 8, pp. 4–29.

O'Riordan, T. (2000) *Environmental Science for Environmental Management*, Harlow: Pearson Education.

Orwell, G. (1949) *1984*, London: Secker & Warburg.

Owens, S., Rayner, T. and Bina, O. (2004) 'New agendas for appraisal: reflections on theory, practice and research', *Environment and Planning A*, Vol. 36, pp. 1943–59.

Parker, D. J. (1995) 'Floodplain development policy in England and Wales', *Applied Geography*, Vol. 15, No. 4, pp. 341–63.

Pastor, M. R., Bullard, J. K., Fothergill, A., Morello-Frosch, R. and Wright, B. (2006) 'Environment, disaster and race After Katrina', *Race, Poverty and the Environment*, Vol. 13, No. 1, pp. 21–6.

Peck, J. (2003) 'Geography and public policy: mapping the penal state', *Progress in Human Geography*, Vol. 27, pp. 222–32.

Peet, R. (1985) 'The social origins of environmental determinism', *Annals of the Association of American Geographers*, Vol. 75, pp. 309–33.

Pepper, D. (1996) *Modern Environmentalism*, London: Routledge.

Pike, A. Dawley, S. and Tomaney, J. (2010) 'Resilience, adaptation and adaptability', *Cambridge Journal of Regions, Economy and Society*, Vol. 3, pp. 153–67.

Pinker, S. (2002) *The Blank Slate: The Moral Denial of Human Nature*, New York: Penguin.

Pitkin, H. F. (1972) *Wittgenstein and Justice: On the Significance of Ludwig Wittgenstein for Social and Political Thought*, Berkeley, CA: University of California Press.

Pitt, M. (2008) *Learning Lessons from the 2007 Floods: An Independent Review by Sir Michael Pitt*, London: Cabinet Office.

Platt, H. L. (2005) *Shock Cities: The Environmental Transformation and Reform of Manchester and Chicago*, Chicago: University of Chicago Press.

Plato (2008 [360]) *Critias*, trans. B. Jowett. Available at: http://www.gutenberg.org/files/1571/1571-h/1571-h.htm; accessed 26 August 2014.

Pliny (2012 [77–79]) *Natural History*, trans. H. Rackham, London: Folio Society.

Plunkett, J. (2010) 'Daily Star pulled from airports over volcanic ash splash', *The Guardian*, 21 April. Available at: http://www.guardian.co.uk/media/2010/apr/21/airports-pull-daily-star; accessed 6 April 2014.

Polanyi, M. (1958) *Personal Knowledge: Towards a Post-Critical Philosophy*, London: Routledge & Kegan Paul.

Polanyi, M. (1962) 'The republic of science: Its political and economic theory', *Minerva*, Vol. 1, pp. 54–74.

Poore, B. and Chrisman, N. R. (2006) 'Order from noise: toward a social theory of information', *Annals of the Association of American Geographers*, Vol. 96, No. 3, pp. 508–23.

Popper, K. R. (1968) *The Logic of Scientific Discovery*, 2nd edn (revd), New York: Harper Torchbooks.

Popper, K. R. (1972) *Objective Knowledge*, Oxford: Oxford University Press.

Popper, K. R. (2002) *Conjectures and Refutations*, London: Routledge.

Porritt, J. (1984) *Seeing Green: Politics of Ecology Explained*, Oxford: Basil Blackwell.

Proctor, J. (1998) 'The social construction of nature: relativist accusations, pragmatist and critical realist responses', *Annals of the Association of American Geographers*, Vol. 88, No. 3, pp. 352–76.

Proust, M. (1992) *In Search of Lost Time: Volume V*, London: Chatto & Windus.

Pulido, L. (2000) 'Rethinking environmental racism: white privilege and urban development in Southern California', *Annals of the Association of American Geographers*, Vol. 90, No. 1, pp. 12–40.

Ravetz, J. R. (2004) 'The post-normal science of precaution', *Futures,* Vol. 36, No. 3, pp. 347–57.

Rawls, J. (1971) *A Theory of Justice*, Cambridge, MA: Belknap Press of Harvard University Press.

Rhodes, R. A. W. (1994) 'The hollowing out of the state: the changing nature of the public service in Britain', *The Political Quarterly*, Vol. 65, No. 2, pp. 138–51.

Richards, D. and Smith, M. J. (2002) *Governance and Public Policy in the UK*. Oxford: Oxford University Press.

Rittel, H. and Webber, M. (1973) 'Dilemmas in a general theory of planning', *Policy Sciences*, Vol. 4, pp. 155–69.

Roberts, R. (1956) 'Science: One big greenhouse', *Time*, Vol. 67, No. 22, 28 May. Available at: http://www.time.com/time/magazine/article/0,9171,937403,00.html; accessed 6 April 2014.

Robinson, J. (1980) *Collected Economic Papers 1951–1980, Volume II*, Cambridge, MA: MIT Press.

Robson, B. (1999) 'Vision and reality: urban social policy' in J. B. Cullingworth (ed.), *British Planning: 50 Years of Urban and Regional Policy*, London: Athlone Press, pp. 168–83.

Rousseau, J.-J. (1923 [1762]) *The Social Contract and Discourses by Jean-Jacques Rousseau*, London/Toronto: J. M. Dent.

Rueschemeyer, D., Rueschemeyer, M. and Wittrock, B. (eds) (1998) *Participation and Democracy, East and West: Comparisons and Interpretations*, London: M. E. Sharpe.

Russell, B. (1962) *Essays in Skepticism*, New York: Philosophical Library.

Russell, B. (2006 [1930]) *The Conquest of Happiness*, New York: W. W. Norton & Company.

Rydin, Y. (2003) *Conflict, Consensus and Rationality in Environmental Planning: An Institutional Discourse Analysis*, Oxford: Oxford University Press.

Rydin, Y. (2004) *Planning, Sustainability and Environmental Risks*, LSE and ERM New Horizons Project for ODPM. Available at: http://webarchive.nationalarchives.gov.uk/20120919132719/www. communities.gov.uk/publications/corporate/planningsustainability; accessed 6 April 2014.

Rydin, Y. (2011) *The Purpose of Planning*, Bristol: Policy Press.

Sagar, T. (1994) *Communicative Planning Theory*, Aldershot: Avebury.

Sandel, M. J. (2009) *Justice: What's the Right Thing to Do?*, New York: Farrar, Straus & Giroux).

Schmithüsen, F. (2013) 'Three hundred years of applied sustainability in forestry', *Unasylva 240*, Vol. 64, pp. 3–11.

Schnaiberg, A. (1980) *The Environment: From Surplus to Scarcity*, Oxford: Oxford University Press.

Schön, D. A. (1983) *The Reflective Practitioner: How Professionals Think in Action*, New York: Basic Books.

Schultz, J. (1998) *Reviving the Fourth Estate*, Cambridge: Cambridge University Press.

Schumacher, E. F. (1973) *Small Is Beautiful*, London: Blond & Briggs.

Sears, P. B. (1964) 'Ecology – a subversive subject', *Bioscience*, Vol. 14, No. 7, July, pp. 11–13.

Selman, P. (2000) *Environmental Planning*, London: Sage.

Semple, E. C. (1911) *Influences of Geographic Environment on the Basis of Ratzel's System of Anthropo-Geography*, New York: Henry Holt & Co.

Sessions, G. (1995) *Deep Ecology for the Twenty-first Century*, Boston, MA: Shambhala Publications.

Shepard, P. (1969) 'Introduction: ecology and man – a viewpoint', in P. Shepard and D. McKinley (eds), *The Subversive Science: Essays Towards an Ecology of Man*, Boston, MA: Houghton Mifflin).

Sierra Club (2012) *From the Current Articles of Incorporation & Bylaws*. Available at: http://www.sierraclub.org/policy/downloads/goals.pdf; accessed 6 April 2014.

Simmie, J. (2012) 'Path dependence and new technological path creation in the Danish wind power Industry', *European Planning Studies*, Vol. 20, pp. 753–72.

Simon, J. L. (1980) 'Resources, population, environment: an oversupply of bad news', *Science*, Vol. 208, No. 4451, pp. 1431–7.

Sinclair, U. (1935 [1994]) *I, Candidate for Governor: And How I Got Licked*, Berkeley, CA and Los Angeles: University of California Press.

Skeffington Report (1969) *People and Planning – Report of the Committee on Public Participation in Planning*, London: HMSO.

Smardon, R. C. (2008) 'A comparison of Local Agenda 21 implementation in North American, European and Indian cities', *Management of Environmental Quality: An International Journal*, Vol. 19, No. 1, pp. 118–37.

Smith, M. R. and Marx, L. (1994) *Does Technology Drive History? The Dilemma of Technological Determinism*, Cambridge, MA: MIT Press.

Smith, N. (1990) *Uneven Development: Nature, Capital and the Production of Space*, Athens, GA: University of Georgia Press).

Snow, J. (1854) 'The Cholera near Golden Square, and at Deptford', *Medical Times and Gazette*, Vol. 9, 23 September, pp. 321–22.

Spretnak, C. and Capra, F. (1984) *Green Politics: The Global Promise*, London: Hutchinson.

Stine, J. and Tarr, J. (1998) 'At the intersection of histories: technology and the environment', *Technology and Culture*, Vol. 39, No. 4, pp. 601–40.

Stoker, G. (1998) 'Governance as theory: five propositions', *International Social Science Journal*, Vol. 50, No. 155, pp. 17–28.

Sutton, P. W. (2007) *The Environment: A Sociological Introduction*, Cambridge: Polity Press.

Swyngedouw, E. (2009) 'The antinomies of the post-political city: in search of a democratic politics of environmental production', *International Journal of Urban and Regional Research*, Vol. 33, No. 2, pp. 601–20.

Tarrow, S. (1994) *Power in Movement: Social Movements, Collective Action, and Politics*, Cambridge/New York: Cambridge University Press.

Taylor, C. (1994) 'Neutrality in political science', in M. Martin and L. C. McIntyre (eds), *Readings in Philosophy of Social Science*, Cambridge, MA: MIT Press, pp. 547–70.

Taylor , D. E. (2009) *The Environment and the People in American Cities, 1600s–1900s*, Durham, NC/London: Duke University Press.

Thaler, R. H. and Sunstein, C. R. (2008) *Nudge: Improving Decision about Health, Wealth and Happiness*, New Haven, CT: Yale University Press.

Tocqueville, A. de (2003 [1835]) *Democracy in America: And Two Essays on America*, trans. G. Bevan, London: Penguin Classics.

Turner, G. M. (2008) 'A comparison of *The Limits to Growth* with 30 years of reality', *Global Environmental Change*, Vol. 18, pp. 397–411.

UNECE (United Nations Economic Commission for Europe) (1998) 'Convention on Access to Information, Public Participation in Decision-making and Access to Justice in Environmental Matters'. Available at: http://www.unece.org/environmental-policy/treaties/public-participation/publications.html; accessed 6 April 2014.

UN-Habitat (2007) *Enhancing Urban Safety and Security: Global Reports on Human Settlements 2007*, London: Earthscan.

United Nations (1992) *Rio Declaration on Environment and Development*, A/Conf.151/26, Rio de Janeiro, Brazil: United Nations Conference on Environment and Development).

United Nations (2007) *World Population Prospects: The 2006 Revision*, New York: United Nations.

United Nations (2009) *Copenhagen Accord: UN Framework Convention on Climate Change* United Nations, 18 December. Available at: https://unfccc.int/meetings/copenhagen_dec_2009/items/5262.php; accessed 6 April 2014.

United Nations (2011) *World Population Prospects: The 2010 Revision,* New York: United Nations.

United Nations Environment Programme (2012) '21 Issues for the 21st century: results of the UNEP foresight process on emerging environmental issues', Nairobi, Kenya: United Nations Environment Programme. Available at: http://www.unep.org/publications/ebooks/foresightreport/Portals/24175/pdfs/Foresight_Report-21_Issues_for_the_21st_Century.pdf; accessed 6 April 2014.

United States Energy Information Administration (2013) *International Energy Outlook 2013,* Washington, DC: Office of Communications.

United States Environmental Protection Agency (2010) 'Seven priorities for the EPA's future, Memorandum'. Available at: http://blog.epa.gov/administrator/2010/01/12/seven-priorities-for-epas-future/; accessed 6 April 2014.

US Department of Defense (2002) *DoD News Briefing – Secretary Rumsfeld and Gen. Myers,* 12 February. Available at: http://www.defense.gov/transcripts/transcript.aspx?transcriptid=2636; accessed 22 August 2014.

US General Accounting Office (1983) *Siting of Hazardous Waste Landfills and their Correlation with Racial and Economic Status of Surrounding Communities* (Washington, DC: Government Printing Office).

Vinten-Johansen, P., Brody, H., Paneth, N., Rachman, S. and Rip, M. (2003) *Cholera, Chloroform and the Science of Medicine: A Life of John Snow,* Oxford: Oxford University Press.

Walker, G. (2012) *Environmental Justice: Concepts, Evidence and Politics,* London: Routledge.

Walker, G., Mitchell, G., Fairburn, J. and Smith, G. (2005) 'Industrial pollution and social deprivation: evidence and complexity in evaluating and responding to environmental inequality', *Local Environment,* Vol. 10, No. 4, pp. 361–77.

Walker, J. and Cooper, M. (2011) 'Genealogies of resilience: from systems ecology to the political economy of crisis adaptation', *Security Dialogue* Vol. 43, No. 2, pp. 143–60.

Wall, D. (1994) *Green History: A Reader in Environmental Literature, Philosophy and Politics,* London: Routledge.

Weber, M. (1978 [1922]) *Economy and Society,* trans. G. Roth and C Wittich, Oakland, CA: University of California Press.

Weber, M. (1949) *On The Methodology of the Social Sciences,* trans. and ed. E. A. Shils and H. A. Finch, Glencoe, IL: The Free Press.

Whatmore, S. (1999) 'Culture nature', in P. Cloake, P. Crang and M. Goodwin (eds), *Introducing Human Geographies,* London: Arnold, pp. 4–11.

Wells, H. G. (1914) *The World Set Free*, London: Macmillan.

Wells, H. G. (1933) *The Shape of Things to Come*, London: Hutchinson.

White, I. (2008) 'The absorbent city: urban form and flood risk management', *Proceedings of the Institution of Civil Engineers: Urban Design and Planning*, December (DP4, pp. 151–61.

White, I. (2010) *Water and the City: Risk, Resilience and Planning for a Sustainable Future*, London: Routledge.

White, I. (2013) 'The more we know, the more we don't know: reflections on a decade of planning, flood risk management and false precision', *Planning Theory and Practice*, Vol. 14, No. 1, pp. 106–14.

White, I. and Howe, J. (2004) 'The mismanagement of surface water', *Applied Geography*, Vol. 24, 261–80.

White, I. and O'Hare, P. (2014) 'From rhetoric to reality: which resilience; why resilience; and whose resilience in spatial planning?', *Environment and Planning C*. Advance online publication: doi:10.1068/c12117.

White, L. Jr. (1967) 'The historical roots of our ecological crisis', *Science*, Vol. 155, pp. 1203–7.

Wildavsky, A. (1973) 'If planning is everything, maybe it's nothing', *Policy Sciences*, Vol. 4, pp. 127–53.

Williams, R. (1980) *Problems in Materialism and Culture*, London: Verso.

Wisner, B., Blaikie, P., Cannon, T. and Davis, I. (2004) *At Risk: Natural Hazards, People's Vulnerability and Disasters*, London: Routledge.

Wittgenstein, L. (1953) *Philosophical Investigations*, Oxford: Basil Blackwell.

Wondolleck, J. M. and Yaffee, S. L. (2000) *Making Collaboration Work: Lessons from Innovation in Natural Resource Management*, Washington, DC: Island Press.

Wong, C. (2006) *Indicators for Urban and Regional Planning*, London: Routledge.

Wood, C. (1999) 'Environmental planning', in B. Cullingworth (ed.), *British Planning: 50 Years of Urban and Regional Policy*, London: Athlone Press.

World Commission for Environment and Development (WCED) (1987) *Our Common Future*, Oxford: Oxford University Press.

Worster, D. (1977; 1994 2nd edn) *Nature's Economy: A History of Ecological Ideas*, Cambridge: Cambridge University Press.

Wynne, B. (2009) 'Uncertainty and environmental learning: reconceiving science and policy in the preventative paradigm', in R. E. Lofstedt and A. Boholm (eds), *The Earthscan Reader on Risk*, London: Earthscan.

Wynne-Jones, J. (2007) *Floods are Judgement on Society, Says Bishops*, *Daily Telegraph*, 1 July. Available at: http://www.telegraph.co.uk/news/uknews/1556131/Floods-are-judgment-on-society-say-bishops.html; accessed 22 August 2014.

Udall, S. (1963) *The Quiet Crisis*, New York: Holt Rinechart & Winston.

Žižek, S. (1999) *The Ticklish Subject – The Absent Centre of Political Ontology*, London: Verso.

Index

CPI Antony Rowe
Eastbourne, UK
October 11, 2019